# THE INVISIBLE CRISIS OF CONTEMPORARY SOCIETY

# Advancing the Sociological Imagination
## A Series from Paradigm Publishers

**Edited by Bernard Phillips and J. David Knottnerus**

*Goffman Unbound! A New Paradigm for Social Science*
By Thomas J. Scheff (2006)

*The Invisible Crisis of Contemporary Society: Reconstructing Sociology's Fundamental Assumptions*
By Bernard Phillips and Louis C. Johnston (2007)

*Understanding Terrorism: Building on the Sociological Imagination*
Edited by Bernard Phillips (2007)

*Struggles before* Brown: *Early Civil Rights Protests and Their Significance Today*
By Jean Van Delinder (2008)

*Postmodern Cowboy: C. Wright Mills and a New 21st Century Sociology*
By Keith Kerr (2008)

*The Treadmill of Production: Injustice and Unsustainability in the Global Economy*
By Kenneth A. Gould, David N. Pellow, and Allan Schnaiberg (2008)

## Forthcoming

*Ritual as a Missing Link within Sociology: Structural Ritualization Theory and Research*
By J. David Knottnerus (2009)

# The Invisible Crisis of Contemporary Society

## Reconstructing Sociology's Fundamental Assumptions

*Bernard Phillips and Louis C. Johnston*

Routledge
Taylor & Francis Group

LONDON AND NEW YORK

First published 2007 by Paradigm Publishers

Published 2016 by Routledge
2 Park Square, Milton Park, Abingdon, Oxon OX14 4RN
711 Third Avenue, New York, NY 10017, USA

*Routledge is an imprint of the Taylor & Francis Group, an informa business*

Library of Congress Cataloging-in-Publication Data
Phillips, Bernard S.
  The invisible crisis of contemporary society : reconstructing sociology's fundamental assumptions / Bernard Phillips and Louis C. Johnston.
    p. cm.
  ISBN-13: 978-1-59451-371-8 (hc)
  ISBN-13: 978-1-59451-372-5 (pbk)
 1. Social problems. 2. Applied sociology. 3. Sociology. I. Johnston, Louis C. II. Title.
  HN29.5.P47 2007
  301.01—dc22

                                                              2006037208


Designed and Typeset by Straight Creek Bookmakers.

ISBN 13: 978-1-59451-371-8 (hbk)
ISBN 13: 978-1-59451-372-5 (pbk)

To David Christner

for his long-term and enthusiastic commitment

# Contents

# Preface

THE SIGNIFICANCE OF THE FOLLOWING PAGES is yet to be assessed. Will it communicate effectively to contemporary sociologists and their students? To other social scientists? To a broader reading public? Will it succeed in opening the door to a rethinking of the metaphysical and epistemological assumptions prevalent throughout the social sciences as well as contemporary society? Will it help to usher in the development of alternative paradigmatic assumptions which promise to help resolve basic contradictions between present ideals and practices within the academic world and beyond? More concretely, will it help academicians and others to develop a scientific method which follows scientific ideals and, as a consequence, penetrates deeply into the complexity of human behavior and into urgent social problems? Will we social scientists learn how to use that broad scientific method in our everyday lives? And can we succeed in demonstrating to others how knowledge can be put to work to solve problems, and how such partial solutions can in turn yield greater understanding?

Our grandiose aims for this book are implied by the above questions. We earnestly believe that the times call for such optimism about the possibilities of the social sciences, given the threatening problems facing the human race in our new century. Yet at the same time we are aware of the incredible difficulties involved in developing the changes called for by positive responses to those questions. However, despite current highly threatening events, and despite a prevailing pessimism throughout the social sciences, we have never lost our commitment to the Enlightenment dream of societies based on reason and, we would add, a scientific method that promises to continually and rapidly extend our understanding of human behavior without any limit. We hope that this book will succeed in helping to open the door to the development of such a method along with the metaphysical stance or worldview that will make this possible.

We would like to thank David Christner, to whom this book is dedicated, for his continuing and enthusiastic encouragement and insights during the development of this manuscript. As an early participant within the Sociological Imagination Group—described in the Introduction—he joins us in our optimism about the possibilities of the social sciences. We also wish to thank Harold Kincaid for his close reading and many suggestions that have yielded numerous additions to the manuscript. Much the same is true for David Knottnerus's reading of the entire manuscript and his many insights. Thomas J. Scheff has also contributed most substantially, both through his development of a methodology which has become a key portion of our own approach to the scientific method as well as through his reading of parts of the manuscript. And we are most grateful to Dean Birkenkamp, president of Paradigm Publishers, for his continuing support for our efforts along with important suggestions. In addition, we extend our thanks to other individuals who identify with the Sociological Imagination Group and who have been most encouraging: Hans Bakker, Stephen Baran, Martha DeWitt, Kevin Fox Gotham, Paul D. Johnson, Alan Kahn, John Livingstone, Michael Lynch, John Malarkey, Neil McLaughlin, Adam Rafalovich, Suzanne Retzinger, Hilarie Roseman, Sandro Segré, Robert Stebbins, Emek Tanay, Jonathan Turner, Jean Van Delinder, and Todd Powell-Williams.

Finally, our long list of references indicates individuals and their work who formed the backbone of this book. That list includes Marx on alienation, Durkheim's *Suicide,* Mills' *White Collar* and *The Sociological Imagination,* Kuhn's *Structure of Scientific Revolutions,* Gouldner's *Coming Crisis of Western Sociology,* Kincaid's *Philosophical Foundations of the Social Sciences* and Scheff's *Emotions, the Social Bond, and Human Reality: Part/Whole Analysis.*

*Bernard Phillips and Louis C. Johnston*

# PART I

# Introduction

Upon this gifted age, in its dark hour
Rains from the sky, a meteoric shower
  Of facts ...
They lie unquestioned, uncombined.
Wisdom enough to leech us of our ill
Is daily spun, but there exists no loom
  To weave into fabric.
                    —Edna St. Vincent Millay

## Social Science and Metaphysics

Al Qaeda's assault on the American people on September 11, 2001, accompanied by increasing concerns over the deadly nature of nuclear, chemical and biological weapons of mass destruction, has dramatically increased a sense of insecurity and fear for the future throughout the world. Martin Rees, England's Astronomer Royal and a professor at Cambridge University, has examined such problems in *Our Final Hour: A Scientist's Warning.* Rees claimed that "The 'downside' from twenty-first century [biological and chemical] technology could be graver and more intractable than the threat of nuclear devastation that we have faced for decades" (2003: vii). Yet we should not minimize nuclear threats. As we move into the twenty-first century the "club" of nations with nuclear capability will, in all probability, continue to expand along with the nuclear capabilities of terrorist groups. At the same time, there appears to be no corresponding expansion of the ability to understand and control whatever forces are making for an increasingly dangerous world.

At this time in the twenty-first century we appear to be losing a race between biophysical technologies that are unleashing ever more powerful weapons of mass destruction and social science technologies for controlling the use of those weapons. Some would argue that our problems in this century are nothing really new, and that there is no need to be frightened by "prophets of doom and gloom." For the human race has managed, somehow, to overcome many earlier threats to its continuing existence. This was dramatized by Thornton Wilder in his play, "The Skin of Our Teeth," referring to the many very narrow escapes throughout human history. Yet science

1

has taught us that what has occurred in the past yields no guarantee as to what will occur in the future. The accurate prediction of future events must be based not on commonsense convictions as to the repetition of phenomena but on scientific understanding. Without such understanding we continue to live in a dream world of unrealistic optimism if we assume that once again we will escape disaster by the skin of our teeth. All the while that we continue to fiddle and avoid confronting the realistic problems we face, Rome is burning, yet our understanding of what is happening to us and what we can do about it remains drastically limited.

Why do we appear to be losing this race between forces that will yield destruction and forces for achieving understanding? Is it inevitable that the former will overtake the latter? Does our basic problem lie with the biophysical scientist? With the social scientist? With human nature? Or does it lie to a large extent—as we believe—with our fundamental assumptions or paradigm, that is, our metaphysical stance as to the nature of reality? In other words, are we to a large extent the victims of our own worldview or Weltanschauung, which provides a foundation for all of our behavior as individuals and societies from one moment to the next, granting the existence of other forces as well? From this perspective, the solution to our contemporary problems would require not merely limited changes in contemporary society but fundamental changes in every single one of our institutions along with corresponding changes in the individual's patterns of thought, feeling and action.

Suppose, for example, that our present metaphysical stance or worldview as to the fundamental nature of reality builds on the idea that human behavior is not nearly as complex as it actually is. And since our metaphysical assumptions are the basis for our epistemology or methods for discovering the nature of reality, we would then expect that our approach to the social sciences has been far too simplistic. For example, we would not be surprised if social scientists proceeded to divide up the pie of human behavior into distinct pieces to be investigated by anthropologists, economists, historians, political scientists, psychologists and sociologists who generally fail to communicate their findings to one another despite scientific ideals calling for such communication. That would be an example of a metaphysical assumption or worldview as to the simplistic nature of human behavior trumping scientific ideals calling for openness to the full range of phenomena relevant to a given problem. This is assuming that any given problem is sufficiently complex so as to require that we bring to bear on it the range of social science knowledge.

This is in fact what appears to have actually occurred. The situation of a lack of integrated understanding of human behavior is far worse than most of us imagine, all apparently based on an oversimplified worldview or metaphysical stance. For example, there are no less than forty-four distinct Sections—and counting—of the American Sociological Association, with only limited communication across these Sections. But the situation is even worse than this. The five-volume *Encyclopedia of Sociology* (Borgatta and Montgomery, 2000) lists 397 specialized topics within sociology, and once again the overall situation appears to be one of limited communication across these specialized fields. The result is that sociological understanding—and understanding within the social sciences in general—is based on bits and pieces of knowledge that have not been pulled together so as to provide the comprehensiveness essential to penetrate the complexity of human behavior. This leaves us all relatively helpless in the face of threatening problems such as terrorism. Successes in the far simpler realms of physical and biological phenomena appear to have influenced social scientists to see human behavior in much the same way. And the resulting failure of social scientists to make much headway is not traced back to their simplistic assumptions about the fundamental nature of reality—that is, their worldview or metaphysical stance—which make such headway almost impossible.

Just as there is specialization with limited communication throughout the social sciences, so is there specialization with limited communication dividing all academic disciplines as well as applied fields. Specialization, when it is accompanied by communication among specialists so as not to lose the forest for the trees, can be a most useful procedure. But specialization without such communication can easily yield partial knowledge that fails to address adequately the problem at hand. As the saying goes, a little learning can be a dangerous thing. Particularly important is the separation between philosophy, which is much concerned with metaphysics or worldviews, and the social sciences. William James, one of the founders of the philosophy of pragmatism, put forward his view of the importance of philosophy for all of us, quoting from an essay by G. K. Chesterton:

> There are some people—and I am one of them—who think that the most practical and important thing about a man is still his view of the universe. We think that for a landlady considering a lodger, it is important to know his income, but still more important to know his philosophy. We think that for a general to fight an enemy, it is important to know the enemy's numbers, but still more important to know the enemy's philosophy (1907/1995: 1).

James went on to claim that, within the new philosophy of pragmatism, "Science and metaphysics would come much nearer together, would in fact work absolutely hand in hand" (20). His view of metaphysics was shared by the original founder of pragmatism, Charles Peirce. Peirce claimed that "metaphysics, even bad metaphysics, really rests on observations, whether consciously or not," contradicting "the common opinion ... that metaphysics ... is intrinsically beyond the reach of human cognition" (1898/1955:

310–311). Even today the "common opinion" among social scientists is that metaphysics, and philosophy in general, is much like angels dancing on the head of a pin, and that the scientific revolution over the past centuries was achieved by rejecting philosophical "speculation" and substituting concrete evidence for untested ideas. Yet this narrow view of the nature of the scientific method ignores the fundamental role of metaphysical assumptions in shaping how scientists—and everyone else—go about their work. As illustrated above, when we assume that human behavior is no more complex than physical or biological phenomena, the result is our present bits and pieces of un-integrated knowledge, which fail to yield substantial understanding of human behavior and fail to provide a basis for solving problems. To illustrate further, such a simplistic assumption appears to have yielded throughout history what Robert Merton has called "the unanticipated consequences of purposive social action" (1936; see chapter 3). As one of a great many examples, Southern sheriffs using cattle prods and police dogs on civil rights demonstrators did not anticipate the consequence that televised footage of their behavior would help to create a moral outcry that influenced the passage of civil rights legislation. Those sheriffs had adopted an oversimplified view of their behavior, failing to allow for the impact of television.

Apparently, an understanding of our metaphysical stance or worldview is incredibly powerful in yielding insights into our current problems. For this one aspect of our worldview, our assumptions about the simplicity or complexity of human behavior, yields a profound critique of almost every one of the studies in the social sciences that has ever been undertaken. For those very studies, based as they are on a narrow worldview or metaphysical stance, yield partial information, and there is little awareness of this limitation. And in turn that partial information can be a dangerous thing when it comes to using it in efforts to solve the full range of our problems, whether large-scale problems or personal problems. This has to do with the efforts of professionals like politicians, educators, social workers, criminologists and psychotherapists. It also has to do with the understandings employed by the rest of us, including journalists, business people, those in the arts, biophysical scientists, engineers, doctors and nurses, lawyers, and everyone else.

Yet how are we to uncover the nature of our worldview, given the overriding importance of our doing so at this time in history? For example, should we turn to the academic philosophers who have been writing about metaphysics for many years? Karl Mannheim, a sociologist who attempted to penetrate the nature of our worldview, has this to say in an essay he wrote, "On the Interpretation of Weltanschauung":

> Is it possible to determine the global outlook of an epoch in an objective, scientific fashion? Or are all characterizations of such a global outlook

necessarily empty, gratuitous speculations? ... theoretical philosophy is neither the creator nor the principal vehicle of the Weltanschauung of an epoch; it is merely only one of the channels through which a global factor ... manifests itself.... If, on the other hand, we define Weltanschauung as something a-theoretical with philosophy merely as one of its manifestations, and not the only one, we can widen our field of cultural studies ... our search for a synthesis will then be in a position to encompass every single cultural field. The plastic arts, music, costumes, mores and customs, rituals, the tempo of living, expressive gestures and demeanour—all these no less than theoretical communications will become a decipherable language, adumbrating the underlying unitary whole of Weltanschauung (1952: 9, 13-14).

Following Mannheim's argument, philosophers do not have the answers on the nature of our worldview or metaphysical stance, granting their concern with this issue. For it takes very broad studies of "every single cultural field" to uncover assumptions which underlie and shape our entire way of life. Perhaps, then, we should turn to social scientists, who have indeed investigated all of these phenomena. Yet here again we come up against a brick wall. As we have noted, social scientists have shied away from efforts to understand something as broad as a worldview or metaphysical stance. Given their oversimplified understanding of human behavior, they have divided it up into literally thousands of watertight compartments. And the result is that almost all we have are what Edna St. Vincent Millay has called "a meteoric shower of facts" which remain largely unrelated to one another. It would take an alternative worldview that fully recognizes human complexity to begin to link those pieces to one another, a worldview that has yet to be understood and employed.

Our pursuit of the fundamental assumptions guiding sociologists and others should not neglect the work of Thomas Kuhn, the historian of science whose *The Structure of Scientific Revolutions* (1962) has been having an enormous influence not only on the social sciences but also throughout the academic world up to the present time. His concept of "paradigm" has many meanings, yet one of them points to the importance of the basic assumptions that underlie a given science and that must be challenged by an alternative paradigm if indeed that science is to undergo a revolution. Kuhn saw such revolutions as "changes of world view" and not merely the substitution of one theory for another, suggesting that this process might be extended to basic changes in culture or society as well. Kuhn's idea here—to be elaborated in chapter 3—is that a basic change requires a new set of fundamental assumptions (or paradigm) which promises to resolve the problems or contradictions within the former assumptions (or paradigm). The widespread attraction of his book can, then, be partially explained as deriving from the interest of academicians in a theory of change as well as their interest in uncovering basic assumptions. Our own rethinking of sociology's paradigmatic assumptions involves not just the raising up of assumptions to full view. It also involves the presentation of alternative assumptions which promise to resolve contradictions within the previous ones. And it also points toward basic changes in the scientific method along with basic changes in society, since those assumptions are by no means limited to those of us in the academic world.

## The Web and Part/Whole Approach to the Scientific Method

There is indeed a way to begin a journey that employs a scientific method for understanding human behavior along with a worldview that confronts the complexity involved. Sociologists need not give up on the possibility of fulfilling the Enlightenment dream of Auguste Comte. The approach we shall adopt builds, first and foremost, on the incredible potential of the human being. Given the range of problems that we humans have not yet been able to solve, and given their threatening nature, it is easy to lose sight of that potential and to adopt a pessimistic view of our future. Our potential is based very largely on our complex language, which sharply distinguishes us from all other forms of life. It is language which twentieth-century research has discovered to be absolutely central to an understanding of human behavior. It is language which has been the fundamental basis for the development of human civilization. It is language that will continue to be the basis for our further development. It is language which is our most powerful tool for solving problems. And it is language which ushered in the creation of our second most powerful problem-solving tool—the scientific method—which has been much of the basis for the industrial revolution and the process of modernization over the past four centuries. In this book we shall focus on both language and the scientific method.

It was the eighteenth-century Enlightenment era which, based on scientific achievements in the seventeenth century, developed the optimism about the possibilities of the human being which became much of the foundation for the development of the social sciences. That optimism and faith in the scientific method influenced Auguste Comte in the nineteenth century to develop his vision of sociology as a new and wide-ranging "science of society." And it also motivated classical sociologists like Marx, Durkheim, Weber and Simmel to carry that vision much further, proceeding far more systematically and empirically. It is a combination of the breadth of classical sociology—coupled with the breadth of some modern sociologists together with the specialized achievements of contemporary sociology—which is much of the basis for the present approach.

Two twentieth-century sociologists in particular have influenced our own orientation: C. Wright Mills and Alvin W. Gouldner. Although we shall examine their contributions in chapters 6 and 2, respectively, an introduction to their work is in order. Despite Mills's short life—from 1916 to 1962—and his preference to work alone with no following, his *The Sociological Imagination* (1959) was rated in a 1997 survey of the members of the International Sociological Association as the second most influential book for sociologists published during the entire twentieth century (Phillips, 2004). It preceded works by Merton, Berger and Luckman, Bourdieu, Elias, Habermas, Parsons, and Goffman. It was in that book that Mills developed his image of the breadth of perspective required to penetrate the depths of human behavior:

> The sociological imagination ... is the capacity to shift from one perspective to another—from the political to the psychological; from examination of a single family to comparative assessment of the national budgets of the world; from the theological school to the military establishment; from considerations of an oil industry to studies of contemporary poetry. It is the capacity to range from the most impersonal and remote transformations to the most intimate features of the human self—and to see the relations between the two (1959: 7).

It was in *The Sociological Imagination* that Mills developed a direction for actually achieving such breadth, namely "to shuttle between levels of abstraction" (1959: 34). Instead of remaining at a high level of abstraction ("grand theory") or at a low level of abstraction ("abstracted empiricism"), the social scientist should move up and down the "ladder" of abstraction. It is such movement that addresses the long-standing conundrum of how to link abstract or general theory with concrete empirical research that has been plaguing the social sciences. Metaphorically, by moving up language's ladder of abstraction we gain the height that enables us to see far and wide, linking those phenomena when we come down that ladder. And by moving very far up that ladder, we can even encounter our metaphysical assumptions and alter them as needed. In an early article analyzing social science textbooks, Mills (while still a graduate student) criticized their authors—including his own department chair—for their rejection of the importance of philosophy and emphasizing instead "lower levels of abstraction" (1943: 168). Mills's own doctoral dissertation demonstrated another possibility by focusing on the concrete origins of the abstract ideas developed by the originators of the philosophy of pragmatism (1964).

Alvin W. Gouldner carried forward Mills's breadth in his *The Coming Crisis of Western Sociology* (1970). It was there that he emphasized the importance of the sociologist's "background assumptions" which are "world hypotheses," that is, "primitive assumptions about the world and everything in it. World hypotheses ... are what are sometimes called "'metaphysics'." It was through his exploration of metaphysical assumptions that Gouldner was able to emerge with his emphasis on the importance of a "Reflexive Sociology," an orientation which challenges fundamental, although largely invisible, assumptions held by contemporary sociologists:

> What sociologists now most require from a Reflexive Sociology, however, is not just one more specialization, not just another topic for panel meetings at professional conventions.... The historical mission of a Reflexive Sociology as I conceive it, however, would be to transform the sociologist, to penetrate deeply into his daily life and work, enriching them with new sensitivities, and to raise the sociologist's self-awareness to a new historical level.... A Reflexive Sociology means that we sociologists must—at the very least—acquire the ingrained habit of viewing our own beliefs as we now view those held by others (1970: 489).

If social scientists make the basic assumption that they must avoid any focus on themselves as they proceed with their investigations, Gouldner implies that they are avoiding an examination of their own impact on the research process. A reflexive approach makes for much more complex research, yet it also opens up to vital factors which must be taken into account in order to understand what is in fact going on. In a discussion of his book after it was published, Gouldner brought forward another idea that is central to the focus of the present book on addressing the fundamental assumptions of sociologists along with the rest of us. It has to do with the sociologist's usage of language:

> The pursuit of ... understanding, however, cannot promise that men as we now find them, with their everyday language and understanding, will always be capable of further understanding and of liberating themselves. At decisive points the ordinary language and conventional understandings fail and must be transcended. It is essentially the task of the social sciences, more generally, to create new and "extraordinary" languages, to help men learn to speak them, and to mediate between the deficient understandings of ordinary language and the different and liberating perspectives of the extraordinary languages of social theory.... To say social theorists are concept-creators means that they are not merely in the knowledge-creating business, but also in the language-reform and language-creating business. In other words, they are from the beginning involved in creating a new culture (Gouldner, 1972: 16).

It is, then, both language and the scientific method—the two most powerful tools of the human being—which will also be our own two most important tools in this effort to probe the social scientist's fundamental assumptions and come up with an approach that addresses human complexity. And it is the work of Mills and Gouldner—coupled, of course, with the work of a great many others—which guides our own orientation. That orientation finally broke into print in a systematic way with *Beyond Sociology's Tower of Babel: Reconstructing the Scientific Method* (Phillips, 2001). It was based on applying recent developments in the philosophy of social science (Duhem, 1954; Quine and Ullian, 1970; Kincaid, 1996) to sociological research so as to take into account the web of phenomena surrounding any given isolated hypothesis. Those new developments point toward the web of phenomena which make up the entire context of a given investigation, versus centering on whatever can be approached mathematically. From the perspective of methods in sociology, those developments open up to the importance of qualitative, no less than quantitative procedures, for research. This broader approach to the scientific method, in the spirit of Mills, Gouldner and Kuhn, is illustrated by the work of Willer and Webster, 1970; Phillips, 1972, 1979, 1985, 1988, 1990; Scheff, 1990, 1994, 1997; Lauderdale, McLaughlin and Oliverio, 1990; and Wallerstein, 1980, 1991.

This "Web Approach" to the scientific method was continued in a volume with ten authors, *Toward a Sociological Imagination: Bridging Specialized Fields* (Phillips, Kincaid and Scheff, 2002). The topics ranged widely, indicating the possibility that this approach to research might be applied to the full range of topics within sociology and even throughout the social sciences. Topics included the process of secularization, small-group experiments, explaining inequality, the transition from feudalism to capitalism, prejudice, aspects of mental illness and working-class emotions and relationships. The methodological approach accepted by the authors included a commitment to the importance of a very wide range of phenomena in any effort to investigate a given problem, granting that this was an ideal more than something that the authors generally were able to achieve. That wide range of phenomena includes physical structures, biological structures, social structures, personality structures, the momentary scene and long-term history. It also encompasses the cognitive, emotional and active or interactive aspects of human behavior. Metaphorically, we can see these three aspects as stressing the "head," the "heart" and the "hand."

The "Web Approach" to the scientific method presented in those two books—*Beyond Sociology's Tower of Babel* and *Toward a Sociological Imagination*—includes five components (Phillips, 2001, especially chapter 1):

1. *definition of the problem,*
2. *movement up language's ladder of abstraction,*

3. *movement down that ladder;*
4. *integrating knowledge, and*
5. *reflexive analysis and interactive worldview.*

Those components are not different from our ideals for the scientific method, which specify openness to all phenomena relevant to a given defined problem. Yet they differ substantially from near-universal practices, which ignore reflexivity and severely limit attention to the other components of the Web Approach. As a result, the range of phenomena that are seen as relevant to any given problem also becomes quite limited, as illustrated by extreme specialization with limited communication among specialists. We may note here the importance of Mills's work with reference to (2) "shuttling" up and (3) down language's ladder of abstraction as well as (4) integrating knowledge. We may also note that (3) movement down that ladder includes not just using more concrete concepts but also the testing of abstract propositions in order to present evidence toward their verification or falsification. And in addition we may note Gouldner's contribution to (5) with his emphasis on a reflexive sociology. But let us not forget Gouldner's contribution to the centrality of our tool of language on which the scientific method itself is based. We might also look to Kuhn's concern with paradigmatic assumptions as pointing in the direction of (5) worldviews. As for (1), the other four components of the scientific method help the researcher to define any given problem in a very broad way. And that breadth in turn transforms apparently trivial problems into important ones. Mills is admired largely for his ability to confront the fundamental problems of contemporary society.

Over the next few years there was progress in developing more systematic and thorough explanations along with further illustrations. For example, Robert Stebbins used the Web Approach to analyze the nature of the Protestant work ethic in his *Between Work and Leisure: The Common Ground of Two Separate Worlds* (2004). Thomas Scheff's *Goffman Unbound!: A New Paradigm for Social Science* (2006) not only provided another illustration of the approach but also carried further an explanation of the importance of moving down language's ladder of abstraction. He had developed his Part/Whole Approach to the scientific method in three earlier monographs (1990, 1994 and 1997). Just as a novelist can write about the momentary details involved within any given human situation—such as the play of emotions, the thoughts of those involved and the specific actions that take place—so can the social scientist do the same. In Scheff's 2006 publication he was able to combine the Web Approach (and its detailed illustrations of shuttling up the ladder of abstraction) with the Part/Whole Approach (and its detailed illustrations of shuttling down the ladder of abstraction). The result is what came to be called the "Web and Part/Whole Approach." The change is not a shift in direction but a matter of giving equal emphasis to Mills's call for shuttling both up the ladder and down the ladder.

Another contribution to the Web and Part/Whole Approach was a volume collecting the papers given at the fourth annual conference of the Sociological Imagination Group in August, 2004, in San Francisco: *Understanding Terrorism: Building on The Sociological Imagination* (Phillips, 2007). The senior author had organized that group with the help of Harold Kincaid—a philosopher of social science—and Thomas J. Scheff. The group's first conference in 2000 had been the basis for the volume edited by Phillips, Kincaid and Scheff and described above. Publications and other materials of the Sociological Imagination Group can be found on its website, www.uab.edu/philosophy/sig

The Web and Part/Whole Approach aims to capture the breadth of our ideals for the scientific method by providing a framework broad enough to encompass the full range of social science research. This breadth might be illustrated by its links to a variety of contemporary sociological theories, each of which also strives for comprehensiveness. For example, there is Jeffrey Alexander's emphasis on the importance of culture and language, building on the earlier work of Talcott Parsons. This is exemplified by an analysis of "binary discourse" in civil society, with its focus on a dichotomous emphasis within culture—by contrast with the inclusion of a gradational orientation—that treats the in-group favorably and the out-group very negatively (2001: 193–201). We also have Nicholas Luhmann's concept of "autopoiesis," referring to the importance of self-reference or self-consciousness in human behavior, which links to the idea of reflexivity and makes possible the continuation of social structures (1984/1995). This idea is paralleled by Anthony Giddens's concept of "recursivity," emphasizing the feedback between structure and agency that is based on the agency's conscious anticipation of the outcome of any action. His approach, in common with that of the Web and Part/Whole Approach, sees "structuration" as linking momentary actions to long-term structures, emphasizing the importance of momentary actions and viewing structures dynamically (1979, 1984).

To illustrate further such links to contemporary sociological theory, the approach's emphasis on language as well as on a contrast between egalitarian and stratified structures overlaps with Jürgen Habermas's concept of an "ideal speech community" (1984). It also overlaps with Erik Olin Wright's efforts to build on the Marxist tradition with his focus on the importance of stratification, the ideal of equality and history as well (1992). And if we move from stratification within a given nation to international stratification—along with the importance of history—then we also have an overlap with the work of Immanuel Wallerstein on world-system analysis (1974, 1979). Yet this openness to international stratification by no means rules out the importance of the political processes taking place within any given nation, as illustrated by the work of Theda Skocpol (1979). One additional example has to do with the role of biology, as illustrated in Jonathan Turner's view of its role in interpersonal behavior (2002). The Babel book includes illustrations of human perception as a key aspect of the impact of human biology on our behavior.

The Babel book, with its focus on the Web Approach to the scientific method, distinguished among the languages of social science, biophysical science and literature (Phillips, 2001: 21-23). We might carry further our understanding of the role of language in human affairs by seeing these languages as emphasizing, respectively, three capacities of language: dichotomy, gradation or number, and figurative language or imagery. The social sciences have emphasized dichotomies, such as the distinction between equality and hierarchy or conformity and deviance. This goes back to the fundamental nature of all languages: their division of the world into two categories. There is the phenomena denoted by a given word, on the one hand, and all other phenomena, on the other hand. Such a dichotomous perspective also appears to be the emphasis within everyday speech and thought.

The biophysical sciences, by contrast with the social sciences, have emphasized the gradational component of language. Here, we might see just about everything as a matter of degree, and we might even go so far as to designate a given phenomenon with a number and use that number as a basis for making predictions about the occurrence of that phenomenon. Following the title of a book by Tobias Dantzig, *Number: The Language of Science* (1954), the development of mathematics has been essential in the development of the biophysical sciences. For example, it is the calculus which became the basis for much of the ability of engineers to make use of physical science knowledge in their procedures for building public works and developing means for transportation and communication. It is indeed difficult to imagine the development of physical science without the tool of mathematics with its gradational orientation.

Literature, by contrast, emphasizes imagery or figures of speech, which uses language to represent sense experiences. This takes us back to biological or perceptual experiences so fundamental that they precede the development of language, granting that language shapes those experiences and is in turn shaped by them. In chapter 2 of this book we examine a book by John Berger, based on the British Broadcasting Corporation's television series, *Ways of Seeing*. Berger begins his book with these words:

> "Seeing comes before words. The child looks and another sense in which seeing comes before words. It is seeing which establishes our place in the surrounding world; we explain that world with words, but words can never undo the fact that we are surrounded by it" (1985: 7).

Images from literature are, potentially, powerful means of communication. They can help the scientist to understand what he or she has learned, and they can also help the scientist communicate that knowledge.

It is a focus on only one of these capacities of language—whether dichotomy, gradation, or imagery—which is a basis for a narrow, or what might be called a stratified, worldview or metaphysical stance. By contrast, a focus on all three is a basis for a broad, or what might be called an interactive, worldview. Given an effort to include all three capacities of language, this should not imply that a new worldview will automatically be in play. For it is possible to compartmentalize one's approach to those three capacities and, thus, continue with the narrow orientation to phenomena that characterizes a stratified worldview. Consciousness of the limitations of that worldview together with awareness of an alternative worldview appear to be essential in order to escape from that compartmentalized perspective.

The sociologist's paradigmatic assumptions include not just a metaphysical stance or worldview but also an epistemological stance or an approach to the scientific method. It is that epistemological stance—the nature of our broad approach to the scientific method—which has been our focus within the preceding section on the Web and Part/Whole Approach to the scientific method. That stance, although not as high up on language's ladder of abstraction as a metaphysical stance, is nevertheless higher than specific theories. Given that height—which enables epistemology to trump theories in violation of scientific ideals—we can expect a more scientific epistemology to help social scientists develop a much broader approach to theory and thus move toward integrating their knowledge and their usage of language's three capacities. But to do this requires illustrations of the Web and Part/Whole Approach to the scientific method. There are a great many within the chapters of this book, but an illustration is also called for in this Introduction. It will be an example that returns us to the threatening problems examined at the beginning of this Introduction.

## The Invisible Crisis of Contemporary Society

Daniel Lerner, a political scientist, initiated an international study half a century ago to learn about the transition from preindustrial to contemporary society (Lerner, 1958: especially 23-25). That study unearthed a very broad problem linked to the modernization process, and this is the problem that we shall examine. As part of that study Tosun B., an interviewer who lived in Turkey's capital city, Ankara, embarked on a two-hour drive on the dirt road connecting Ankara with the small village of Balgat. After locating the village chief, Tosun asked the chief how satisfied he was with life. The chief replied: "What could be asked more? God has brought me to this mature age without much pain, has given me sons and daughters, has put me at the head of my village, and has given me strength of brain and body at this age. Thanks be to Him."

The only non-farming person in Balgat was the village grocer. His response was markedly different from that of the chief:

> I have told you I want better things. I would have liked to have a bigger grocery shop in the city, have a nice house there, dress nice civilian clothes.... I am born a grocer and probably die that way. I have not the possibility in myself to get the things I want. They only bother me.

The grocer had made many trips to Ankara, with visits to shops and moviehouses. He had seen in a film the shop that he wanted, with "round boxes, clean and all the same dressed, like soldiers in a great parade." Yet the villagers of Balgat looked down on this shopkeeper, who was not a farmer like them. They also saw him as rejecting the worth of his own community, and even the supreme authority of Allah.

Tosun asked both men what they would do as president of Turkey. The chief would attempt to obtain "help of money and seed for some of our farmers." As for the grocer, his answer was not limited to helping the villagers of Balgat: "I would make roads for the villagers to come to towns to see the world and would not let them stay in their holes all their life." Yet another difference between the two men's responses to Tosun had to do with this question: "If you could not live in Turkey where would you want to live?" The chief's response was "Nowhere. I was born here, grew old here, and hope God will permit me to die here." Yet the grocer could imagine himself living outside of Turkey, as shown by this response: "America, because I have heard that it is a nice country and with possibilities to be rich even for the simplest persons." Yet the grocer's dreams were never fulfilled, for he died in Balgat several years later.

It was Lerner's study that was fundamental to the focus on the aspirations-fulfillment or expectations-fulfillment gap throughout the previous publication, *Beyond Sociology's Tower of Babel* (Phillips: 2001). It was there that the senior author introduced a schematic diagram (figure I.1), which is reproduced here with some modifications (2001: 20). This diagram, "The Invisible Crisis of Contemporary Society," is not based on any one specific study, but rather derived from many different studies suggesting the nature of the change from preindustrial to contemporary society. The top curve of rising expectations or aspirations illustrates the great difference between the chief's aspirations on the left-hand side (preindustrial society) and the grocer's aspirations on the right-hand side (contemporary society). As for the lower curve, fulfillment of expectations, we see that curve gradually moving toward the horizontal. As a result, the two curves are close to one another within preindustrial society and increasingly further apart as we

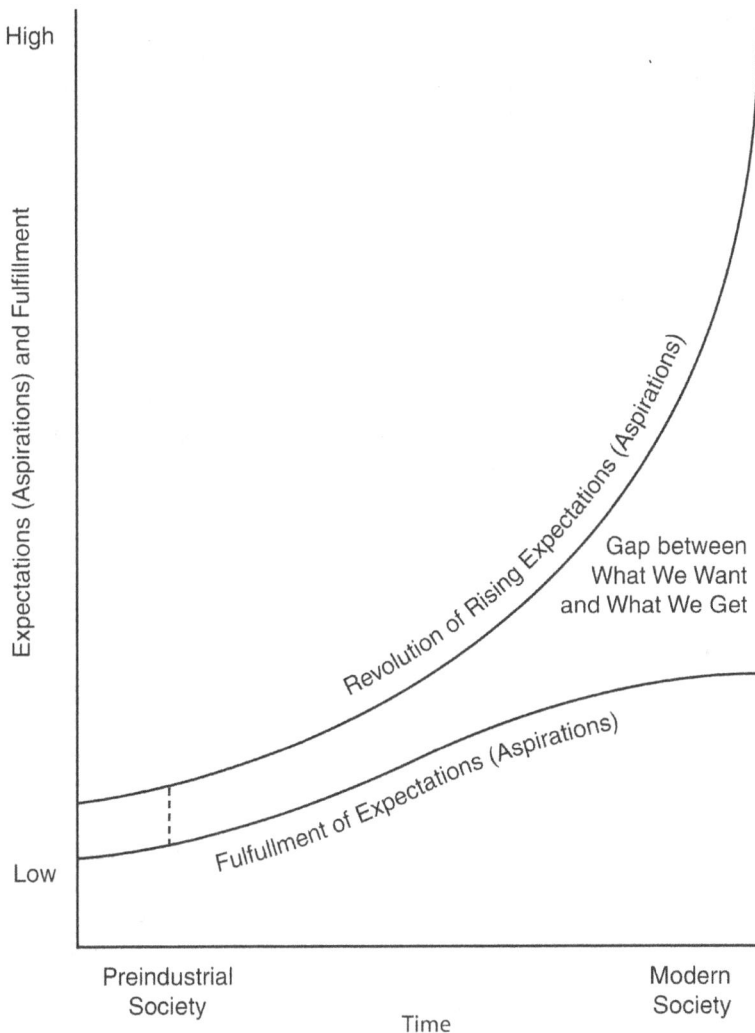

Figure I.1. The invisible crisis of contemporary society.

move into contemporary society, illustrating an increasing "gap between what we want and what we are able to get." We may see the chief as located on the left or preindustrial side off figure I.1 where the gap between the two curves is small ("What could be asked more?"). And we can see the grocer as located on the right or contemporary side of figure I.1, where the gap is very large ("I have told you I want better things"). These two individuals, taken together, suggest a long-term trend from preindustrial to contemporary society. The scientific and industrial revolutions beginning in the seventeenth century and continuing to the present day not only have transformed the physical world. They have also yielded what has been called a "revolution of rising expectations," where the modern individual has learned to want more and more yet has been unable to fulfill those accelerating desires to an increasing extent.

Both material and nonmaterial goals or values are involved in this revolution of rising expectations or aspirations. For example, the grocer not only wants "a bigger grocery shop in the city, have a nice house there, dress nice civilian clothes." He also would like to "make roads for the villagers to come to towns to see the world and would not let them stay in their holes all their life." His desire to help others is linked to fundamental and widely shared nonmaterial or intangible goals associated with political revolutions that accompanied the scientific and industrial revolution. For example, the American revolution pointed toward a government "of the people, by the people, and for the people," in Lincoln's words. And the French revolution emphasized the ideals of "liberty, equality, and fraternity." Those revolutions illustrate a great change: from an emphasis on hierarchy in government and elsewhere to a concern for equality and the worth of every individual.

Yet just as the grocer experienced hierarchy in his own village, where the farmers saw him as the lowest of the low, so do we all experience continuing hierarchy or social stratification in almost every aspect of life, despite our egalitarian ideals or values. This is a finding of modern social scientists that is backed up by literally thousands of studies. Persisting hierarchy is to be found not only in the world of work, where almost every occupation reflects it. We find it as well in the school, in church, in the family, in friendship groups, and in informal and fleeting relationships. Looking at figure I.1, the persistence of such hierarchies in all walks of life helps us to understand the failure of that lower curve—of the fulfillment of expectations or aspirations—to rise up to meet the upper curve of expectations or aspirations. It appears to be the case that patterns of social stratification or persisting hierarchy generally work to prevent the individual from fulfilling expectations. We can see from the limited rise of the bottom curve that there has indeed generally been some increase in that fulfillment, but that increase does not prevent a widening gap. Yet we must bear in mind that figure I.1 is no more than a schematic diagram, and that we will be gathering evidence on its validity throughout this book.

The English poet Robert Browning had something to say about this aspirations-fulfillment gap: "Ah, but a man's reach should exceed his grasp, Or what's a heaven for?" Browning is arguing that if we fail to create some gap between what we want and what we already have, then we drastically reduce our basic motivations. And it is those very motivations which are basic to our ability to fulfill our highest ideals. This suggests the idea that our curve of aspirations or expectations should indeed be above our curve of fulfillment in figure I.1, working to pull up that curve of fulfillment. Yet if we examine figure I.1 we find a much different situation, where the gap between the two curves continues to increase with no evidence that the upper curve is succeeding in pulling up the lower curve. Thus, what Browning suggests is an ideal situation which we might, hopefully, move into once we learn how to move our curve of fulfillment close to our curve of aspiration. We must first discover the nature of the forces preventing our fulfillment from moving up. As a result of those forces, we often choose to give up on our aspirations, coming to believe—as did the grocer of Balgat—that we cannot fulfill them. An alternative is to keep hope alive, which is a basis for the optimism of the scientific method.

The historian Daniel Boorstin published *The Image: A Guide to Pseudo-Events in America* (1961) a few years after Lerner's *The Passing of Traditional Society* appeared. Boorstin emphasized this problem of the aspirations-fulfillment or expectations-fulfillment gap:

> We expect anything and everything. We expect the contradictory and the impossible. We expect compact cars which are spacious; luxurious cars which are economical. We expect to be rich and charitable, powerful and merciful, active and reflective, kind and competitive. We expect to be inspired by mediocre appeals for "excellence," ... to eat and stay thin, to be constantly on the move and ever more neighborly ... to revere God and to be God. Never have people been more the masters of their environment. Yet never has a people felt more deceived and disappointed. For never has a people expected so much more than the world could offer (1961: 3-4).

This expectations-fulfillment gap that Boorstin describes has implications far beyond our resultant feelings of disappointment at not having a compact car that is spacious, not staying thin while eating, and not being ever more neighborly while being constantly on the move. There are also our expectations for peace and love in a world full of war, violence and prejudice; for safety in a world with increasingly deadly weapons, for equality in a world of hierarchy; for the well-being of the human race in a world of poverty and disease; and for institutions and people governed by reason in a world full of ignorance. These are some of the aspirations-fulfillment or expectations-fulfillment gaps referred to in the first paragraph of this Introduction. They are also contradictions between our ideals or cultural values and our actual practices which fail to help us fulfill those ideals. And this is the broad problem—linked to a great many specific problems—that will be our focus throughout this book.

It is the Web and Part/Whole Approach which enabled us to locate this broad problem. For one thing, that approach opens up to long-term historical situations, and this problem has been developing over at least the four centuries of the scientific and technological revolutions. Also, the Web and Part/Whole Approach opens up to both cultural values or aspirations (top curve of figure I.1) and patterns of social organization like stratification and bureaucracy that limit their fulfillment (bottom curve), phenomena usually kept separate and studied by different specialists. In addition, we have both the use of gradational language (emphasized in figure I.1) as well as dichotomous and metaphorical language (emphasized in the story of the grocer and the chief), suggesting the importance of both quantitative and qualitative research. Still further, it is an interactive rather than a stratified worldview or metaphysical stance which has enabled us to develop this epistemology or approach to the scientific method.

As for the title of this book, if we assume that the aspirations-fulfillment gap is increasing, then this suggests the development of a genuine crisis, indicating the ever greater frustration of fundamental cultural values and individual goals. It is the stuff that can easily lead to individual violence against others or against oneself. And all of this—given the highly abstract nature of cultural values or individual aspirations as well as the long-term genesis of this problem—remains relatively invisible. That invisibility makes the crisis all the more dangerous. For how are we to confront what we fail to see? In a war the enemy is concrete and we can thus more easily learn how to defend ourselves and also how to carry out offensives. But how do we fight what remains invisible?

Is this idea of an "invisible crisis" no more than hype to get an audience to pay attention to these ideas? Is it a piece with "gloom-and-doom" scenarios, designed to create fear in an audience? Does it have little relevance to the concrete day-to-day issues that all of us must face in everyday life? We think not. As for invisibility, how often do we look back at our own entire past, thinking of our myriad experiences as we proceed in everyday life? How frequently do we think of what happened in the nineteenth century, let alone during a stretch of four centuries? How often do we think of the entire history of the human race and to our potential future? How often do we blot out problems in the present and potential problems in the near future because we have no clue as to how they might be solved? How often is our awareness captured by the daily news cycle of the mass media with its focus on the last twenty-four hours of minor tragedies and minor accomplishments, all the while avoiding the big picture?

As for the presumably threatening nature of the aspirations-fulfillment gap and its possibly increasing size, to understand it more clearly we might compare it to Marx's thesis of a growing contradiction between the "forces of production" and the "relations of production" (Marx, 1849/1964: 147). With respect to the forces of production, Marx never emphasized the importance of culture, and it has been modern anthropology and sociology which have taught us its power and reach. We see that power and reach in a continuing revolution of rising expectations associated with the scientific and industrial revolutions. We see it also in ethnic conflicts in the Middle East that spawn terrorism, conflicts based on far more than concerns for a higher standard of living. Granting the heightening of materialistic expectations, there are also heightened nonmaterial expectations, as illustrated by the American civil rights movement, the women's movement and the gay/lesbian movement. Yet people generally fail to see how this powerful revolution of rising expectations or aspirations threatens all of us to the degree that it remains far from being fulfilled. That gap between the two curves of figure I.1 remains invisible, given its long-term and abstract nature. Marx's own historical perspective was, unfortunately, tied to a theory of inevitable class conflict. That idea certainly has not stood the test of time, although class conflict remains a most important phenomenon in contemporary society.

The relations of production have to do with the social organization of productive activities, including such universal patterns as social stratification and bureaucracy. Marx saw the impact of those relations on the individual worker in his essay on alienation, to be examined in chapter 4. He saw the phenomenon of alienation as encompassing all of the structures experienced by the worker: physical, biological, social and personality. And he saw that phenomenon as stretching far beyond the workplace to impact all aspects of society. A conclusion Marx drew, which has worked to discredit his powerful insights on alienation, was the necessity of a violent revolution that would establish a supposedly temporary dictatorship of the proletariat. Yet that conclusion is by no means essential to his argument for the alienating impact of patterns of stratification in the workplace. This is what the aspirations-fulfillment gap depicted in figure I.1 is all about. And Marx's view of it as affecting all structures parallels our own analysis of it as a child of a stratified worldview or metaphysical stance. Instead of a violent revolution that will unseat the bourgeoisie from power, what we appear to require is a cultural revolution—based on a more effective epistemology or scientific method—that will address our fundamental problems like alienation. Apparently, nothing less than such a revolution could succeed in closing the aspirations-fulfillment gap depicted in figure I.1's schematic diagram. Failing such a vast change in contemporary society, it appears that our "invisible crisis" may continue to become ever more threatening, just as figure I.1's aspirations-fulfillment gap continues to increase.

## The Plan of This Book

The chapter headings reflect an effort to build on key concepts developed within the literature of sociology and, to a lesser extent, psychology. We have, for example, the concepts of interaction, social relationships, social stratification, cultural values, anomie, alienation, labeling and conforming behavior. From psychology we have perception and reinforcement. Of course, many other concepts from the social sciences as well as philosophy are employed within the various chapters. We see this approach of building on existing literatures as essential to scientific ideals and also to our own approach. These basic concepts have often been abandoned by contemporary social scientists in their efforts to distance themselves from what they see as the simplistic contents of introductory textbooks, and generally in their attempt to become highly specialized as a basis for climbing the ladder of success. Yet we see those concepts—linked to a broad framework encompassing structures and the situation—as providing a backbone that can enable us to integrate highly specialized findings. Our argument is not against such specialization but rather against parts of a vast body of social science findings that remain unattached to one another.

The headings of chapters 1–11 all have the same dichotomous format, such as "Isolation versus Interaction" and "Outward versus Inward-Outward Perception." This reflects our interest in emphasizing both language's dichotomous and gradational potentials as well as our metaphysical assumptions. We see the left-hand side of these titles ("Isolation," "Outward Perception") as linked to a stratified worldview or metaphysical stance, with the right-hand side ("Interaction," "Inward-Outward Perception") linked to an interactive metaphysical stance. And we see the possibility of moving, gradationally, from the left-hand side to the right-hand side with respect to the phenomena discussed in each of these chapters. Realistically, we believe that presently we are all more or less close to the left-hand side or to a stratified worldview, and it is that metaphysical stance which prevents us from understanding the existence of our large aspirations-fulfillment gap. And we attach a sense of urgency to the idea of moving toward an interactive metaphysical stance, as suggested by the right-hand side of these chapter headings. Such movement will also take us away from our overemphasis on language's dichotomous potential and work to include language's gradational potential.

As for language's metaphorical potential, that is illustrated by references to "head," "heart" and "hand" in the headings of chapters 3–11. We see a lack of serious attention to metaphor—or, more generally, figures of speech—throughout the social sciences as a very serious failing. Our ideals for the scientific method call for effective communication to others as well as for the understanding by social scientists themselves of the significance of their own work. Yet this lack of attention to communication and understanding, which includes a lack of interest in the achievements of literature and the arts, compromises those ideals. It is a species of what C. P. Snow argued in his *The Two Cultures* (1959): "Literary intellectuals at one pole—at the other scientists." A key ideal of democracy is an educated electorate, and this requires communication between academics and ordinary folk. Lack of attention to figures of speech with its resulting lack of effective communication goes against that democratic ideal, making it difficult for the public to educate those in power to their responsibilities and to educate the sociologist about human behavior.

A central metaphor for this book as a whole, one that is not to be found in the table of contents, is figure I.1's schematic diagram with its increasing gap between the curves of aspiration and fulfillment. This is the problem on which all of the chapters are focused, with each chapter except the final one exploring one aspect of this problem. It is one thing to write about this accelerating gap, yet it is quite another thing to depict that gap with its ominous increase from preindustrial to contemporary times. We know of the importance of geometry within the history of mathematics as well as the importance of analytic geometry for the development of modern mathematics. It is visual representations, akin to figures of speech, which have helped mathematicians throughout the ages move up language's ladder of abstraction to their abstract ideas. And such images are no less important for social scientists grappling with the complexities of human behavior. Yet it remains for us to provide evidence that this gap is in fact increasing.

As for the contents of the various chapters, we might note the importance of imagery in the selections listed in the table of contents. For one thing, we have a number of pieces of fiction represented: Abbott's *Flatland* (chapter 1), Hesse's *Magister Ludi* (chapter 5), Orwell's *Nineteen Eighty-Four* (chapter 8), Hoyle's *The Black Cloud* (chapter 9), and Van Vogt's *The Players of Null-A* (chapter 10). Yet images are by no means limited to those fictional examples, for many of the pieces of nonfiction convey powerful images. For example, Ivan Illich presents in his *Deschooling Society* (chapter 8) a vision of social stratification throughout society as a kind of "schooling," where we all learn a "hidden curriculum" of conformity to the powers that be, just as children learn to conform to the desires of their teachers. His idea of "deschooling," then, is nothing less than a direction for getting rid of social stratification or persisting hierarchy in all of our institutions. This image of schooling suggests the immature nature of our societies. Illich's images of schooling and deschooling thus enable us to see more clearly the nature and implications of the abstract concept of social stratification.

A more well-known and influential example can be taken from Nietzsche's *The Gay Science* (chapter 6), where he developed the idea that God is dead. When we understand that metaphor as invoking not just religious hierarchy but also patterns of persisting hierarchy or social stratification throughout society, then we can see it as constituting a powerful force for reinforcing sociological knowledge of the near-universality of those patterns. But there are many other examples of metaphorical power within the nonfiction books examined here. For example, there is Chua's title of her book, *World on Fire* (chapter 7). There is Lundberg's image of a governmental official attempting "to fly the modern stratoliner without an instrument board or charts" (chapter 11). There is Levin's image of human relationships as a kind of "see-saw" (chapter 3). There is Marx's view of the workplace as producing workers who are "crude and misshapen," who are "slave[s] of nature," who live in "hovels," and who exhibit "cretinism" (chapter 4).

Our argument in the above pages pointed toward the existence of an increasing gap between expectations and their fulfillment in contemporary society. Yet we view that argument as no more than an introduction to this idea of a growing gap, rather than providing substantial evidence for its existence. We wished to establish an intuitive basis for the hypothesis that will be tested within the following chapters, the first of the two basic hypotheses in this book:

1. *The gap between aspirations and their fulfillment is in fact increasing in contemporary society.*

Evidence supporting this hypothesis would indicate that we are in fact threatened by an invisible crisis at this time in history. Such evidence would help us to understand the breadth and fundamental nature of the threat we are facing. And as a result we could learn to convert our invisible crisis into a visible one as a basis for confronting it effectively. The overall result would be much the same as an early warning system for the emergence of a monster tsunami, a wave large enough to threaten contemporary society as a whole. Presently, the social sciences have failed us in providing such an early warning system, and the results may well prove to be catastrophic.

Yet evidence for the existence of such an invisible crisis is not evidence bearing on how it might be confronted effectively, and that has to do with our second hypothesis:

2. *To the degree that a worldview or metaphysical stance is stratified versus interactive, there will be a large gap between aspirations and their fulfillment.*

This has been our argument in the above pages as well as in prior publications, and the time has come to develop more systematic and comprehensive evidence bearing on it. Of course, a worldview or metaphysical stance is by no means the only factor behind a large aspirations-fulfillment gap, and we hope that this study will encourage others to investigate such factors as well to corroborate the findings presented here. But a worldview or metaphysical stance appears to be the most invisible factor involved as well as the one that is most difficult to measure. And it may well prove to be the most important force operating to widen the gap between aspirations and their fulfillment, given its fundamental nature with its implications for every aspect of contemporary society.

Yet how can such extremely broad propositions be tested? Surely not with the traditional and highly specialized approach that conforms to a stratified worldview. For example, we are dealing with an extremely long stretch of time. Further, the gap has to do with both culture and patterns of social organization like stratification, two fields of knowledge that generally are kept very far apart by sociologists. And we must pay attention to physical, biological and personality structures, to social structure and also to the momentary situation as well as long-term history, fields of knowledge kept even further apart throughout the academic world. It is by shifting to the Web and Part/Whole Approach to the scientific method that we aim to carry forward scientific ideals into the complex realm of human behavior and link all of these phenomena. That approach also implies a metaphysical stance or worldview: an interactive versus a stratified worldview. It also involves a central ideal of the scientific method: addressing, over time, more and more of the forces relevant to the defined problem. The promise of this approach is not simply for the problem at hand but for all social science research. If it indeed proves to be effective, then it provides a direction for carrying forward scientific ideals into the range of complex problems that we humans face.

The practical difficulties involved in testing our two extremely broad hypotheses, even with the aid of the Web and Part/Whole Approach, dictate that we make them more manageable. Our focus will be on the kinds of aspirations or expectations that are associated with existing cultural values throughout contemporary society, given that those values summarize the aspirations that are widely shared by individuals. For example, there are the cultural values of equality, freedom, individual worth and democracy. Thus, unique or idiosyncratic aspirations by particular individuals are not involved here. As for the fulfillment of expectations, our focus will be on the degree to which patterns of social stratification or persisting hierarchy exist throughout society. Such stratification, which contrasts with egalitarian interaction, restricts the fulfillment of people-oriented cultural values like equality, freedom and democracy. Also, stratification restricts the fulfillment of work-related cultural values—like achievement and success—for most individuals, given its invidious nature. As for the nature of "contemporary" society, our focus will be on the past four centuries, which have seen the origins and development of the scientific and industrial revolutions along with the continuing development of technologies primarily based on biophysical science.

In our effort to avoid a narrow approach to our two hypotheses in this book, we have centered on secondary analyses of previously collected data—or previous theoretical, philosophical or literary arguments or examples—from thirty-three different works, three for each of the following eleven chapters. Such an approach is unusual but by no means unprecedented inside or outside of the social sciences. For example,"meta-analysis" procedures in preventive medicine collate thousands of studies and therapies in order to reach overall conclusions within a reasonable period of time. Within sociology the secondary analysis of data sets from a variety of archives—such as that for the U.S. Census—is a well-established procedure. Yet a major problem within secondary analysis is that the original data were collected for purposes other than those of the secondary analyst. Thus, the measurements employed within secondary analysis must make do with data not specifically designed for the purposes of the secondary analyst. Balancing this defect, however, is the credibility deriving from the use of multiple studies.

However, what is new in our own approach to secondary analysis is an emphasis on the abstract conclusions of the author or investigator rather than on the specific data collected in a given study. For those conclusions often carry the author's central images by contrast with the specific data obtained, granting the importance of such data. And it is those images, illustrating a key potential of language that social and biophysical scientists generally neglect, which are no less important than language's dichotomous and gradational potential for helping us to understand the complexities of human behavior. This is also why the thirty-three selections in this book include the work of philosophers and literary figures along with social scientists, for we desperately need their contributions to imagery in order to understand our situation as human beings and the problems we are facing at this time in history. This is not at all a question of viewing those authors as second-class citizens who have been given grudging permission to be heard. Rather, their ideas are absolutely essential if we are to understand the invisible crisis of contemporary society, and they provide balance to the sociologist's orientation to dichotomy and—to a lesser extent—to gradation.

Of course, tests of our two hypotheses on the basis of new studies involving primary data would be most welcome. Such studies might develop measurement procedures that would help to shed light on these hypotheses. Our own focus on secondary analysis was not at all a rejection of the importance of primary data. Rather, our dominant aim was to demonstrate how to make use of the knowledge that is presently available in bits and pieces throughout diverse literatures, and we saw secondary analyses of existing works as most appropriate relative to this aim. It is indeed possible to connect those dots by means of secondary analyses without mounting new studies, granting that the measurements involved are far from ideal. To the extent that we can demonstrate the fruitfulness of secondary analyses, we will make it easier to follow the scientific ideal of opening up to all phenomena relevant to a given problem. Thus, for example, we can work toward building bridges connecting the specialized and subspecialized fields throughout the social sciences. As such integration proceeds, a platform of knowledge of human behavior can be built which pulls together what has already been learned. Such a platform could, then, become a far better basis for basic and applied work than specialized efforts based on limited knowledge of the complexities of a given problem. Such work need not await some long-term goal of completing the construction of such a platform, but rather could proceed as soon as that platform demonstrates its possibility of including a wide range of knowledge.

It is crucial that the data presented in this book allow for us to falsify these hypotheses. Ideally, the works in this book should have been selected by means of a probability sample of the "population" of all work that has ever been published bearing on the gap between aspirations or expectations and their fulfillment. More realistically, we might have chosen all published books in English over the past two centuries that are available on loan from American libraries, granting that important books and especially articles would be missed. If this had been done, then the works selected for inclusion in our secondary analysis could have been viewed as representative of that large population. In other words, conclusions about the "internal validity" of the hypothesis, based only on the analysis of the studies included here, would also have constituted conclusions about that hypothesis's "external validity," namely, the applicability of that hypothesis to that entire population, taking into account some margin for error. However, developing such a probability sample would not have been a practical undertaking, despite its ideal nature. For we would have had to construct a complete listing of that population, and we would have had to read every book in order to assess its relevance for hypothesis (1) before a probability sample could have been drawn on the basis of that list. That would have involved a great many years of work by a great many researchers.

Instead, we chose a research design that is a "purposive or judgmental sample," which is a type of non-probability sample chosen so as to utilize theoretical insights and practical concerns (Phillips, 1985: 191–192). As such, there is no longer an excellent basis for falsifying the hypothesis by concluding that its internal validity—resulting from the analysis in these pages—is the same as its external validity. Nevertheless, there are several reasons to believe that the hypothesis has been given at least a fair chance to be falsified. Our first consideration was to include studies which ranged very widely over the basic phenomena studied within the social sciences, as indicated by the headings of chapters 1–11. Those studies include physical and biological phenomena, and they emphasize personality structures, social structures and the situation. Within each of those latter three categories that have been emphasized, we felt it important to include studies focusing on the intellectual, emotional and active or interactive components of human behavior. This approach is fundamental to our Web and Part/Whole

Approach to the scientific method. Such breadth yields a wide range of opportunities for discrediting our hypothesis.

Our rationale for examining this diversity of studies is that an understanding of aspirations or expectations and their degree of fulfillment—along with a worldview—should be reflected in the study of any aspect of human behavior whatsoever, given the breadth of our hypotheses. Concerning the particular studies selected, our focus was on choosing those classical and contemporary studies that appeared to bear most directly on the hypotheses and that had the greatest credibility among social scientists, philosophers and literary people. This included, for example, work by Boorstin, Durkheim, Freire, Goffman, Gouldner, Horney, Hesse, Illich, Kuhn, Marx, Mead, Merton, Mills, Nietzsche, Orwell, Peirce and Simmel. Also, it was not practical to examine entire books, given the number of studies involved, and we had to make do with excerpts from those books. This by no means guarantees the external validity of those studies, yet it does provide at least some evidence for external validity.

A basic aspect of the Web and Part/Whole Approach is reflexivity—as suggested by Alvin Gouldner—where the researcher includes an analysis of self and his or her own impact on every stage of the investigation. In this way, the reader will be able to take that impact into account in assessing the study. Accomplishing this involves a full-blown additional study that would be particularly difficult because of the researcher's inability or unwillingness to confront personal limitations. Such a study—which is extremely rare—has not been undertaken here, and this limits our own usage of the Web and Part/Whole Approach and should be taken into account with reference to the conclusions to be drawn. We believe that it is most important for social scientists to move in this direction. We openly confess our own belief in the utility of the Web and Part/Whole Approach as well as in an interactive worldview. We believe in the importance of our two hypotheses, although we have attempted to make at least some room for their being falsified.

A key problem in this analysis is the fact that none of the excerpts from the studies examined in this book provided an illustration of all eleven of the factors we conceived of as linked to a given worldview or metaphysical stance. And the fact that we had no measurements constructed specifically for those factors, given the secondary nature of our analyses, made it difficult to infer the stance of a given author. As a result, we decided to focus on only one of those eleven factors for each study. Yet those eleven factors are all inferred from the same epistemological analysis of a contrast between a traditional approach to the scientific method and the Web and Part/Whole Approach oriented to scientific ideals. Further, they all are linked to a contrast between a narrow approach to language and one that builds on language's imagery along with its dichotomous and gradational potential. Still further, these eleven factors are all linked to a given worldview.

Consequently, we assume that commitment to either the stratified or the interactive part of any one of those eleven pairs will constitute at least partial evidence for commitment to its associated worldview.

As for the organization of this book, we divide those eleven factors into four parts—beginning with part II of the book—focusing on (II) physical and biological structures, (III) personality structures, (IV) social structures and (V) the situation. Yet the ideas within the chapters in each part are such as to avoid isolation from the ideas in the other parts, following our Web and Part/Whole Approach. At the end of each chapter in the section on "Some Implications," we examine the implications of the three studies presented in that chapter for our two hypotheses. And we pay special attention to the figures of speech to be found within the chapter. It is there that we also briefly examine those hypotheses in relation to the literature of sociology and—to a limited extent—to the literature of other social sciences. By so doing we suggest directions for building bridges connecting diverse pieces of those literatures which otherwise would remain isolated. And in a final chapter in part VI on conclusions and implications, we focus on integrating what we've learned about our two hypotheses, and we carry their implications further.

As we proceed to chapter 1, let us not lose sight of the problem that we are addressing: the invisible crisis of contemporary society. We might compare this problem to that of the 1918 influenza virus that killed between 20 million and 50 million people, and to the present threat from the H5N1 bird flu virus, taking into account the three-fold increase in the world's population. Those problems are at least visible ones and thus can at least be confronted. An increasing aspirations-fulfillment gap is very largely invisible, and thus requires successful efforts to make it visible before it can be confronted. As a result of the present study we can at least (1) begin to make the aspirations-fulfillment problem visible, (2) begin to understand whether that gap is increasing, and (3) begin to learn whether our worldview or metaphysical stance is working to generate that gap. The threatening potential of an increasing gap, should it exist, extends to the entire world population, given that gap's involvement in the range of fundamental problems throughout contemporary society. Let us not forget that it is our sense of problem—the first and most important step of the scientific method—which is our fundamental basis for learning about and solving the invisible crisis of contemporary society. This involves attention to the "heart" no less than the "head" and the "hand." The resulting balance can help the sociologist—and everyone else—weave "our meteoric shower of facts" into a "fabric" that can confront our invisible crisis.

# PART II

# Physical and Biological Structures

Few social scientists emphasize the importance of physical and biological structures in their analysis of human behavior. Yet a broad approach to the scientific method demands that those structures be included within any comprehensive analysis of human behavior. This view does not require that every research project undertaken at this time must include those structures. From the pragmatic perspective of Charles Sanders Peirce, we have the dictum—"Do not block the way of inquiry"—which is a perspective that we shall examine in chapter 6. That dictum points us toward our continuing development of an understanding of human behavior without any limits. Whatever the limits within present investigations, they conform to Peirce's advice insofar as they point toward improving that understanding in the future. And that improvement includes seriously addressing the role of physical and biological structures.

Physical and biological structures appeared long before our social and personality structures. By taking them into account we are also going far back in history, even to the origins of the universe. The dimension of time is involved no less than broad attention to all structures. Yet, one might ask, are those structures really so important? Although attention to them might satisfy some abstract ideal for comprehensiveness and a long-term perspective, are they genuinely relevant to our understanding of human behavior, given so many other factors that should be taken into account? It is exactly such questions that we shall explore in part II.

At this point, however, we can at least begin to examine the relevance of physical and biological structures for an analysis of human behavior. It is difficult to imagine a metaphysical stance or worldview which does not include attention to physical and biological structures. It is true that within the history of Western philosophy there has been a turning toward emphasizing the importance of human behavior, as illustrated by the work of the British empiricists, by Marx and Hegel, and by the newer philosophies of pragmatism and existentialism. Yet all of that attention should not take away from the importance of physical and biological structures. A metaphysical stance or worldview must be comprehensive if it is indeed to constitute a worldview. This is important not just for its impact on limiting or opening up our approach to the scientific method. It is also important for reasons that as yet we do not understand, given our limited knowledge of human complexity.

Chapters 1 and 2 emphasize physical and biological structures, respectively. Within sociology the fields of ecology and demography have been oriented to these structures, but they have never succeeded in achieving much integration with the rest of the discipline. The fault lies on both sides of the equation: with the ecologists and demographers, and also with the rest of the tribe of sociologists. And it appears to be a fault not limited to theories, and even not limited to epistemology, but a fault going back to square one: a metaphysical stance that can trump both theory and methods. This current approach to physical and biological structures illustrates a simplistic orientation, for opening up to the importance of physical structures and our biological nature would greatly increase the complexity of any analysis of human behavior.

The dichotomous nature of the two chapter headings reflects contrasting epistemological and metaphysical stances. By viewing the different components of the universe as isolated from one another ("Isolation"), we simplify the task of understanding the nature of the universe. And by limiting our perception to an outer orientation ("Outward Perception"), we avoid the complexity that would accompany our looking both inward and outward. The rationale for attention to the right-hand side of the two headings ("Interaction" and "Inward-Outward Perception") stems from the assumption that human behavior is indeed quite complicated. Yet the choice of a simplistic epistemology and metaphysics flies in the face of that complexity. That choice, which also violates the scientific ideal of openness to all relevant phenomena, apparently is not made deliberately and consciously. Our argument is that by bringing our stratified epistemological and metaphysical assumptions up to the light of day, we can learn to become aware of their problematic nature and move into a position to alter them. Having the alternative epistemological and metaphysical stance suggested by these chapter headings increases the likelihood that we will act on the basis of that awareness.

As for chapter 1, "Isolation versus Interaction," physicists have taught us that our physical universe is of such a nature that no phenomenon can remain in complete isolation from any other phenomenon. Although it is far simpler for us to focus on certain parts of the universe while ignoring everything else, everything else nevertheless is interacting with those particular parts, even if only very indirectly and to an infinitesimal extent. For example, within our physical universe there can be no such thing as a perfect vacuum, for the walls of the vacuum's container would be bombarded by phenomena from the rest of the universe, transmitting energy to the interior of the container. And those walls would also project outward the impact of phenomena from the inside, thus interacting with phenomena outside the container. It is interaction, then, and not isolation, which is programmed into the very nature of the universe.

Apparently the universe is becoming ever more interactive when we consider the huge role that interaction comes to play in organisms, let alone us creatures with language. This suggests the importance not only of a metaphysics emphasizing complexity but of a metaphysics emphasizing the increasing complexity manifested by human beings. Thus, the very nature of the physical universe suggests the importance of human behavior, for we illustrate the direction in which our universe is evolving. And it is the entire history of the universe—stretching over some fourteen billion years—which points toward our own importance and toward the centrality of the process of interaction.

Granting the enormous achievements of biophysical scientists in depicting the nature of the universe, it is essential that we also understand their limitations so that we are able to go beyond those achievements in learning about the nature of human behavior. For example, in chapter 1 we will note the importance of the fields of cybernetics and general system theory as developed by biophysical scientists. Yet we will also note the deficiencies of those fields for penetrating the nature of human behavior when they are not combined with the achievements of social scientists. It has been tempting for biophysical scientists to ignore those achievements, given their own status relative to that of social scientists. And it has been equally tempting for social scientists to emphasize the tools of biophysical scientists—such as mathematics—at the expense of qualitative tools that are often more important at this stage of the development of social science. When qualitative procedures are combined with quantitative ones, we have the best of both worlds, since this generally results in a more comprehensive study. One illustration is our own combining of figure I.1 with the story of the grocer and the chief.

In chapter 2 we focus on a key aspect of our biological nature: how we perceive ourselves and the world. This by no means implies that other aspects of human biology are unimportant. Our focus on perception stems largely from its proximity to our sensory abilities. Images precede language, and we should note the importance of the senses in all forms of life. For example, the idea of "worldview" contains the idea of perception. In our "view"—note the importance of perception as a metaphor within ordinary language—attention to perception will help us to "see" the links between our behavior and our biological nature. This does not mean that biology takes precedence over non-biological aspects of human behavior. Rather, the situation appears to be one of interaction. When we no longer ignore perception, then we gain a basis for understanding the importance of linguistic images and metaphors. This is not a question of biology versus language but rather of biology and language working together. Such interaction also implies change in both patterns of perception and patterns of linguistic usage. And it may well prove to be the case—as suggested by the heading of chapter 2—that we have to learn how we can use language to shift our metaphysical stance so as to move from outward perception toward inward-outward perception.

We might note the considerable literature developed within the field of psychology that bears on the nature of human perception. Given that the emphasis in this book is on sociology, we can do little more in chapter 2 than refer to that literature in passing. Yet a great deal more should be done to examine the relationship between that literature and the central arguments in this book. For example, to what extent does work done in the field of attribution theory support or contradict our two hypotheses? What about work in the general field of cognitive science? How about work in the area of social perception and perception? These are questions that can only be hinted at in this book, yet answers to them might serve to link those literatures far more closely to the literature of sociology. And by so doing they would constitute a further step toward the integration of our knowledge of human behavior.

## CHAPTER 1

# Isolation versus Interaction

*FLATLAND: A ROMANCE OF MANY DIMENSIONS,* a science-fiction novel written in 1884, describes a two-dimensional world invaded by a Sphere who kidnaps a Square and introduces him to the complexities of the three-dimensional world of Spaceland. Yet it is by means of this example that the reader can learn to understand the complexities of our own four-dimensional Timeland. We swim in the present, on the surface of a deep ocean that includes both the history of the world and our own personal history. Apparently we rarely go below that surface, and when we do we do not go down very far. However, we are largely shaped by that ocean of the past, and as a result we remain largely ignorant of where we have come from, who we are and where we are going. These metaphors are certainly not what social scientists are accustomed to emphasizing, given the clear separation between "the two cultures" of science and literature which C. P. Snow has described (1959). Yet they can help us to understand ourselves more fully.

Walter Buckley's *Sociology and Modern Systems Theory* (1967) was written at a time when general systems theory, cybernetics and information theory—ideas emerging from biological and physical science—held out great promise for helping social scientists cope with the complexity of human behavior. Their promise today is more limited, yet it is nevertheless real. For example, the simple idea of "feedback loop" alerts us to far greater complexity in understanding cause-effect relationships among phenomena than is assumed by the common one-way cause-effect relationship emphasized within the social sciences. The problem faced by sociologists is how to integrate that sophisticated orientation with current research.

*Tight Spaces: Hard Architecture and How to Humanize It* is about our small-scale rather than our large-scale architecture. It contrasts "hard architecture"—such as immovable classroom seats in neat rows facing the instructor's desk or podium—with "soft architecture," which makes it easy for people to interact. Soft architecture is illustrated by movable chairs which might be arranged in a circle to give students the opportunity to interact with one another. Yet soft architecture is not enough to achieve such interaction, since the author found that university students arriving before class generally rearranged chairs that they had found to be in a circle into neat rows facing the instructor's podium. Educational ideals generally call for students and instructors to emphasize the importance of interaction. However, apparently there are forces which work against those ideals. In this case it appears to be a stratified worldview emphasizing a pattern of social stratification as between instructor and student that trumps the cultural value of equality along with educational ideals.

## Abbott's *Flatland: A Romance of Many Dimensions*

Edwin A. Abbott was a schoolmaster primarily interested in literature and theology. Here is his description of the two-dimensional world of Flatland and what happened to the Square who was introduced by a Sphere to the three-dimensional world of Spaceland:

> Square: I call our world Flatland, not because we call it so, but to make its nature clearer to you, my happy readers, who are privileged to live in Space. Imagine a vast sheet of paper on which straight Lines, Triangles, Squares, Pentagons, Hexagons, and other figures, instead of remaining fixed in their places, move freely about, on or in the surface, but without the power of rising above or sinking below it, very much like shadows—only hard and with luminous edges—and you will then have a pretty correct notion of my country and countrymen....
>
> Sphere: I have told you I can see from my position in Space the inside of all things that you consider closed. For example, I see in yonder cupboard ... two tablets of accounts. I am about to descend into that cupboard and to bring you one of those tablets. I saw you lock the cupboard half an hour ago, and I know you have the key in your possession....
>
> Square: I rushed to the closet and dashed the door open. One of the tablets was gone. With a mocking laugh, the Stranger appeared in the other corner of the room, and at the same time the tablet appeared upon the floor. I took it up. There could be no doubt—it was the missing tablet (1884/1952: 3, 77–78).

The Square remains unconvinced, and the Sphere takes him on a journey upward out of his plane to enable him to see Flatland through Spaceland eyes. He looks down and is able to see into all of the rooms in his own two-dimensional house, finally coming to believe in the existence of a third dimension. He is enchanted by his new vision of the world as he opens his eyes to wonders he had never expected to see. When the Sphere returns him to Flatland and departs, the Square is anxious to tell his countrymen about his experiences and the reality of a three-dimensional world. But just as the Sphere was unable, initially, to convince the Square of that reality, so is the Square unable to convince anyone in Flatland of a third dimension. As a result of his seditious remarks he is imprisoned for life, voicing this lament:

> Hence I am absolutely destitute of converts, and, for aught that I can see, the millennial Revelation has been made to me for nothing. Prometheus up in Spaceland was bound for bringing down fire for mortals, but I— poor Flatland Prometheus—lie here in prison for bringing down nothing to my countrymen. Yet I exist in the hope that these memoirs, in some manner, I know not how, may find their way to the minds of humanity in Some Dimension, and may stir up a race of rebels who shall refuse to be confined to limited Dimensionality (1884/1952: 102).

If the inhabitants of Flatland remain prisoners of their assumptions about the nature of the world, is this true of us as well? If they refused to accept the possibility of a third dimension, do we see our universe as Spaceland and all the while reject the importance of a fourth dimension of time? If they limited their own personal development by confining themselves to two dimensions, are we largely limiting ourselves by confining ourselves to three dimensions? More specifically, are we in fact creatures of Timeland who neglect to pay much attention to the fourth dimension of time? Do we focus almost exclusively on the knife-edge of the present rather than on the past or the future? Does such a simplified focus also imply a stratified epistemological and metaphysical stance? Our own answers to all of these questions are affirmative.

For example, how frequently do we think about our own past experiences, let alone apply what we've learned in those situations to our present experiences? How frequently do we apply our knowledge of past history to the world problems that exist in the present? And even if we do these things to some extent, just how far back do we go in personal or world history? Do we go back as far as the Middle Ages? To the times of Ancient Rome, Greece and the Middle East? To the times when agriculture was invented? To the eras before human beings learned to write? To the evolution of life before human beings appeared? To the nature of the universe before life began? Do we almost invariably continue to swim on the surface of the ocean of time, centering on the present while ignoring the depths representing the past or the sky representing the future?

The importance for social scientists of paying attention to the distant past is illustrated by Lerner's study of the change from preindustrial to industrial society, as discussed in the Introduction. In order to understand the nature of "the invisible crisis of contemporary society," namely, the gap between aspirations and their fulfillment, it is essential that we go back to a scientific and industrial revolution that stretched over at least four centuries. However, contemporary research in the social sciences almost invariably fails to take into account such long stretches of history. And if this is the case for social scientists, we might expect it to be the case for the rest of us even more so. As a result of this Spaceland versus Timeland perspective, we appear to lose out on understanding the fundamental problems of contemporary society. And in our everyday lives we appear to be much like the Square, whose Flatland perspective prevented him from understanding his location in a Spaceland world. In our own case, we become victims of threatening problems which we fail to understand. As George Santayana claimed, "Those who cannot learn from history are doomed to repeat it."

Flatland illustrates the importance of language's dichotomous, gradational and metaphorical or image-oriented potential. For one thing, we have the sharp and dichotomous contrast between Flatland and Spaceland, as well as between Spaceland and Timeland. For another thing, we have the gradational orientation of the time dimension, alerting us to the potential significance of any given moment, by contrast with a focus solely on the knife-edge of the present moment. And there are also the metaphors of Flatland, Spaceland and Timeland, which give us images of different worlds based on different metaphysical assumptions. We can remember those images more clearly than abstract concepts, and they can thus help us to understand our present situation and future possibilities.

## Buckley's *Sociology and Modern Systems Theory*

Although the physical and biological sciences have largely ignored the complexities of human behavior, they have nevertheless contributed a great deal to social science. Perhaps first and foremost are the enormous achievements of biophysical science in penetrating the mysteries of physical and biological phenomena. The optimism that resulted about the possibilities of the scientific method have encouraged the social sciences from their very beginnings until the present day. There are also specific ways in which those sciences have contributed to an understanding of the scientific method, and Walter Buckley's *Sociology and Modern Systems*

*Theory* (1967) centers on one of them. It was during World War II that new concepts such as "system" and "feedback" began to appear, and it was in the decade after the war that the new fields of general systems theory (Bertalanffy, 1950) and cybernetics (Wiener, 1954) began to be developed. These fields opened up new scientific tools for confronting the complexity of human behavior.

One of those tools has to do with metaphysical assumptions, worldviews or cultural paradigms. Buckley is not very specific about the exact nature of those tools, but he considers them to be most important:

> Scientific work, analytically speaking, goes on at three, not two, distinguishable levels: besides empirical research and logico-deductive theory we have the equally important, though all too implicit, frameworks, models, or philosophies that inform our approach to both of the former (1967: viii).

Following Buckley, the human mind is not, contrary to John Locke, a *tabula rasa*. For example, scientists build theory not simply from whatever is observed but also on the basis of metaphysical assumptions.

We noted in the above discussion of *Flatland* the potential importance of the time dimension for understanding human behavior, contrasting a Flatland focus on the knife-edge of the present with a Timeland orientation to the past, the present and the future. Buckley builds on this idea by going back into the process of biological evolution and contrasting the far greater complexity of human beings with the complexity of other organisms. It is we humans with the aid of language, and no other organism, who can look far back into the past, even to the very origins of the universe. It is also we humans who can gaze far forward into the future, even much further than our own personal deaths, and even into the death of the earth and far beyond. We are able to bring the past and the future into the knife-edge of the present moment. Buckley sees that the complexity of physical systems is as nothing compared to that of biological systems and that the complexity of biological systems is as nothing compared to that of socio-cultural systems.

What has been the reaction of sociologists in devising research methods that take that complexity into account? Buckley has some critical words to say:

> During most of the present century, sociology has devoted its energies to the establishment of basic propositions showing that one part or aspect of society is related to another part or aspect: religion is related to voting, solidarity is related to suicide, education is related to class, delinquency is related to group association, and so forth.... Now that the groundwork has been laid, however, we have begun to ask much

more complete questions and to seek to understand the more detailed mechanisms underlying the development, maintenance, and change of the established societal interrelationships. On the theoretical level, the notion of society as a system has been around for some time, but it has been unable ... to carry us very far toward an adequate analysis of the more complex questions. It has rightly insisted that at least many parts of a social system are related to many other parts, but the theory—especially as interpreted by the functionalists—has failed to offer any program of research that does more than admonish us to go out there and trace the interrelations of all the parts or even more narrowly, to trace out the "consequences" of any part for any other part. And research methodology has hardly begun to think beyond relatively simple, traditional statistical techniques to the methods needed to get at a system of complexly interacting parts (1967: 66–67).

Sociological theory may well call for a methodological approach that takes into account the complexity of "a system of complexly interacting parts," but the fact is that methodology fails to fulfill that requirement. Is this still the case after two generations since Buckley's book was published? Apparently so, despite the emergence of many sophisticated techniques of multivariate analysis. A key problem seems to be that the sociologist's conformity to a simplistic worldview has hardened the separation between the specialized areas of theory and methodology, where the two orientations are not located within the same individual and where methodologists and theorists communicate only too rarely. Largely as a result, Buckley's challenging book fell on deaf ears.

However, developments by Jay Forrester, an engineer who joined the Sloan School of Management at MIT in the 1960s, carried forward earlier ideas from general systems theory and cybernetics. Forrester and his colleagues developed a computer simulation software package—known as "system dynamics"—which provided highly sophisticated methodological procedures for taking into account the complexity called for by Buckley. Forrester addressed management problems, teaching graduate students with no physical science background to use such procedures as part of an M.B.A. program. He described his approach in an initial book, *Principles of Systems* (1968), and then he and his colleagues proceeded to apply them to urban problems (1969) and world problems (1971; Meadows et al., 1972). Just as in the case of earlier work on general systems theory, cybernetics and information theory, there were high hopes that the new methodology would solve fundamental problems. This time, however, it was problems of human behavior which were addressed and not simply physical or biological problems.

Yet the problem of understanding human complexity proved to be far more difficult than the system dynamics group had anticipated. For example, we find almost no references to the social science literature in the books they produced, revealing a narrow approach to the scientific method. Instead of paying attention to the hard-won insights producing such concepts as "social stratification," "cultural values," "definition of the situation," "anomie," "alienation," "social interaction" and "self image," the group was content to work with concepts from everyday speech located at a low level of linguistic abstraction. Instead of finding ways to obtain the many measurements which their complex models demanded, they satisfied themselves by multiplying their assumptions. And instead of moving up language's ladder of abstraction to confront their own metaphysical assumptions, they continued with assumptions that paid little attention to what social scientists had discovered, all the while that the complexity of human behavior required something better. For example, their worldview did not alert them to the importance of including the behavior of system dynamics consultants within the business models that they developed, thus failing to assess investigator effect (Phillips, 1980).

Nevertheless, the work on system dynamics will not have been in vain provided that bridges are built connecting that work with social science knowledge. The dream of Walter Buckley for a methodology that will address the complexity of human behavior can indeed come to be fulfilled, for system dynamics does not require an all-or-none approach. Rather, one can move in stages toward the complexities of computer simulation. For example, Forrester's colleagues have developed a detailed description of those stages, which include the relatively simple procedure of developing a "causal-loop diagram" (Roberts, et al., 1983). Such diagrams need not involve a large number of concepts or variables along with a large number of assumptions. Since they involve feedback loops and systems, they point the investigator away from the simplistic one-way analyses of selected elements of a system, which constitutes the bulk of quantitative research within the social sciences. Most important, such analyses are not limited to using concepts from the vernacular, since they can easily employ fundamental concepts from the literature of sociology. The senior author has used such causal-loop diagrams in *Beyond Sociology's Tower of Babel* (Phillips, 2001: 32, 36, 127, 205), and a colleague has used them in *Toward a Sociological Imagination* (Jacobsen, 2002: 68–84).

## Sommer's *Tight Spaces: Hard Architecture and How to Humanize It*

If we are interested in the contrast between physical isolation and interaction, then small-scale physical structures are no less important than the large-scale ones illustrated by the design of cities. Hard architecture, like benches in a park that cannot be moved into the shade, or immovable chairs in a classroom that all face toward a podium at the front of the room, is designed to resist any human imprint along with the possibility of vandalism. At the same time, however, hard architecture gets in the way of human interaction, such as students interacting with one another. Robert Sommer, the author of *Tight Spaces,* focuses on the classroom in this excerpt from his book:

> We turn now to the second phase of the study to learn whether or not a rearrangement of the room would appreciably increase the amount of student participation. In these sessions, the observer arrived at the room just as the previous class was leaving. He then quickly converted the straight rows into a circular arrangement, an operation that took less than 60 seconds. At the time he rearranged the chairs, the observer did not know which particular class would be using the room in the next hour.
>
> The data here were not what we expected. We had hoped to compare participation in the circular arrangement with participation in sessions when the chairs were in straight rows. In this case, we found that twenty of the twenty-five classes rearranged the chairs back into straight rows before the class began! This was true for small classes as it was for larger ones, and for social science classes as well as natural science classes. What was most discouraging was that students were often the instigators in returning to row arrangements, sometimes before the instructor even arrived. In several cases the instructor made negative remarks and the students practically jumped to rearrange the room according to his wishes....
>
> The most encouraging finding was the high frequency of participation among all participants in the laboratory sessions.... Abstracting from the study of laboratory situations what seem to be essential characteristics of high-interaction situations, one finds: (1) the existence of a specific problem or task that necessitates involvement for its solution; (2) an instructor who allows the assigned task to generate its own questions, which motivates students to find answers to concrete questions; (3) a physical environment that facilitates movement among participants ... (1974: 87–88, 99–101).

Sommer found the results of his rearrangement of chairs from straight rows to circles "discouraging," stating that "We were disheartened at the reaction to the guerrilla-type rearrangements" (98). On their own initiative, many of the students rearranged the chairs before the instructors appeared on the scene. And instructors themselves were often not happy with the circular rearrangement. The result was that in no fewer than twenty of the twenty-five classes the chairs were returned to their original straight-row arrangement. Added to this, Sommer found that instructors monopolized forty or more minutes of the class time during the fifty-minute period, granting that students in small classes had slightly more time to present their own ideas. This was for him a "depressing" finding. It illustrates the large gap or contradiction between our ideals for egalitarian interaction and actual patterns of hierarchy within contemporary society. Chairs in a circle encourage interaction among students and get away from a hierarchy between instructor and students.

Sommer's observation of laboratory sessions was "the most encouraging finding" of his study. Those laboratories included physical-science laboratories (physics, biology, zoology, botany and bacteriology) and art laboratories, such as textile design and painting. Interaction was defined as "a verbal exchange directed to a specific person(s)." And the resulting finding was an "extreme" contrast between interaction in laboratories and classrooms. Students were free to come and go as they liked, and they could even leave before the scheduled period was over. What they decided to do was their own choice. Student-instructor interactions in laboratories averaged about 24 percent of the time, by comparison with 12 percent in the classrooms. More significant, however, is the fact that interactions were occurring among students throughout the entire period, interactions which were rare in the classrooms. On the average, more than 70 percent of the students participated in student-student interactions and 65 percent in student-teacher interactions.

It is most significant that the laboratories far more than the classrooms not only illustrated interaction but also the use of the scientific method. It was there, following Sommer's discussion of his findings in the last paragraph quoted above, that the classes centered on "a specific problem or task that necessitates involvement for its solution." And it was there that we frequently find "an instructor who allows the assigned task to generate its own questions, which motivates students to find answers to concrete questions." Here again we note the importance of that first step of the scientific method: the definition of a problem. We might also note that the sense of problem must be transferred from the instructor to the individual student. Students in those classes were exposed by their instructors and by reading materials to general directions for how to solve the problems they faced in the laboratories. This has to do with further steps of the scientific method: bringing to bear existing knowledge relevant to that problem, and taking appropriate actions to make progress in solving that problem.

Sommer concludes that the physical environment is a necessary but not a sufficient condition for student involvement and—more generally—effective education: "By itself no single change, including carpeting, decorations, portable chairs, reduced class size, or open-air surroundings is going to revolutionize American education, but without these changes no improvement is likely." Thus, the physical environment is indeed a significant factor, but it is only one of a number of factors. It is this same broad approach to problems that is illustrated by Buckley's approach to the scientific method. Yet just because problems have complex causes and require complex solutions is no excuse for giving up on them or for rejecting a very limited approach to them.

## Some Implications

With respect to *Flatland,* through Abbott's criticism of the limitations of the assumptions of Flatlanders that a two-dimensional world is the only possible world, he is suggesting that we too may have limiting assumptions about our own world. This appears in fact to be the case. By our failure to take very seriously the dimension of time, we are also failing to understand the nature of our Timeland world. Abbott's tale may then be seen as an allegory suggesting first, a gap between our aspiration to understand our world and our inability to fulfill that aspiration. Also, Abbott's allegory implies that this gap is in turn derived from our fundamental assumptions or metaphysical stance as to the nature of our world. Thus, although Abbott has nothing to say relative to hypothesis (1) about an increasing gap, he supports hypothesis (2) by implying that our own worldview yields much of the basis for that aspiration-fulfillment gap with respect to our understanding.

Buckley's section on systems theory gives us a history of efforts to move beyond the simplistic approach to methodology which characterizes most social science research. We saw this initially in the introductory chapter, where we were introduced to the general failure of such research to account for the complexities of human behavior. At this point in time, procedures do exist for moving beyond such oversimplification of human behavior. Yet adoption of such procedures apparently requires awareness of the enormous gap between the social scientist's scientific ideals and his or her practices. Although Buckley does not address hypothesis (1), he illustrates one kind of gap, as portrayed in figure I.1: between our aspirations for scientific ideals and the limited degree to which we are fulfilling them. As for the cause of that gap, Buckley claims that scientific work includes not just theory and research but also "frameworks, models, or philosophies" that are all too implicit. And with this he implies that it is our philosophical framework—we would say our worldview or metaphysical stance—that is responsible for that gap, thus supporting hypothesis (2).

Robert Sommer describes an additional gap: between physical structures (classroom chairs in a circle) illustrating egalitarian ideals and physical structures (chairs facing the instructor's podium) illustrating hierarchical practices. This gap is yet another example of the general gap between aspirations and their fulfillment depicted in figure I.1. Most of the students rearranged their chairs from a circular to a hierarchical pattern, perhaps exemplifying the power of a stratified worldview. And all this despite the cultural value of equality. In common with Abbott and Buckley, Sommer does not address hypothesis (1), the question of whether or not the gap is increasing. However, Sommer is convinced of the existence of a large gap with respect to nothing less than the cultural value of equality. Since such a basic gap invokes the fundamental nature of society, and since Sommer sees any change in education as requiring a very broad framework, he implicitly supports hypothesis (2).

Our examination of these contributions with reference to hypotheses (1) and (2) has emphasized language's dichotomous and gradational capacities. In addition, we might look to their use of language's metaphorical or image-oriented capacities. Abbott's images of Flatland and Spaceland, suggesting our own failure to understand our present situation in Timeland, works to contrast a stratified worldview with an interactive worldview, helping us to see those worldviews more clearly. Buckley's use of "feedback loop" helps us to see more clearly just how interaction works, by contrast with a one-directional relationship between two factors. As for Sommer, his distinction between "hard architecture" and "soft architecture" is well illustrated by movable classroom chairs and rigid chairs facing the instructor's podium. It is a distinction that we can learn to apply to the array of physical structures we encounter in our own everyday lives.

It is of course possible to look far beyond the above three selections to other literature from the social sciences that bears on our two hypotheses, as indicated in the introduction to part II. We might also mention one work of unusual importance: Jane Jacobs's *The Death and Life of Great American Cities* (1961). Just as in the case of Sommer's *Tight Spaces,* Jacobs was concerned with how physical structures affect people's everyday interactions with one another. For example, she emphasized the importance of short blocks in cities in order to encourage such interaction, with long blocks encouraging individual isolation. She sees such isolation as illustrative of a huge gap between her ideals or aspirations for what cities should be like and the actual way in which cities have generally taken shape. Jacobs argued that it is not long blocks alone which foster this gap but many other factors, such as the lack of diversification of shops and services within any given area of a city.

## CHAPTER 2

# Outward versus Inward-Outward Perception

OUR INTEREST IN THE IMPORTANCE OF LINKING an understanding of human biology with the social sciences and the humanities is shared by the contemporary biologist Edward O. Wilson. He sketches a direction for the "consilience" or jumping together of these fields, which he believes is essential for building on the broad orientation of Sir Francis Bacon and fulfilling Enlightenment ideals: "true reform will aim at the consilience of science with the social sciences and the humanities in scholarship and teaching" (1998: 62). It is most important to emphasize the unification of knowledge, as Wilson does. And he is able to justify that integration on the basis of serious social problems. Yet how are we to move beyond this aspiration, given the actuality of shattered and isolated disciplines and sub-disciplines? What will it take to connect our disparate fragments of knowledge? Wilson is contributing toward defining a serious problem, and this is the most important step within the scientific method. How, then, are we to move toward a solution? One way of doing so, in our view, is to return to our fundamental assumptions. For we believe that it is those assumptions which constitute a key force preventing us from fulfilling Wilson's ideal and our own.

The process of perception is no more than one aspect of our biological structure, yet it is a fundamental aspect. Our biological nature has been developing over billions of years, a past that we Timeland creatures cannot afford to ignore. In this chapter we contrast two alternative emphases on how we structure our process of perception: outward perception, linked to a stratified worldview or metaphysical stance, and inward-outward perception, associated with an interactive worldview. For example, we hypothesize that it is the former emphasis that encourages social scientists to ignore the process of investigator effect and thus fail to work toward understanding our own impact on the research process. Emphasizing outward perception moves us counter to what Alvin Gouldner's *The Coming Crisis of Western Sociology* called for, as suggested in the Introduction and to be examined in this chapter: a "reflexive sociology."

Within the literature of cognitive science, with its emphasis on the field of social psychology, perception generally is viewed as involving the individual no less than the external world. For example, P. N. Johnson-Laird writes: "We seem to perceive the world directly, not a representation of it. Yet this phenomenology is illusory: what we perceive depends on both what is in the world and what is in our heads—on what evolution has 'wired' into our nervous systems and what we know as a result of experience" (1993: 470–471). It is a similar idea pointing toward an interactive worldview that was a major conclusion of Alfred Korzybski, the founder of the field of general semantics (1933). What we see abstracts from what is in fact out there, versus reproducing what is out there. Thus, we need to become "conscious of abstraction," learning that we interact with what we see. We can go further back in time and find a similar idea within the philosophy of Immanuel Kant, who emphasized the idea that the individual's mind works to structure whatever the individual perceives, by contrast with the British empiricists with their idea that the mind is what John Locke called a *tabula rasa*. And we can come forward to the work of the American psychologist, George Kelly, also to be discussed in this chapter.

Our first illustration of perception is based on George Kelly's two-volume work, *The Psychology of Personal Constructs* (1955). Organisms, and not just human beings, are able "to represent the environment, not merely to respond to it." And because we organisms can do this, we can do something about the environment if it does not suit us. Organisms without language are limited both in their ability to represent the environment and in what they are able to do. But we humans have incredible potential for learning how to do a better and better job of representing and responding to the environment, for language appears to give us the capacity to continue to learn throughout our lives. We can come to see ourselves as the creatures that we in fact are with that potential for learning, and not as the helpless prisoners of a world with increasing problems that cannot be solved. To accomplish this, however, appears to require us to change the way we see the world and ourselves from one moment to the next. Kelly illustrates that change by referring to a possible change in our self image: "Let us then, instead of occupying ourselves with *man-the-biological organism* or *man-the-lucky-guy*, have a look at *man-the-scientist*."

This view of the human being as a kind of scientist in everyday life, looking for causes and effects as a basis for solving problems, has been carried forward within the contemporary literature on "attribution theory" in social psychology. Fritz Heider, the founder of the approach, believed that individuals attempt to understand, predict and control phenomena in their own everyday lives just as scientists do these things within their investigations (1958). Further, he believed that they emphasize enduring causes or structures by contrast with momentary phenomena. We might note here that the Web and Part/Whole Approach includes both enduring structures (physical, biological, social and personality) and situational phenomena. Influential work in attribution theory by Harold Kelley (1967, 1973), Edward Jones and Keith Davis (1965), and Edward Jones and Daniel McGillis (1976) carries further Heider's analysis of structures with efforts to identify more clearly the nature of those structures. Judith A. Howard and Danielle Kane provide a more current review of the literature on attribution theory (2000).

Alvin Gouldner, in his *The Coming Crisis of Western Sociology* (1970), has given social scientists the advice to be "reflexive," just as Socrates has given all of us the advice to "know thyself." In telling social scientists that they should apply their ideas to their own lives, he is saying: "Doctor, heal thyself." For if social science ideas are indeed worthwhile in helping people to understand themselves and the world, social scientists should be the first to use those ideas in their own lives. Yet it appears that just as in the case of what became of Socrates' advice, social scientists applaud Gouldner for his remarks and then quickly move on to other things. For apparently the advice of Socrates and Gouldner runs counter to a stratified worldview linked to outward perception by contrast with inward-outward perception. How are we, then, to take seriously Socrates' and Gouldner's advice? In our view, one direction is to open up to the nature and impact of our biological structure in general and our patterns of perception in particular.

Our final example bearing on perception has to do with advertising as a device which has changed our perception of the world and ourselves. John Berger was instrumental in creating the British Broadcasting Corporation's television series *Ways of Seeing.* His book with the same title begins with the sentence, "Seeing comes before words." Berger centers on the negative impact of advertising on our lives. We learn to imagine that our lives will be transformed if only we would buy this product or that one. In this way our own aspirations accelerate, thus yielding an ever-widening gap—as advertising becomes ever more pervasive—between those aspirations and our ability to fulfill them. Further, advertising emphasizes narrow materialistic expectations rather than expectations for a broader way of life. Yet all the while that we remain prisoners of our illusions and unrealistic dreams, the world outside may be continuing to change in destructive ways, as suggested by figure I.1. And it is our outward perception that teaches us to pay attention to advertising and encourages its growth. Without that outward emphasis it is probable that we would have a marked reduction in the number of our couch-potatoes.

## Kelly's *The Psychology of Personal Constructs*

George A. Kelly was a clinical as well as an academic psychologist who published his theory of personality in the middle of the twentieth century (1955, 1963). More than any other psychologist, Kelly focused on language, which helps to make his theory ultra-modern. We begin by returning to the quote from Kelly in the introduction to this chapter: organisms, and not just human beings, are able "to represent the environment, not merely to respond to it." Thus, all organisms are vastly different from non-living objects in that they have some degree of "creative capacity." If their representation of the environment does not suit them, they can act to change their situation. Given that all living things are indeed creative, the human being with language is endowed with incredible potential for creativity. For language opens up the human being's capacity to perceive phenomena to a fantastic extent, far beyond what any other organism has been able to achieve. However, when social scientists look at the human being in a highly specialized way, their guiding assumption is what Kelly called "accumulative fragmentation." That is the assumption that we can arrive at truth by coming up with small pieces of the truth and then combining them. But those small pieces are much too tiny to open up to understanding human creativity, which requires the full range of the human being's capacity to think, feel and act on a given problem. Namely, it requires us to see the human being as a kind of scientist, and scientists can continue to learn without limit.

Kelly saw the human being in this way:

> The long-range view of man leads us to turn our attention toward those factors appearing to account for his progress rather than those betraying his impulses. To a large degree—though not entirely—the blueprint of human progress has been given the label of "science." Let us then, instead of occupying ourselves with *man-the-biological organism* or *man-the-lucky-guy,* have a look at *man-the-scientist....* [E]very man is, in his own particular way, a scientist.... Might not the individual man ... Assume more of the stature of a scientist, ever seeking to predict and control the course of events with which he is involved? Would he not have his theories, test his hypotheses, and weight his experimental evidence? (1963: 4).
>
> What I think this view of man as the paradigm of the scientist—and vice-versa—does mean is that the ultimate explanation of human behavior lies in scanning man's undertakings, the questions he asks, the lines of inquiry he initiates and the strategies he employs, rather than in analyzing the logical pattern of the events with which he collides. Until one has grasped the nature of man's undertakings, he can scarcely hope to make sense out of the muscular movements he observes or the

words he hears spoken. In dealing with human behavior we inevitably find ourselves confronted with the human ingenuity it expresses. And that is the point of confrontation at which most psychology breaks down (quoted in Bannister and Fransella, 1971: 82).

Kelly viewed the individual as an organism who, in fundamental ways, acts like a scientist. Starting with what is generally the first step of the scientific method, awareness and definition of a problem, Kelly saw all of us as oriented to altering our future if the present does not suit us. The title of a key book that explains Kelly's ideas is *Inquiring Man* (Bannister and Fransella, 1971). We human beings are far more than simply another species of biological organism. We cannot be understood simply by examining bits and pieces of our behavior. A broader approach to our behavior must be adopted. In Kelly's words, we must scan "man's undertakings, the questions he asks, the lines of inquiry he initiates and the strategies he employs." Yet much of the discipline of psychology adopts a very narrow approach to human behavior and thus misses out on our capacities. That approach is much like giving a rat the narrow choice of pressing a bar or suffering an electric shock. The rat has a great deal more capacity for learning than such narrow experiments allow for. Yet such experiments will not be able to tap that capacity.

If we should view the human being as a scientist, then we should also view the scientist as a human being. As a result we should take into account the impact of the investigator when analyzing any research project: "[P]sychologists should be regarded as human beings who interact with the actual experiment they are trying so hard to keep under careful control" (Fransella and Thomas, 1988: 28). There appears to be a lack of concern for such "investigator effects" in almost every example of social science research. This is exactly what Fransella and Thomas, who are explaining Kelly's ideas, refer to in this quote. Not just psychologists but all social scientists avoid treating the scientist as a human being who would like to see certain outcomes of the experiment, and whose feelings may easily be conveyed to the subjects of an investigation. People generally have very limited ability to prevent their emotions from showing themselves in one way or another. An alternative procedure, which would require that the researcher be treated as a human being along with the subjects or respondents, is that the impact of the researcher on the investigation be studied along with the research project.

To get at the human being's capacities, it is essential to focus much of our attention on the individual's linguistic abilities:

There are many different scientific strategies which psychologists use.... One of these is to relate the person's behaviour and experience to physical things, especially the structure and function of the nervous system and the chemistry of the body.... However, there is quite a different strategy ... It is to regard man as a *categorizing* animal. All perception involves categorizing. If you see something you have never seen before you will already have categorized it as "something I have never seen before." At birth (and before) stimuli are categorized in the sense that the nervous system deals differently with light and sound stimuli, and so on. At the other extreme, in complex social behaviour, categorizing is very evident. A person reacts to others depending on how he has categorized them. Probably the most general dichotomous social category is "Us versus Them" (Bannister and Fransella, 1971: 7).

Kelly has emphasized the importance of language in any effort to understand the human being. This meshes very well with Kelly's belief in the human being's enormous creative capacities as well as his view of the individual as a scientist. For it is language which opens up our creative capacities, and it is the scientific method which has enabled us to build on those capacities. Let us note the example that Bannister and Fransella use in the above quote: the individual's use of the dichotomy "Us versus Them." Kelly was a psychotherapist as well as an academic psychologist, and he and his students were much concerned with applying his theory to help his patients solve their problems. He saw the importance of helping people to change their ways of thinking, or the linguistic categories they were using, so as to help them open up to the complexity of human behavior and thus improve their understanding of themselves and others. "Us versus Them" illustrates a very simplistic way of thinking, and it can easily yield antagonism to those defined as "Them."

Kelly used the term "construct" rather than idea or hypothesis to emphasize the idea that each individual constructs a personal interpretation of any given idea. Thus, the subtitle of Bannister's and Fransella's *Inquiring Man* is *The Theory of Personal Constructs*. They illustrate in the following passage how the individual might learn to develop a more scientific way of using language and, thus, of dealing with the complexity of human behavior:

> Kelly ... classified constructs ... into *pre-emptive, constellatory* and *propositional.* A pre-emptive construct is a construct which pre-empts its elements for membership in its own realm exclusively. This is in effect saying that if this man is a homosexual he is *nothing but* a homosexual.... [I]t is essentially a denial of the right of other people and ourselves to re-view, re-interpret and see in a fresh light some part of the world around us.
>
> A *constellatory* construct is a construct which fixes the other realm membership of its elements. This is essentially stereotyped or typological thinking and says in effect that if this man is a *homosexual* then he

must *be effeminate, artistic, degenerate* and *a menace to society.* Again, it reduces our chances of elaborating or re-viewing our outlook—it is a kind of intellectual package deal.

Finally, Kelly talked of *propositional* constructs, which are those constructs which carry no implications regarding the other realm membership of their elements. These are ... constructs where we are prepared to recognize that we can look upon person X *as a homosexual* and thereby make sense out of a lot of what he says and does. But we are recognizing that this is only *one* way of viewing him and is not some final, absolute or all-comprehending truth. We can equally regard him *as a friend* or *as a chess player.* The more propositional our constructs the richer becomes our world and the less likely we are to become irretrievably trapped into a conflict which arises out of the rigidity of our viewpoint (1971: 31–32).

The achievements of the scientific method are based on the capacity of scientists to be cumulative or to continually advance their knowledge by "standing on the shoulders of giants." This cumulative capacity is much the same as the capacity for learning throughout our lives that language gives each of us. By contrast, when we construe ideas in a "pre-emptive" way, we limit drastically our movement on a path of learning or inquiry. We engage in gross stereotyping, ignoring most of the distinctive characteristics of an individual. This procedure treats the individual as almost completely invisible. And our use of "constellatory" constructs is only somewhat better, for it also assumes that we are already in possession of the truth and are closed to new knowledge. A "propositional" orientation, by contrast, is closest to the scientific method. For it leaves the individual open to further learning. If we recall our analysis of the dichotomous, gradational and metaphorical potential of language in the Introduction, then we can see Kelly's approach to language as adding to that discussion. Pre-emptive and constellatory constructs emphasize language's dichotomous potential, for such categorizations denote fixed phenomena by contrast to gradation's orientation to change. By contrast, a propositional orientation does not fix our characteristics and thus is oriented to language's gradational potential. As for metaphor, Kelly's view of man-the-scientist is a most powerful image.

Kelly does not employ the concept of "worldview," but his analysis can help us to understand the enormous power that a worldview exerts over every aspect of our behavior:

A person's construction system is composed of complementary superordinate and subordinate relationships. The subordinate systems are determined by the superordinate systems into whose jurisdictions they are placed.... The changes that take place, as one moves toward creat-

ing a more suitable system for anticipating events, can be seen as falling
under the control of that person's superordinating system. In his role
identifying him with his superordinating system, the person is free with
respect to subordinate changes he attempts to make. In his role as the
follower of his own fundamental principles, he finds his life determined
by them. Just as in governmental circles instructions can be changed
only within the framework of fixed directives, and directives can be
changed only within the framework of fixed statutes, and statutes can be
changed only within the framework of fixed constitutions, so can one's
personal constructs be changed only within subsystems of constructs
and subsystems changed only within more comprehensive systems....
[O]ne does not learn certain things merely from the nature of the stimuli
which play upon him; he learns only what his framework is designed to
permit him to see in the stimuli (Kelly, 1963: 78-79).

Kelly refers here to the power which superordinate or general
constructs have over subordinate or more specific constructs. The latter
can be changed if the former is sufficiently "permeable" to permit this.
For example, the U.S. Constitution includes as its first amendment the
right to freedom of speech. And this superordinate system can overrule
laws or statutes which the Supreme Court determines are in violation of
this amendment. Fortunately, constitutions and laws are quite visible, and
we can thus learn to develop the kinds of constitutions and laws which
closely follow our own ideals and values. However, a worldview—such
as the stratified worldview—is a superordinate system which is relatively
invisible. As a result it can violate our ideals, say, for egalitarian relationships,
without our even becoming aware of its existence. Further, the breadth
of a worldview enables it to shape the individual's every thought, feeling
and action. Thus, even if we attempt to relate to others in egalitarian ways,
following our democratic ideals, those attempts may remain subordinate
to our superordinate stratified worldview, which will trump them.

It is from this perspective that we can hypothesize why scientists
have failed to follow scientific ideals calling for openness to the full range
of phenomena relevant to a given problem. Instead, they limit themselves
to only those phenomena falling within their own narrow specialties. It is
also from this perspective that we can hypothesize why scientists fail to
take into account their own impact on the research process despite the
scientific importance of doing so, since that impact requires an interactive
inward-outward worldview rather than a stratified outward worldview. Following Kelly, the stratified worldview is a construct that is superordinate
to the scientist's construction of the scientific method. In turn, the social
scientist's construction of the scientific method is superordinate to the
many specific theories of human behavior within the social sciences. We
have, then, a hierarchy from a metaphysical stance to an epistemological

stance to theories. As a result, those theories almost universally suffer from a failure to pay attention to the social scientist's epistemology and metaphysics.

To illustrate further, as we read through a number of the 400-odd articles in the *Encyclopedia of Sociology* (Borgatta and Montgomery, 2000), we are absolutely amazed at the general failure of those authors to pay the least bit of attention to their own epistemological and metaphysical assumptions. This naïveté is an example of what Johnson-Laird suggested—as quoted in the introduction to this chapter: an understanding of perception as a direct representation of the world rather than as an interaction between ourselves and our environment. It is also an example of what Korzybski called—also mentioned in that introduction—a failure to achieve "consciousness of abstraction." In addition, it is an example of what Gouldner saw as a lack of reflexivity. Yet social scientists no less than the rest of us apparently are deeply influenced by a Spaceland or stratified worldview which teaches us all a simplistic understanding of phenomena.

What, then, does Kelly's theory imply about figure I.1's hypothesized growing gap between expectations and their fulfillment in contemporary society? He views each of us as a kind of scientist with the potential for what goes along with scientific thought: propositional by contrast with pre-emptive or constellatory constructs. And his clinical work suggests the existence of large gaps within individuals between the scientific ideal of propositional constructs and the actuality of pre-emptive and constellatory constructs. He does not, however, make the claim that this gap is nearly universal, and he does not focus on historical changes in the size of that gap. But he does imply that this linguistic gap is substantial in contemporary society. Further, he helps us to understand how a worldview or metaphysical stance might shape an epistemology or approach to the scientific method, and also how the latter might shape a scientific theory. His own approach suggests an interactive metaphysical stance or worldview along with an interactive epistemology or approach to the scientific method, given his view of man as a scientist with the potential for developing propositional constructs.

## Gouldner's *The Coming Crisis of Western Sociology*

Alvin W. Gouldner, a sociologist whose work overlapped with and followed that of C. Wright Mills, was able to carry further Mills's advice to his students that they "do not split their work from their lives" in *The Sociological Imagination* (1959), to be discussed in chapter 6. At the end of his *The Coming Crisis of Western Sociology* (1970) he writes about the importance of a "reflexive sociology," a message directed to his sociological colleagues: "*Sociologists are no more ready than other men to cast a cold eye on their own doings....Yet, first and foremost, a Reflexive Sociology is concerned with what sociologists want to do and with what, in fact, they actually do in the world"* (1970: 488). Gouldner illustrates the gap in figure I.1 between aspirations and their fulfillment by applying it to sociologists in particular.

Gouldner is aiming at something fundamental: nothing less than the sociologist's worldview or metaphysical stance. If outward perception is linked to a stratified worldview and inward-outward perception is tied to an interactive worldview, then Gouldner is asking his colleagues to challenge their own stratified worldview and move toward an interactive worldview where they look at themselves as well as others. By writing that "sociologists are no more ready than other men to cast a cold eye on their own doings," he is suggesting that sociologists are no closer to an interactive worldview than anyone else. Yet regardless of the difficulties involved, it is important for them to move in that direction. Those difficulties are enormous, given the fact that looking inward to any depth is closely tied to shifting one's worldview or metaphysical stance.

Gouldner shows awareness of the magnitude of what he is asking as he details what he means by a "Reflexive Sociology":

> What sociologists now most require from a Reflexive Sociology, however, is not just one more specialization, not just another topic for panel meetings at professional conventions.... The historical mission of a Reflexive Sociology as I conceive it, however, would be to transform the sociologist, to penetrate deeply into his daily life and work, enriching them with new sensitivities, and to raise the sociologist's self-awareness to a new historical level.... A Reflexive Sociology means that we sociologists must—at the very least—acquire the ingrained habit of viewing our own beliefs as we now view those held by others....
>
> The core of a Reflexive Sociology, then, is the attitude it fosters toward those parts of the social world closest to the sociologist—his own university, his own profession and its associations, his professional role, and importantly, his students, and himself—rather than toward only the remotest parts of his social surround. A Reflexive Sociology is distinguished by its refusal to segregate the intimate or personal from the public or collective, or the everyday life from the occasional "political" act.... A Reflexive Sociology is not a bundle of technical skills; it is a conception of how to live (1970: 487, 493, 504).

Gouldner is asking for nothing less than that sociologists transform their lives in fundamental ways. If indeed sociologists are convinced that their professional knowledge is important, then there is every reason for them to use that knowledge to help them to transform their own lives. He refers not just to the intellect or the "head" but also to emotional life or the "heart": "The character and quality of such knowing is molded not only by a man's technical skills or even by his intelligence alone, but also by all that he is and wants, by his courage no less than his talent, by his passion no less than his objectivity." What he is asking is that the sociologist's emotions be called into play if an effective science is to be achieved. And even the "hand" in addition to the "head" and the "heart" must be involved: "A Reflexive Sociology is not a bundle of technical skills; it is a conception of how to live."

Earlier in *The Coming Crisis of Western Sociology*, Gouldner develops an argument similar to that of Thomas Kuhn's analysis of scientific revolutions, to be discussed in chapter 3. Just as Kuhn wrote about the scientist's commitment to a "paradigm" which involves very general assumptions, Gouldner writes about the scientist's commitment to "background assumptions" which are not explicitly stated and can be quite general. Just as Kuhn suggested that scientific revolutions require not merely evidence for a new theory but also the development of a new scientific paradigm that can replace the old one, so does Gouldner suggest that new background assumptions are required for the acceptance of a new theory. Following Kuhn, we can see this in the shift from Newton's laws of motion to Einstein's special theory of relativity, where Einstein put forward not just evidence but also a new scientific paradigm or new background assumptions. We also can see the slowness of that shift, given traditional and personal commitments of physicists to the Newtonian scientific paradigm, commitments that were based on their acceptance of Newton's laws throughout their entire lives.

Gouldner reveals his understanding of the kinds of background assumptions which are of the most general type, namely, those which are worldviews or metaphysical stances:

Background assumptions ... influence the social career of a theory, influencing the responses of those to whom it is communicated. For, in some part, theories are accepted or rejected because of the background assumptions embedded in them.... Background assumptions come in different sizes, they govern domains of different scope. They are arranged, one might say, like an inverted cone, standing on its point. At the top are background assumptions with the largest circumference, those that have no limited domain to which alone they apply. These are beliefs about the world that are so general that they may, in principle, be applied to any subject matter without restriction. They are, as Stephen Pepper calls them, "world hypotheses." Being primitive presuppositions about the world and everything in it, they serve to provide the most general of orientations, which enable unfamiliar experiences to be made meaningful. They provide the terms of reference by which the less general assumptions, further down the cone, are themselves limited and influenced.

World hypotheses are the most pervasive and primitive beliefs about what is real.... World hypotheses—the cat may as well be let out of the bag—are what are sometimes called "metaphysics" (29-31).

Few modern social scientists pay any attention to metaphysical assumptions, worldviews or "world hypotheses." Yet by making use of Gouldner's work and paying attention to the nature of language, we can gain further understanding of their nature. For Gouldner, moving toward those assumptions is—metaphorically—movement toward the rim of a cone that contains our metaphysical assumptions. Gouldner claims that these assumptions "provide the terms of reference by which the less general assumptions, further down the cone, are themselves limited and influenced." Gouldner's idea that our metaphysical assumptions influence or trump the ideas below them strengthens our own idea that our world-view shapes our approach to the scientific method, and that approach in turn shapes the theories we develop in trying to understand phenomena and solve problems. Worldviews, then, are our most general background assumptions, assumptions that are not reported explicitly when research is published or theories are advanced. Rather, they remain hidden from view, yet their importance cannot easily be overestimated. Thus, Gouldner saw the importance of such general assumptions in much the same way that George Kelly saw the relationship between superordinate constructs like the U.S. Constitution and subordinate constructs like specific laws. General background assumptions—or one's metaphysical stance—shape one's approach to the scientific method just as the Constitution shapes the laws that are enacted. If we want to follow scientific ideals, then we had better learn the nature of our metaphysical stance or worldview. If it opposes our scientific ideals then we had better change it.

If we wish to take seriously Gouldner's advice to become reflexive, then we would do well to pay close attention to literatures from disciplines other than sociology. For example, Quinn and Holland (1987), following Lakoff (1987), distinguish between "image schemas" and "proposition schemas." "Schemas" are representations or models of phenomena, and they work to shape what we perceive and what we understand when we experience phenomena. Attention to schemas enables us to avoid the naïve approach to perception where we fail to understand its interactive nature or, in Korzybski's words, "fail to" attain consciousness of abstraction. Thus, the idea of a worldview or metaphysical stance or an epistemological stance is an example of a schema. "Image schemas" are abstract visual representations, whereas "proposition schemas" are abstract language-based representations. Both kinds of schemas are based on the potentials of language, as discussed in the introduction to this book, with image schemas closer to language's image-oriented or metaphorical capacity and propositional schemas closer to language's dichotomous and gradational capacities. We might note here the loose link between the nature of language and the schemas that we employ to understand, predict and control our experiences.

We might also note that schemas can be quite specific by contrast with general schemas like metaphysical or epistemological stances. For example, Taylor and Crocker define schemas as organized structures of cognitions pertaining to social objects such as the self, other persons, groups, roles and events (1981). Given this situation where the individual develops both very general schemas like worldviews and very specific schemas such as one about "college professors," then what we have is enormous complexity introduced to any given behavior of the individual. As a result, Gouldner's advice for the sociologist to become reflexive no more than scratches the surface of what it takes to become reflexive. Yet from a pragmatic perspective we can do no better than take one step at a time within the research process. We would do well to focus initially on those schemas which have the most profound and broadest effects on our behavior: the ones that are most superordinate, following Kelly. These have to do with our metaphysical and epistemological assumptions. Granting that other schemas with more limited impact on our behavior are involved in what we think, feel and do, we might do well to begin by understanding our superordinate schemas.

Gouldner became somewhat more specific about language and the role of social scientists when he discussed his *The Coming Crisis of Western Sociology* two years after it was published as quoted in the Introduction:

> The pursuit of … understanding, however, cannot promise that men as we now find them, with their everyday language and understanding, will always be capable of further understanding and of liberating themselves. At decisive points the ordinary language and conventional understandings fail and must be transcended. It is essentially the task of the social sciences, more generally, to create new and "extraordinary" languages, to help men learn to speak them, and to mediate between the deficient understandings of ordinary language and the different and liberating perspectives of the extraordinary languages of social theory.... To say social theorists are concept-creators means that they are not merely in the knowledge-creating business, but also in the language-reform and language-creating business. In other words, they are from the beginning involved in creating a new culture (Gouldner, 1972: 16).

Gouldner recognizes here the centrality of language for effective problem-solving as well as the particular importance of the "extraordinary" languages of social science. He commits himself to the overriding importance of communicating those extraordinary languages outside of the academic world so as "to help men learn to speak them, and to mediate between the deficient understandings of ordinary language and the different and liberating perspectives of the extraordinary languages of social theory." Thus, Gouldner joins Kelly in probing how language works in order to penetrate the depths of human complexity. Our own book, with its emphasis on key social science concepts in the headings of each chapter, also illustrates a commitment to the vital importance of language in penetrating human behavior. Granting that those headings are dichotomous, they also suggest the importance of moving—gradationally—from a stratified to an interactive worldview. Further, our usage of literary selections such as *Flatland* attests to the importance of language's metaphorical potential.

## Berger's *Ways of Seeing*

John Berger in his BBC television series and his book focuses on the power of visual advertising on television as well as in the print media to create dissatisfaction within the individual along with patterns of stratification throughout society:

> The spectator-buyer is meant to envy herself as she will become if she buys the product. She is meant to imagine herself transformed by the product into an object of envy for others, an envy which will then justify her loving herself.... [T]he publicity image steals her love of herself as she is, and offers it back to her for the price of the product.
>
> Publicity speaks in the future tense and yet the achievement of this future is endlessly deferred. How then does publicity remain credible—or credible enough to exert the influence it does? It remains credible because the truthfulness of publicity is judged, not by the real fulfillment of its promises, but by the relevance of its fantasies to those of the spectator-buyer. Its essential application is not to reality but to daydreams.
>
> Publicity turns consumption into a substitute for democracy. The choice of what one eats (or wears or drives) takes the place of significant political choice. Publicity helps to mask and compensate for all that is undemocratic within society. And it also masks what is happening in the rest of the world (1972: 134, 146, 149).

Following Berger's argument, "the publicity image steals her love of herself as she is, and offers it back to her for the price of the product." But love of self is never actually recovered, as the individual is continually bombarded with many other messages throughout the day that succeed in stealing her love of herself as she is. Without that love of self, the individual is in a worse position to think for herself, to express herself emotionally and to commit to personal goals, and also to act effectively in the pursuit of those goals. Instead of helping us to understand, commit to and work toward realistic goals, advertising influences us to enter a world of fantasy. As a result, we individuals in such a world will have difficulty in interacting with others or with our environment in a realistic, confident and effective way.

Further, advertising works to emphasize patterns of hierarchy or stratification with their stereotypical focus on material goods and separation of the "haves" from the "have-nots." We learn to envy those with material wealth and, correspondingly, to think little of those who are poor. This comes about not just because advertisers generally want to sell material products. It is also because we can *see* such products in the media, but we would have great difficulty *seeing* intangibles. In addition, advertisers are not in a position to sell the intangibles that people want, such as love or self-confidence. Berger also argues that advertising works against political democracy, which points toward an opening up of the individual's possibilities for effective actions. In place of important political choices, advertising offers the individual trivial choices, such as between this toothpaste and that one. The individual learns to substitute such insignificant choices for significant political choices. Part of the problem here is that political leaders have difficulty in developing significant choices, given the complexity of social problems and their failure to understand how to solve them.

Berger's analysis meshes closely with figure I.1, for he is claiming that advertising encourages us to continually raise the top curve of aspirations or expectations. But at the same time, advertising tends to influence that bottom curve of fulfillment to remain low, given its general emphasis on stratification or persisting hierarchy. As a result, advertising works to increase the gap between what we aspire to and can actually attain, creating an unrealistic situation for all of us. Its lack of realism is further illustrated by its equating something quite trivial—such as a choice among different kinds of toothpaste—with genuine democracy. Yet advertising succeeds because politicians and social scientists generally have offered the individual no way to close the gap between aspirations and their fulfillment. In this situation, the individual has little choice but to remain in a fantasy world where awareness of that gap does not emerge. Otherwise, the individual would move into an intolerable situation: awareness of fundamental yet unfulfilled aspirations coupled with no direction or even hope for fulfilling them.

Berger is by no means the only analyst of contemporary society who has come up with this conclusion about the fantasy world we have created in contemporary society, where expectations far exceed their fulfillment. Here we might think of Durkheim's analysis of anomie and suicide, to be presented in chapter 7. We might also consider the argument of the historian Daniel Boorstin, who was quoted in the Introduction:

In this book I describe the world of our making, how we have used our wealth, our literacy, our technology, and our progress, to create the thicket of unreality which stands between us and the facts of life.... [E]ach of us individually provides the market and the demand which flood our experience. We want and we believe these illusions because we suffer from extravagant expectations. We expect too much of the world....

We expect anything and everything.... For never has a people expected so much more than the world could offer.... To discover our illusions will not solve the problems of our world. But if we do not discover them, we will never discover our real problems. To dispel the ghosts which populate the world of our making will not give us the power to conquer the real enemies of the real world or to remake the real world. But it may help us discover that we cannot make the world in our image (1961: 3-4, 6).

Boorstin distinguishes between dreams and illusions. Dreams, like Martin Luther King's dream of a world without racial prejudice and discrimination, give us a direction for solving real problems. Illusions, by contrast, take us away from the real world, as illustrated by extravagant aspirations that can never be fulfilled. For Boorstin, it is the individual who must somehow learn to turn away from extravagant aspirations and see the world as it is and not as he or she would like it to be. For it is the individual who "provides the market and the demand" for the illusions "which flood our experience." By engineering an escape from illusions, the individual will not have solved personal and world problems but will have taken an important step in that direction.

## Some Implications

Both Gouldner and Kelly add to our understanding of the nature of metaphysical stances or worldviews. But exactly what do we now know? For one thing, there is support for the analysis of worldviews or metaphysical stances. There is also support for a link between a stratified worldview and a limited approach to the scientific method that fails to follow scientific ideals. This supports hypothesis (2), since that failure is an instance of a gap, as depicted in figure I.1. But this does not bear directly on hypothesis (1), which specifies an increasing gap. Kelly suggests the existence of another gap: between propositional thinking and our pre-emptive and constellatory modes of thought. As for Berger, he clearly sees advertising yielding the increasing gap that figure I.1 depicts, with a specific emphasis on materialistic desires, thus supporting (1). Also, he sees the materialistic orientation of advertising as not only clashing with broad cultural ideals but also producing the increasing gap that figure I.1 depicts, thus lending affirmation to (2).

Beyond this examination of our two hypotheses, we can also look to the images and metaphors of these authors. Kelly's image of "man the scientist" opens up to new ways of thinking about human behavior, ways that emphasize the broad potential of every human being. This points squarely toward the importance of an interactive worldview to open up to that potential. Gouldner's ideal of a "reflexive sociology" also points toward that worldview. And it suggests as well an epistemology that is far from what is practiced at this time. Berger's portrayal of the "publicity image," with its huge gap between aspirations and the possibilities for fulfilling them, shows a key source of our increasing gap between aspirations and their fulfillment, or the invisible crisis of contemporary society.

On a more concrete level, the work of Berger and Boorstin point toward the increasing development of a consumption-oriented society closely tied to a materialistic way of life. It is this trend toward consumerism which is what contemporary research in the social sciences has been revealing. We can understand this development from the perspective of a focus on outward-perception versus inward-outward perception. If the individual cannot see a stairway with wide steps that he or she can continue to climb while not competing with others—as might be seen in inward-outward perception—then he or she tends to become reduced to an invidious or competitive view of phenomena. This is illustrated by what Thorstein Veblen called "conspicuous consumption" in his *The Theory of the Leisure Class* (1963) or what has been called in the past "keeping up with the Joneses."

It is crucial that the reader understand the limitations of our three illustrations. For there are large literatures on cognition within other disciplines, especially psychology. We have cited no more than a few publications in those areas, referring for example to attribution theory within social psychology and to schemas within cognitive anthropology as well as social psychology. However, our own focus on epistemological and metaphysical assumptions stands up as a crucial orientation in any effort to understand perception. One problem with other literatures is that they generally fail to focus on the schemas that are very widely shared—perhaps universally shared—throughout society. This is quite understandable, given the focus of psychology on the individual. Our point is not that schemas like worldviews should replace individual schemas, but rather that both can be taken into account. That makes for a much more complex approach to research, yet it appears to be required if indeed we are to move toward the complexity envisaged by the Web and Part/Whole Approach to the scientific method.

# PART III

# Personality Structure

In part III we continue what we began in part II, where we presented two pairs of dichotomies: isolation/interaction, bearing on physical structures, and outward perception/inward-outward perception, having to do with biological structures. In part III we shall put forward three additional pairs of dichotomies, all of them bearing on personality structures. Part III will deal with social structures and part IV with the situation. In the Introducton we outlined the importance of taking into account both long-term structures and momentary situations as a basis for understanding the process of change along with the complexity of human behavior. Our focus on structures in parts II, III and IV, and on the situation in part V, is thus only a matter of emphasis, since each part along with each chapter and even each section within any chapter must take into account both structures and situations. And we must not ignore what we have learned about physical and biological structures as we proceed.

Let us also note the division of each of parts III, IV and V into three chapters having to do with—metaphorically—"head," "heart" and "hand," just as is indicated in the table of contents and just as was outlined in the Introduction. We see thinking or speaking ("head"), feeling or expressing emotions ("heart") and acting or interacting ("hand") as key components of human behavior, whether by an individual, by what is shared within a group of individuals, or with respect to a momentary scene. Just as we must take into account both structures and momentary situations simultaneously to get at the complexity of human behavior, so must we do the same for "head," "heart" and "hand" for the same reason. Those chapters oriented to "head," "heart" or "hand" have to do with no more than an emphasis on one of these three components of human behavior. Indeed, we see human behavior as sufficiently complex so that ideas from all of these chapters—along with chapters 1 and 2—are needed in order to make progress in explaining it. By opening up to the potential language and by making use of its dichotomous, gradational, and metaphorical tools, we point toward addressing that complexity. Those tools help us, following the work of C. Wright Mills along with our understanding of the scientific method, to shuttle far up and down language's ladder of abstraction from the very abstract to the very concrete.

The specific concepts we have chosen to highlight in part III—just as those in parts IV and V—are by no means the only ones that might have been chosen, given the breadth of these categories of "head," "heart" and "hand." Our focus in this book is on the literature of social science with particular emphasis on sociology. Employing a Web and Part/Whole Approach to the scientific method so as to open up to the very broad range of phenomena invoked by our hypotheses, we want to move far up language's ladder of abstraction to concepts which can encompass a very wide range of phenomena. Further, we want to put forward paired concepts which we believe are key components of a stratified versus an interactive worldview or metaphysical stance. Yet our own decision to emphasize those specific paired concepts over others within the social science literature should by no means limit the development of a great many other concepts in investigating the sources of gaps between aspirations and their fulfillment.

## CHAPTER 3

# "Head"

## Stratified versus Interactive Beliefs

BELIEFS INCLUDE IDEAS, opinions, assumptions and worldviews. "Stratified beliefs" emphasize hierarchies among individuals or groups, whereas "interactive beliefs" emphasize egalitarian ideas. Our more specific focus in this chapter is on extremely broad beliefs or fundamental assumptions, namely, worldviews or metaphysical stances. This is no more than one kind of belief, granting its importance. It is also the kind of belief that is very widely shared, although our focus in part III is on the individual. It is in part IV, Social Structures, that we emphasize widely shared beliefs.

Thomas Kuhn's *The Structure of Scientific Revolutions* appears to have been so influential throughout academia because, as a historian of science, Kuhn was able to explain a good deal about how the scientific method actually works. Without a solid social science background, he had somehow managed to develop an explanation of scientific revolutions which took into account a good deal of what social scientists had discovered. For example, he was able to take into account the importance of subcultural traditions within a given science. And he did not fail to include in his analysis the importance of personality structures. As a result, he was able to uncover crucial factors which impede the development of scientific revolutions and which are also involved in ordinary scientific research. It is possible to take his central concept, "scientific paradigm," and use it to help us understand the nature of a metaphysical stance or worldview.

Jack Levin's doctoral dissertation, focusing on the causes of prejudice, uncovered the central importance of an individual's worldview. In an experiment with Boston University students he set up a situation which was a microcosm of modern society, with its patterns of hierarchy and prejudice coupled with what we believe to be its stratified worldview.

He discovered that those students with even a slight orientation toward an interactive worldview—by contrast with the other students—were able to resist reacting to personal frustrations by increasing their levels of prejudice. His procedures for measuring an individual's worldview yielded insights into the basis for a worldview that support the contrast in chapter 2 between an outward and an inward-outward orientation.

Among his many works, Robert Merton wrote about "the unanticipated consequences of purposive actions." For example, Britain attempted to prevent Indian independence by violently suppressing the Gandhian movement. This stirred the British and Indian conscience to give greater support to the independence movement, which ultimately led to its success. The result illustrates the narrowness and inadequacy of our stratified worldview relative to the complexity of human behavior. Since our understanding of any given problem is far more limited than we realize, we have little control over "the unanticipated consequences" whenever we use "purposive actions" in an effort to solve that problem. We might hypothesize that moving toward an interactive worldview would open us up to a deeper understanding of problems along with greater control over the results of our actions.

## Kuhn's *The Structure of Scientific Revolutions*

Thomas S. Kuhn's *The Structure of Scientific Revolutions* (1962) took the academic world by storm during the 1960s and beyond. Here was a historian of science who was very well-read in science yet was also blessed with a broad perspective on social science. The process of change, whether inside or outside of academia, is extremely complex, and Kuhn offered academics of all kinds a direction for understanding how change occurs with his narrower focus on scientific revolutions. He looked beyond the specifics of particular contradictions or problems in a science by going back to fundamental assumptions, worldviews or what he called "paradigms"—a concept that he succeeded in popularizing as illustrated by the publisher of this book. Kuhn's dominant concern was not with ordinary change in science or "normal science" but rather with "revolutionary science" or fundamental change, such as the shift from Newton's explanation of motion to Einstein's explanation. And he suggests that our approach to the history of science is far too narrow, failing to explain how such revolutions occur. Thus, Kuhn's sense of history points toward a long-term historical orientation, which is one aspect of an interactive worldview.

In the chapter "Revolutions as Changes of World View" he emphasizes the importance of the scientist's "world view" or paradigm for understanding fundamental change. This parallels our own emphasis on worldviews as basic to understanding whether or not social scientists follow the ideals of the scientific method. In both cases, we must learn to see scientific research as resting on metaphysical assumptions. Following Kelly (chapter 2), those assumptions are superordinate to scientific theories, which are subordinate. Following Gouldner (chapter 2), those "background assumptions" or metaphysical assumptions shape the scientist's theories. When those superordinate, background or metaphysical assumptions change, the result is much like the opening up of a new world. For example, our Spaceland world might suddenly seem limited indeed once we move to a Timeland or an interactive worldview where all of the past suddenly opens up to us. Our very way of perceiving the world might change from outward perception to inward-outward perception. Following Berger (chapter 2), we might learn to see advertising not as a relatively harmless although necessary nuisance but rather as a force that increases our personal and world problems. We might come to see the lack of communication between Snow's scientific and literary cultures not as merely an unfortunate circumstance but rather as a life-or-death problem that we all must face and solve if we wish to survive as a human race.

To understand more fully Kuhn's view of paradigms, we must probe how he contrasts them with the scientific interpretation of specific findings, for here he is distinguishing between revolutionary science and normal science:

> What occurs during a scientific revolution is not fully reducible to a reinterpretation of individual and stable data.... Paradigms are not corrigible by normal science at all. Instead, as we have already seen, normal science ultimately leads only to the recognitions of anomalies and to crises. And these are terminated, not by deliberation and interpretation, but by a relatively sudden and unstructured event.... Scientists then often speak of the "scales falling from the eyes" or of the "lightning flash" that "inundates" a previously obscure puzzle, enabling its components to be seen in a new way that for the first time permits its solution (1962: 120–121).

A change in a scientific paradigm opens up a great many other changes. If the fundamental assumptions which underlie a science change, then much of that science will change along with that paradigmatic change. This breadth of scientific paradigms is equally a characteristic of our own concept of worldview. Kuhn wrote about the "parallelism" between scientific revolutions and political revolutions, thus getting closer to our own approach. For the idea of changes in a worldview includes both scientific and political revolutions, and a great deal more. He saw political revolutions as "inaugurated by a growing sense ... that existing institutions have ceased adequately to meet the problems posed by an environment that they have in part created" (1962: 91). Here, then, is a gap between views of what existing institutions *should* be doing and what in fact they *are* doing. Thus, both political and scientific revolutions are based on awareness of that gap, which has much in common with a first step of the scientific method: awareness of a problem. Further, political revolutions require a basic change in society's institutions, just as scientific revolutions require a new scientific paradigm to replace the old one. That change promises to resolve the political problems that led to the political revolution, just as a new scientific paradigm promises to resolve the problems within the old scientific paradigm. This argument parallels our own idea that a change in worldview requires an alternative worldview which promises to solve the problems of the old worldview.

One illustration of a scientific revolution is the sweeping changes in the field of physics that accompanied Albert Einstein's development of his special theory of relativity. Albert Michelson and Edward Morley were American physicists who measured the speed of light in 1881 by means of a series of mirrors located miles apart, with light ricocheting off one mirror after another. Their startling finding was that light travels at the same speed in any direction, whether that direction follows the earth's motion while rotating or is at right angles to the direction of the earth's rotation. This finding directly contradicted Newton's laws of motion—published in his *Principia Mathematica* in 1687—which require a greater speed of light in the former than in the latter case, because the speed of the earth supposedly should be added to the speed of light. Yet it took many years before physicists, having lived their entire lives taking for granted the adequacy of Newton's laws, could bring themselves to question those laws despite mounting evidence like the Michelson-Morley experiment. It also took an alternative theory—Einstein's special theory, published in 1905—which explained the Michelson-Morley finding and also could achieve what Newton's laws of motion achieved.

Einstein proceeded from a perspective far different from that of Newton, or—in the language of Kuhn—from an alternative scientific paradigm. He accepted the results of the Michelson-Morley experiment by starting with the assumption that light travels at the same speed in any direction, leading him to a number of strange hypotheses. For example, individuals who are moving away from the earth and traveling a considerable distance at speeds near that of light would have their aging processes largely suspended, and they would return to earth long after everyone they knew had died. Einstein's special theory not only was able to deal with the inadequacy of Newton's laws of motion but also was able to yield more accurate predictions of motion than Newton's laws. Nevertheless, following Kuhn's analysis, factors like tradition, hierarchy or social stratification as well as the personality structure of scientists stood in the way of the scientific revolution that Einstein initiated. The ideals of the scientific method had to take a back seat to those factors for many years. We might note here that Kuhn was drawing on fundamental knowledge from social science: the importance of culture, of social organization, and of individual or personality structures.

Kuhn fully recognized the great difficulty of changing a scientific paradigm:

> The difficulties of conversion have often been noted by scientists them-selves. Darwin ... wrote: "Although I am fully convinced of the truth of the views given in this volume ... I by no means expect to convince ex-perienced naturalists whose minds are stocked with a multitude of facts all viewed, during a long course of years, from a point of view directly opposite to mine.... But I look with confidence to the future, to young and rising naturalists, who will be able to view both sides of the question with impartiality." And Max Planck ... remarked that "A new scientific truth does not triumph by convincing its opponents and making them see the light, but rather because its opponents eventually die, and a new generation grows up that is familiar with it" (151).

Kuhn's analysis of how scientific paradigms change and how scientific revolutions occur raises serious questions about how we might proceed to shift from a stratified to an interactive worldview or metaphysical stance, assuming a parallel between a scientific revolution and a cultural revolution. For example, how are we to alter the forces of tradition embedded within culture? How can we possibly change fundamental patterns of social organization like social stratification? What about the deep-seated commitments of the individual located within personality structure? These questions have to do with nothing less than fundamental structures that guide the individual from one moment to the next. And if they work against changes in scientific paradigms we can expect them to be far more effective when it comes to worldviews or metaphysical stances that are far more deeply embedded in our way of life.

Yet Kuhn's analysis does at least suggest hypotheses about what might be required for a change of worldviews, granting the incredible difficulty and complexity of such a process. To start, we might become aware of a fundamental problem, such as an increasing aspirations-fulfillment gap in modern society as stated in hypothesis (1). Such awareness would not be easy to develop, since a stratified or Spaceland worldview would point us toward a far more simplistic view of phenomena that would not take into account any long-term historical process like the change from preindustrial to contemporary society. Many smaller steps might have to be involved in order to take this step, such as awareness of a gap between aspirations and fulfillment in different areas of life. The social scientist might, for example, have to become aware of the failure of traditional epistemology, or a stratified approach to the scientific method, in order to follow the scientific ideal of opening up to all relevant factors relative to a given scientific problem. But jumping from that awareness to a general consciousness of the failure of institutions other than that of science to fulfill expectations—for example, political, economic and religious ones—would constitute additional steps that might be required.

As a next step, we might come to see our existing stratified worldview as in part responsible for that general gap between our aspirations or expectations and their fulfillment, as stated in hypothesis (2). One serious problem here is that presently we know very little about the nature of the worldview or metaphysical stance which is widely shared. Philosophers, psychologists, sociologists and anthropologists have done little to analyze and document the nature of a metaphysical stance which we all share. What is required here is systematic research in this direction. Yet if our epistemology is indeed guided by a stratified or Spaceland worldview, then it would be difficult to embark on such research.

Also, we must have an alternative worldview—just as Einstein's special theory of relativity provided an alternative to Newton's laws of motion—which promises to solve the problems within that stratified worldview. Here, we also rely on hypothesis (2), which puts forward an interactive worldview as an alternative to a stratified worldview. That hypothesis includes eleven ideas as to the more specific aspects of an interactive worldview which may provide us with that alternative. Yet once again we know precious little about such an alternative worldview or those eleven aspects of it, and research on such broad phenomena would tend to be trumped by the narrowness of a Spaceland or stratified worldview.

In addition, that alternative worldview must be tested and be found to solve the problems within the initial worldview and also prove to be at least as effective as that initial worldview, just as Einstein's special theory was tested and found to be supported by available evidence. Such testing would have to encompass a wide range of our institutions if indeed we are to emerge with an alternative worldview that works better than our existing one. This would of course involve a great deal of research by investigators familiar with a wide variety of areas of knowledge.

A further problem is that we know very little about scientific revolutions, and this of course limits our understanding of cultural revolutions. Kuhn wrote about the "invisibility" of scientific revolutions:

> Textbooks ... have to be rewritten in the aftermath of each scientific revolution, and, once rewritten, they inevitably disguise not only the role but the very existence of the revolutions that produced them....

The depreciation of historical fact is deeply, and probably functionally, ingrained in the ideology of the scientific profession, the same profession that places the highest of all values upon factual details of other sorts (1962: 136–137).

This invisibility of scientific revolutions illustrates, in our view, the power of our stratified worldview or metaphysical stance. The disguising of scientific revolutions works against understanding the complexity of historical events, and it occurs in the face of scientific ideals requiring no such distortions.

Given all of these problems that might be involved in changing a worldview that Kuhn's work suggests, is it even realistic to consider this possibility? Should we conform to the idea that attempting such change is indeed a hopeless venture? Here we can fall back on the optimism to be found within the history of biophysical science. Once a problem has been brought up to the light of day and been defined scientifically, history indicates that it almost invariably has been solved. From the perspective of the Web and Part/Whole Approach to the scientific method, that definition of a problem appears to be the most important step in the scientific method. For it motivates the investigator to come up with a solution, and the scientific method furnishes the tools required for moving toward that solution.

Kuhn gives us a hint about the nature of a stratified versus an interactive worldview close to the end of his book:

All the well-known pre-Darwinian evolutionary theories ... had taken evolution to be a goal-directed process. The "idea" of man and of the contemporary flora and fauna was thought to have been present from the first creation of life, perhaps in the mind of God. That idea or plan had provided the direction and the guiding force to the entire evolutionary process. Each new stage of evolutionary development was a more perfect realization of a plan that had been present from the start. For many men the abolition of that teleological kind of evolution was the most significant and least palatable of Darwin's suggestions. The *Origin of Species* recognized no goal set either by God or nature.... Even such marvelously adapted organs as the eye and hand of man—organs whose design had previously provided powerful arguments for the existence of a supreme artificer and an advance plan—were products of a process that moved steadily *from* primitive beginnings but *toward* no goal (1962: 170–171).

The idea of "evolution from" is an interactive idea, by contrast with the hierarchical emphasis in the idea of "evolution toward," which has a fixed direction for evolution. And since biological evolution itself follows this interactive versus stratified worldview, this is indeed evidence for the importance of an interactive worldview for the human being. Yet the idea of "evolution toward"—with its link to "creationism"—remains a very popular idea despite all of the evidence on biological evolution that is now available. This illustrates the force of our stratified worldview.

In his closing paragraph Kuhn poses this question: "What must the world be like in order that man may know it?" If the physical universe were not interactive, by contrast with the discussion in chapter 1, then its parts could be completely isolated from one another, and its complexity would be severely limited. In that situation a stratified worldview with an accompanying highly specialized approach to science could succeed in uncovering the nature of the universe. Then it would go no further in yielding understanding, by contrast with our ideal of a scientific method which continues to yield ever more understanding. But with the incredible complexity of an interactive universe, by contrast, we appear to require an interactive science—supported by an interactive worldview—with the ability to penetrate ever more deeply into those complexities. They include the interaction between the scientist or the individual and the universe, and the individual does not remain static as his or her understanding increases. To answer Kuhn's question, we hypothesize that the world itself must be interactive if we are to know it with a scientific method that follows the scientific ideal of yielding ever increasing understanding.

## Levin's Experiment on Prejudice

Jack Levin's doctoral dissertation in sociology at Boston University, "The Influence of Social Frame of Reference for Goal Fulfillment on Social Aggression," was not designed to measure alternative worldviews, but it succeeded in doing so (Levin, 1968; see also Phillips, 1979: 185–187; 2002: 199–226). Its title might well have been simplified to "The Influence of Worldview on Prejudice." Although Levin centered on prejudice, his experiment has implications for aggression in general.

Levin's approach was quite broad. He began with a review of what is known as the "frustration-aggression hypothesis": the idea that individuals who are frustrated, say, by the actions of a bully, will react with hostility to the aggressor or to some easier target. This idea can be traced back to the work of Sigmund Freud, whose earlier writings regarded frustration as resulting from the blocking of pleasure-seeking or pain-avoidance. Freud along with more recent investigators emphasized the idea that aggression can be "displaced" to someone other than the source of the frustration. However, there are other possibilities, such as a victim's coming to blame self instead of becoming aggressive to others.

A number of studies which Levin reviewed emphasize the idea of "relative deprivation," where the individual comes to feel deprived relative to others. Levin gives this illustration:

> The appearance of relative evaluation among Negro Americans may be having profound effects on the character of the civil rights movement in the United States and on the expectations which Negro Americans have about it. Even though the actual gains of Negroes have been occurring faster since 1940 than during any other period of Negro American history, the position of Negro Americans assumes a desperately deprived character when contrasted with the typical conditions of contemporary white Americans.... The result has been a keen sense of relative deprivation (1968: 26).

Levin accepted the importance of relative deprivation, but he also opened up to greater complexity in the genesis of prejudice: "[I]t is often overlooked that the performances of other individuals and groups need not be employed as a point of reference, but that the individual may rely upon personal performances as a standard of comparison." He did not dismiss the importance of feelings of relative deprivation just as he did not dismiss the importance of frustration. But something was missing and should be added to the mix of factors producing aggression in general or prejudice in particular. And that something was what he called the individual's "social frame of reference for goal fulfillment," but what we call "worldview." Levin distinguished between two worldviews, corresponding to a stratified worldview and an interactive worldview:

> These alternative frames of reference for goal fulfillment can be identified as *relative evaluation* whereby the individual judges his personal performances relative to the productivity of other persons and groups, and *self evaluation* whereby the individual relies upon his other personal performances, past or present, as a standard of comparison (1968: 20).

Here, then, was a central part of the forces producing prejudice or aggression. Did the individual have a stratified worldview, characterized by "relative evaluation," where the individual looked outward, corresponding to outward perception (chapter 2)? Or did he or she have an interactive worldview, characterized by "self evaluation," with the individual looking inward to at least some extent (chapter 2)? But how was one to measure these alternatives? And how was one to deal with frustration along with relative deprivation? Further, how does one proceed to measure prejudice?

Levin decided that an experiment coupled with a questionnaire would be the best way to address all of these questions, given his situation as a graduate student in sociology. In that way he could begin with an initial measurement of degree of prejudice by using a questionnaire. Later he could launch his experiment, which would assess whether the individuals involved were oriented to a stratified or interactive worldview. It would also differentiate among groups of individuals: some would experience both frustration and relative deprivation, and others would not. He would also include a final measurement of degree of prejudice to assess the impact which worldview, frustration and relative deprivation had on the individual's degree of prejudice. For example, would it take all three factors—a stratified worldview, frustration and relative deprivation—to yield increased prejudice? Would those individuals with an interactive worldview prove to be resistant to such increased prejudice despite their experiencing frustration and relative deprivation?

It is useful for us to examine Levin's specific techniques. Granting that human behavior is exceedingly complex and social research must address that complexity, there are indeed procedures for doing so. Levin's questionnaire and experiment involved 180 freshmen and sophomores enrolled in two sections of introductory sociology at Boston University during the fall semester of 1965. He gave them an initial questionnaire—long before the experiment took place—which included attitudes toward Puerto Ricans measured with a question that followed the format of Osgood's semantic differential (1967). He proceeded as follows:

> Directions: Place an "X" in one position between the adjectives of each scale (e.g., ___ : ___ : ___ ) to indicate how well these adjectives apply in general to Puerto Ricans. Your evaluation should reflect what you believe many of the members of this particular group tend to be (what the average Puerto Rican is like), and not necessarily what 100% of them are.

### Puerto Ricans

| | | |
|---|---|---|
| reputable | ___ : ___ : ___ : ___ : ___ : ___ : ___ | disreputable |
| knowledgeable | ___ : ___ : ___ : ___ : ___ : ___ : ___ | ignorant |
| intelligent | ___ : ___ : ___ : ___ : ___ : ___ : ___ | stupid |
| industrious | ___ : ___ : ___ : ___ : ___ : ___ : ___ | lazy |
| kind | ___ : ___ : ___ : ___ : ___ : ___ : ___ | cruel |
| clean | ___ : ___ : ___ : ___ : ___ : ___ : ___ | dirty |
| straightforward | ___ : ___ : ___ : ___ : ___ : ___ : ___ | sly |
| reliable | ___ : ___ : ___ : ___ : ___ : ___ : ___ | unreliable |

Much later, when Levin launched his experiment, a key measurement had to do with the nature of the student's worldview, where "relative evaluation" indicated a stratified worldview and "self evaluation" indicated an interactive worldview. He administered a questionnaire within the experiment with several series of paragraphs like the one below. Those checking 1 or 2, comparing themselves with others, were seen as illustrating relative evaluation or a stratified worldview. Those checking 3 or 4, comparing themselves with their own previous performances, were seen as illustrating self evaluation or an interactive worldview.

> Mary was in her freshman year of high school and had just received a B on her first algebra examination. Joan, who was Mary's best friend, got an A on the same examination. The class average for the exam was C. Last year in junior high school, Mary had received a C in mathematics. This year, Mary's highest exam grade was an A in French.
>
> Without referring back to the paragraph on the preceding page [where the above paragraph was located] what do you think is the most accurate way to describe Mary's grade on her first algebra examination? (check only one)
>
> 1___Mary's algebra grade was higher than the class average.
> 2___Mary's algebra grade was lower than her best friend's grade.
> 3___Mary's algebra grade was higher than her last year's grade in mathematics.
> 4___Mary's algebra grade was lower than her grade in French.

As for the factor of frustration, students were led to believe that they were taking an aptitude test for graduate school. Actually, it was a bogus test requiring them to identify pairs of words as having either the same or opposite meanings, with a severe penalty for guessing in that an incorrect answer on any item would nullify two correct answers. They were given only 12 minutes to complete a test consisting of 150 items and were informed that less than 120 correct answers would result in automatic failure. Fully 50 of the 150 vocabulary-test items were constructed from nonsense syllables. No student completed more than 100 of the 150 items and, as a result, no one received a passing score. Immediately following this experience, students were once again given questions measuring their attitudes toward Puerto Ricans—the dependent variable—and this "after" measure was compared with the previous "before" measure to assess changes in levels of prejudice.

With respect to the factor of relative deprivation, those feelings were influenced by giving students this note in their test booklets: "In similar groups of undergraduates at Boston College and Syracuse University, the average student was able to correctly complete 143 of the 150 items." Given the fact that no student completed more than 100 items, they were all led to believe that they did substantially worse than the average student at Boston College and Syracuse University. When students were queried after the experiment was over, they stated that they had no idea that they were involved in an experiment.

The results of the Levin experiment strongly supported the importance of the individual's worldview as a factor in the genesis of prejudice. Frustration all by itself did not yield increased prejudice against Puerto Ricans. Feelings of relative deprivation all by themselves also did not yield such increased prejudice. But when these two factors were combined with a stratified worldview, increased prejudice was the result. That outer-oriented worldview influenced them to behave much like being on a see-saw relative to Puerto Ricans. Levin hypothesized that by putting down Puerto Ricans their own self-esteem would rise, if only temporarily, following their frustrating experience. The self evaluators with an interactive worldview, by contrast, would have nothing to gain by putting down—in see-saw fashion—members of a minority group and attempting to raise themselves up as a result. For they are located on their own stairways, looking to their own previous or contemporary performances in an effort to improve on them.

However, we should note that these students did in fact also compare themselves with others: their orientation was in fact inward-outward, and not purely inward. Their illustration of an interactive worldview generally was not substantial. This result supports the hypothesis that a stratified worldview is universal, and that departures from it do not go very far. Yet even a slight shift toward an interactive worldview can have dramatic repercussions.

Levin's experiment may have succeeded in creating a microcosm of the social and personality structures within modern society along with the specific situations we encounter in everyday life. He appears to have created conditions that illustrate figure I.1. By building substantial frustration into his experiment, he created the gap we see in that figure between aspirations and their fulfillment. In this case, expectations had to do with success in graduate school. Feelings of relative deprivation brought forward patterns of hierarchy or social stratification into the momentary scene of the experiment. Hypothesis (2) states that a stratified worldview lies behind figure I.1, with its growing gap between aspirations or expectations and fulfillment. Levin found that his microcosm yields increased prejudice.

Levin recognized in advance the potential importance of a finding that an individual's worldview affects prejudice, and he attempted to explore the implications of this finding with the aid of his questionnaire. He found many differences between the attitudes of individuals with a stratified worldview and those with the beginnings of an interactive worldview. For example, Levin's questionnaire included a 29–item version of the California F Scale, based on earlier studies of authoritarianism (Adorno et al., 1950). Although the F-scale throws together a number of heterogeneous phenomena which take away from its precision, it includes two subscales—"power and toughness" and "conventionalism"—which are homogeneous. The power-and-toughness cluster consists of items such as these, with responses on a five-point scale: "I agree strongly, I agree somewhat, I neither agree nor disagree, I disagree somewhat, I disagree strongly":

> Obedience and respect for authority are the most important virtueschildren should learn.

> No weakness or difficulty can hold us back if we have enough will power.

> Every person should have complete faith in some supernatural power whose decisions he obeys without question.

> An insult to our honor should always be punished.

> Sex crimes, such as rape and attacks on children, deserve more than mere imprisonment: such criminals ought to be publicly whipped, or worse.

> There is hardly anything lower than a person who does not feel a great love, gratitude, and respect for his parents.

> Most of our social problems would be solved if we could somehow get rid of the immoral, crooked, and feeble-minded people.

Levin found that those with a stratified worldview agreed with these statements to a greater extent than those with an interactive worldview. We might see such agreement as linked to a belief in the value of social stratification within society and, thus, bearing on that aspect of a stratified worldview which is the focus of chapter 8, namely, the impact of social stratification on the aspirations-fulfillment gap. Levin also found that those with a stratified worldview tended to agree with the items on the following subscale of conventionalism—also rated on the same five-point scale—by contrast with those students with an interactive worldview:

> Young people sometimes get rebellious ideas, but as they grow up they ought to get over them and settle down.

> If people would talk less and work more, everybody would be better off.

Nowadays when so many different kinds of people move around and mix together so much, a person has to protect himself especially carefully against catching an infection or disease from them.

No sane, normal, decent person could ever think of hurting a close friend or relative.

Nowadays more and more people are prying into matters that should remain personal and private.

The wild sex life of the old Greeks and Romans was tame compared to some of the goings-on in this country, even in places where people might least expect it.

A person who has bad manners, habits and breeding can hardly expect to get along with decent people.

This finding bears on conforming behavior, which is the focus of chapter 11. Levin also found that students with a stratified worldview—by contrast with those with some degree of an interactive worldview—tended to downgrade the capabilities of the human being, based on what he called the DC scale, as illustrated by these questions rated on the same five-point scale:

The degree of intelligence with which any particular child is endowed determines his general efficiency all throughout life and sets an upper limit to what he can successfully perform.

Science has its place, but there are many important things that can never be understood by the human mind.

The nature of man's achievements is predetermined by his heredity.

Nobody ever learned anything really important except through suffering.

This finding appears related to the focus of chapter 6 on the nature of the scientific method, including its optimistic orientation.

In our view Levin's experiment illustrates what social science research has been able to achieve at its best. It builds on the knowledge obtained by previous investigators, it is done in a very careful manner, it includes at least some assessment of the investigator's own impact on the research process (e.g., Levin asked students whether they thought that they were in an experiment), and it is broad enough to take into account a great many of the factors relevant to the problem that is under investigation. Nevertheless, given our assumption of a stratified worldview throughout society as well as the academic world, such research is buried within narrow specialized fields, and social scientists in other fields almost invariably fail to make any use of its implications for the problems that they are addressing.

The Levin experiment gives us a clearer idea of the nature of a stratified worldview as well as an interactive worldview It also gives us some evidence as to the negative impact of a stratified worldview—by contrast with an interactive worldview—on prejudice. And it opens up to aspects of a stratified worldview, such as stratification, conformity and opposition to the scientific method. Perhaps most important, it illustrates ways in which those worldviews might be measured. Given our focus on secondary analyses, we have not addressed the problem of measurement in a systematic way. This will require primary and not just secondary research. Levin's research yields at least one way in which we might proceed.

## Merton's "The Unanticipated Consequences of Purposive Social Action"

Robert K. Merton pointed out the importance of "the unanticipated consequences of purposive social action" in a paper published in 1936. One illustration comes from Robert Michels' 1949 study, *Political Parties,* based on work with Socialist parties and progressive unions in Germany between World Wars I and II. Those organizations changed over time from relatively informal groups to hierarchical or stratified groups organized along bureaucratic lines with a division of labor. It was a change initiated by those groups in order to push their programs more effectively and perpetuate the authority of the leaders. Yet the result was that this changed pattern of organization worked to subvert the egalitarian ideals of those parties and unions, a result that was not anticipated and that was generally resented by the members. A similar example has to do with religious organizations, as studied by David Moberg (1962: 118-125). In its earliest stage a sect or cult generally emphasizes personal spontaneity and the avoidance of ritualism. Yet in order to achieve efficiency at a later time and stabilize the positions of church officials, it places less emphasis on emotion and moves toward ritualism, and this results in the unanticipated loss of meaning and relevance of the church in the eyes of its members.

The idea of unanticipated consequences of purposive social action is particularly useful because it questions the simplistic assumptions accompanying our belief in the overriding effectiveness of human rationality. Rationality works well up to a point, but it cannot make up for our lack of understanding of phenomena, a lack accompanying the enormous complexity of human behavior. Such complexity is illustrated by the limited degree to which we are able to communicate with one another in any given group as well as the repercussions of that limitation. Prisoner's dilemma, a game that is important within the literature of cognitive psychology (see for example Wright, 2000) illustrates the impact of a failure of communication among individuals by setting up a situation where two partners in crime are being interrogated separately. The state has enough evidence to convict them both on a lesser charge, resulting in a one-year prison term for each. But if a prisoner presents evidence against his partner, he will go free while his partner will receive a ten-year sentence. If each presents evidence against the other, then they both will receive a three-year sentence. In this situation, lack of communication will tend to result in both confessing and both receiving a three-year sentence in order to avoid a ten-year sentence. But with communication which might lead to trust, both might avoid confessing and thus receive only a one-year sentence. Granting the artificiality of the game, it does illustrate both the limitations and the importance of communication in society, and also the unintended consequence of receiving a longer sentence than one would with better communication.

We might argue that the negative outcome for the prisoners—a three-year versus a one-year sentence—is linked to a stratified or Spaceland worldview which would constrain them to avoid communicating with and learning to trust one another. The game itself is structured so that no such communication and learning is possible, since the prisoners are interrogated separately and have no ability to communicate with one another. This should be no surprise, since we assume the prevalence of a stratified worldview, and this might well include those who invented the game. In order to test the potential of an interactive or Timeland worldview, the game would have to allow such communication to occur. Then the empirical question might be: under what conditions would they be able to build up sufficient trust so as to avoid confessions and thus receive the minimum sentences. For example, would reflexive behavior—an aspect of an interactive worldview where each was able to express fundamental personal experiences—be conducive to the development of such trust? It would be most interesting to invent a series of games which allow for the possibility of movement toward an interactive worldview. Presently, almost all of our games, including sports of all kinds, are zero-sum games where the gain of one individual or team accompanies the loss of the other. They illustrate a stratified worldview with winners and losers. Multiple-sum games, where both may gain—as illustrated by egalitarian and profound communication between two individuals—apparently are quite rare, yet they do illustrate an interactive worldview or metaphysical stance.

The historian Hilmar Raushenbush has come up with many historical examples of unanticipated consequences of purposive action (1969; see also Phillips, 1979: 228–230), suggesting the widespread and long-term nature of this phenomenon. Looking to ancient times, Athenian leaders tried to force obedience from small Greek towns in order to extend their empire, but this action ultimately contributed to the subversion of Athenian democracy and independence. As another example, Roman aristocrats sought to acquire wealth by confiscating common lands from villagers. But soldiers' pensions came from the income produced by those common lands, and Roman generals confiscated the aristocrats' properties in order to pay those pensions. An example from religion is that early Christians allied themselves and the Church with the Roman Empire in order to give their religion a firmer foundation. But the result was that Christianity absorbed an elitest or hierarchical orientation that conflicted with its ideals for equality and love.

Closer to modern times, after World War I the allies sought to keep Germany weak by forcing it to accept sole guilt for the war and by collecting large indemnities. But this helped Hitler to build up a resentful nationalism, destroy German democratic institutions and create a powerful war machine. Another example of unintended consequences is the result of Britain's attempt to prevent Indian independence by violently suppressing the Gandhian movement. But this stirred the British and Indian conscience to give greater support to the independence movement. The civil rights movement in the U.S. provides another illustration. In attempting to deprive blacks of their civil rights, some Southern sheriffs used cattle prods and police dogs. This was picked up by television cameras and resulted in a moral outcry that helped to insure the passage of civil rights laws. Closer to the present, the invasion of Iraq by the United States was meant to protect the country from weapons of mass destruction. Yet it encouraged an insurgency which threatens not only America's military forces in Iraq but also the U.S. population through the development of links with Al Qaeda.

These examples emphasize major changes in society as a whole, but we can equally note the prevalence of unanticipated consequences in our own everyday lives. For example, parents who are "only trying to help" their children often find that their efforts to change or control their children's lives actually result in making things worse and hurting their relationships with their children. Individuals who wait to find "the perfect mate" often find themselves either with no mate at all or else in a divorce court because the mate finally selected was unable to live up to unrealistic expectations (Farson, 1977). People who postpone working toward the career they want by taking a "temporary job" often find that the temporary job has become permanent and that their wished-for career has completely disappeared as a possibility for them. Taking a drink, a smoke or lots of extra calories "just this once" can work to feed an addiction that becomes ever more difficult to change. We might note that Merton's idea has been extended here to include not only purposive social actions but also purposive actions in general.

Why are unanticipated consequences of purposive actions so common? Why is it so difficult for groups and individuals to act effectively so as to achieve their purposes instead of being faced with unanticipated consequences that go against those purposes? What is the nature of a society where unanticipated consequences occur frequently in groups large and small, and also within the lives of individuals? Are unanticipated consequences somehow basic to human nature? Are there conditions under which that prevalence can be reduced?

We might hypothesize that unanticipated consequences are tied closely to a stratified worldview with its simplistic approach to the complexity of human behavior. By failing to take into account that complexity, it is reasonable to believe that we leave ourselves open to unanticipated consequences resulting from factors which we failed to take into account.

For example, one possible unanticipated consequence of social research which fails to assess investigator effect is that researchers will find evidence supporting their hypotheses—resulting from investigator effect—when in fact their purposes were to be open to other possibilities. An interactive worldview, by contrast, would encourage the measurement of investigator effect and help the investigator to fulfill the purpose of following the ideals of the scientific method.

## Some Implications

The idea of unanticipated consequences opens up to the complexity of human behavior along with the oversimplification behind efforts to solve social problems. Their widespread existence in modern society suggests the possibility of an aspirations-fulfillment gap. More specifically, their existence suggests a large gap between simplistic assumptions—to be found in such applied fields as government, business, education and social work—and the actual complexity of phenomena. Central to this book is the assumption of complexity within an interactive worldview and approach to the scientific method. Equally central to this book is hypothesis (2): that a stratified worldview works to produce that gap. We can see how this works through the oversimplification of complex phenomena, and this analysis of Merton's concept thus indicates his support of hypothesis (2). What this implies is the continuation in the future of unanticipated consequences of purposive action. As for hypothesis (1), namely, an increasing gap, Merton's analysis does not bear on it.

It is indeed tempting to blame social scientists for a state of affairs where social research continues to proceed with an oversimplified approach to human behavior despite substantial evidence to the contrary. For example, Walter Buckley's *Sociology and Modern Systems Theory* (chapter 1) pointed up the complexity of human behavior and even offered a direction for a methodology that would open up to that complexity. Gouldner's discussion of the need for a reflexive sociology (chapter 2) along with evidence about the importance of investigator effect cries out for a more complex view of the research process. Kuhn's analysis of scientific revolutions with its indication of the power of culture, social organization and personality structures in holding off those revolutions is further evidence for complexity, and thus supports hypothesis (2). And Levin's experiment on prejudice provides indirect evidence for the near-universal existence of a stratified worldview with a greatly oversimplified view of human behavior. That experiment also supports hypothesis (1), with its analysis of an increasing gap associated with the civil rights movement, and also supports hypothesis (2) with his finding of increased prejudice associated with a stratified worldview. By contrast, Kuhn joins Merton in not bearing on hypothesis (1).

# Chapter 4

# "Heart"

## Alienation versus Expressive Orientation

In moving from chapter 3 to chapter 4 we are moving from an emphasis on the "head" or ideas to a focus on the "heart," that is, feelings or emotions. "Alienation," linked closely to feelings or emotions—which are closely tied to interests, goals, values, or motives—is a central concept within sociology, so much so that the idea has penetrated popular culture. One of its key meanings has to do with the repression of emotions, and here we contrast this with the expression of emotions. Let us recall the large gap within contemporary society in figure I.1 between the top curve of aspirations or expectations and the bottom curve of fulfillment. Given the existence of that gap within an individual, what is he or she to do? One possibility, emphasized by Vidich and Bensman (chapter 10), is to repress any awareness of that gap so that one can go on with one's day-to-day experiences without having to confront a problem that one does not know how to solve. The result, then, is alienation. An alternative approach might be to use that awareness as a basis for defining that gap as a problem that should and must be confronted. Here, one need not hide from that gap but rather might be free to express one's feelings in relation to the gap. Whereas in the former case the individual narrows his or her perspective in the manner of a stratified worldview, in the latter that perspective is broadened in the manner of an interactive worldview.

In chapter 4 we begin with Karl Marx's 1844 essay analyzing alienation. His focus in that work early in his career was on drawing out the incredible contradiction or gap between ideals for humanity brought forward during the American and French revolutions and the actuality of working conditions and an economic system which he believed trashed those ideals. Since he coupled that awareness with a general direction which he believed would solve that problem, he attempted to influence his audience to join him in developing that awareness coupled with the motivation to change their situation. From the Introduction to this book we might recall a parallel between our own approach to the aspirations-fulfillment or expectations-fulfillment gap and Marx's belief in a growing contradiction between the forces of production and the relations of production. Both approaches emphasize fundamental and growing problems in contemporary society. A key difference is that, while Marx generally ignored the power and breadth of culture in favor of patterns of social organization, we add to Marx's concern with social stratification a concern for a cultural revolution of rising expectations as the key "force of production" which is a basis for those growing problems.

Georg Simmel was deeply concerned, as was Marx, with the fate of the individual in contemporary society, and he was particularly sensitive to our emotional lives. His orientation was even broader than that of Marx, for he believed in the importance of culture in addition to social organization, and he was also much concerned with the individual's emotional life. He did not use the term "alienation," but he was in fact interested in the same kinds of problems facing the individual in contemporary society which Marx addressed. Although some sociologists accused him of pessimism, we believe that he was realistic about what was happening at the end of the nineteenth century. Yet he remained hopeful about human possibilities and committed to the possibilities of sociology to reveal our fundamental problems.

Karen Horney's *The Neurotic Personality of Our Time* was one of those rare books that managed to bridge the divide separating psychology from sociology as well as the divide separating social science theory from practical applications. She wrote in 1937 about the gap depicted in figure I.1, discussing society's production of contradictory tendencies leading to individual neurosis. For example: "The second contradiction is that between the stimulation of our needs and our factual frustrations in satisfying them." As a psychoanalyst, Horney's emphasis on society and culture led her to being largely ruled out of psychoanalytic circles as a traitor to her profession, and she was certainly not welcomed in sociological circles because of her psychological interests. Yet she gave us a taste of the insights awaiting us when we combine those two disciplines along with an interest in solving problems.

## Marx's 1844 Essay on Alienation

Marx wrote these words about the plight of the worker in industrial society just before the Revolution of 1848 in Paris:

We have now considered the act of alienation of practical human activity, labour, from two aspects: (1) the relationship of the worker to the product of labour as an alien object which dominates him ... (2) the relationship of labour to the act of production within labour. This is the relationship of the worker to his own activity as something alien and not belonging to him.... This is self-alienation as against the above-mentioned alienation of the thing.... Since alienated labour: (1) alienates nature from man; and (2) alienates man from himself, from his own active function, his life activity; so it alienates him from (3) the species.... For labour, life activity, productive life, now appear to man only as means for the satisfaction of a need, the need to maintain his physical existence.... [F]ree, conscious activity is the species-character of human beings. (4) A direct consequence of the alienation of man from the product of his labour, from his life activity and from his species-life, is that man is alienated from other men (Marx, 1844/1964: 125–127, 129).

Marx saw the worker's alienation as tied to the nature of industrial society, where the proletariat are pawns of the capitalistic system. In particular, he saw the persisting hierarchy or social stratification between capitalists and workers as basic to generating the worker's alienation. As a result of his experiences within the workplace, the worker is dehumanized (biological structure), has no control of his own activities (personality structure), comes to be divorced from his physical environment (physical structure), and also loses out on relating to his fellow man (social structure). Marx's broad orientation to the idea of alienation yields a definition of alienation as persisting feelings of isolation from self, others, one's own biological structure and the physical universe. That breadth parallels our own treatment within this book of physical, biological, individual and social structures. We have added a focus on the situation, since it is a combination of momentary situational analysis and long-term structural analysis that appears to yield an understanding of change.

It is the combination of Marx's intellectual breadth, emotional commitment and personal investment in taking action on his beliefs and feelings that helps to explain his worldwide political impact. The following passage from his essay on alienation can give us a sense of his ability to express himself emotionally:

The more the worker produces the less he has to consume; the more value he creates the more worthless he becomes; the more refined his product the more crude and misshapen the worker; the more civilized the product the more barbarous the worker; the more powerful the work the more feeble the worker; the more the work manifests intelligence the more the worker declines in intelligence and becomes a slave of nature.... Labor certainly produces marvels for the rich but it produces privation for the worker. It produces palaces, but hovels for the worker. It produces beauty, but deformity for the worker. It replaces labor by machinery, but it casts some of the workers back into a barbarous kind of work and turns the others into machines. It produces intelligence, but also stupidity and cretinism for the workers (1844/1964: 122–124).

Marx achieves his emotional force by making good use of language's capacity to help us to communicate effectively. For example, he builds on the dichotomous emphasis within language to present sharp contrasts, such as the idea of the worker becoming more worthless as he creates more value. He also uses metaphor effectively, as in his contrast between palaces and beauty for the owner but hovels and deformity for the worker. Also, he makes use of language's gradational potential as well, seeing the situation of the worker getting worse and worse as the situation of the owner gets better and better. This gradational approach is much the same as our own depiction of a hypothesized increasing gap between aspirations or expectations and their fulfillment as we move from preindustrial to contemporary society. If work succeeds in dehumanizing us biologically, if it divorces us from control over our own activities, if it divides us from the physical environment, and if it isolates us from our fellow human beings, then we are facing an increasingly unbearable situation.

Fritz Pappenheim, a student of economics, sociology and philosophy, uses different words than our own argument about that increasing gap to argue for increasing alienation from preindustrial to contemporary society:

> In the present stage of history man has means of self-realization at his command which were unknown to him in former periods. The immense advance in science and technology has helped him to understand the forces of nature to such a degree that he is not any longer at their mercy.... Once this concept of the individual's sovereignty has been awakened in the minds of men, a new climate is prepared. The consciousness that man's yearning for self-realization is thwarted becomes a crushing experience which could not have existed in previous stages (1959: 114–115).

Pappenheim uses history just as Marx did over a century earlier to assess the problems of society and the individual. He sees more clearly than Marx the top curve of figure I.1: "The immense advance in science and technology has helped him [the individual] to understand the forces of nature to such a degree that he is not any longer at their mercy." This creates in turn "a new climate" in the minds of men, new aspirations or expectations relating to "man's yearning for self-realization." At the present time in history, then, awareness of a huge gap between those aspirations and their lack of fulfillment would become "a crushing experience," given a lack of any direction for closing that gap. Here, then, is the basis for contemporary alienation. We all seek to avoid that "crushing experience," repressing any awareness of that gap and learning to repress our emotions in general. As a result, if alienation was a central problem in Marx's day, it is far more of a problem at the present time when "man's yearning for self-realization" has increased enormously, as portrayed by the top curve of figure I.1.

Marx's interest in the importance of alienation did not subside after his early analyses of that idea in his *Economic and Philosophical Manuscripts of 1844*. Arguments have been made to the contrary by a number of Marxists—not by Marx himself—who would prefer to focus on the problems within social structures alone and thus oversimplify an interpretation of Marx's ideas. By focusing on social structures like patterns of hierarchy or social stratification, and by addressing as well personality structures like alienation, Marx succeeded in opening up problems which are incredibly difficult to solve. Current research in social science has moved far away from Marx's broad focus on the alienation of the worker—along with the rest of us in contemporary society—to much narrower concerns, such as the alienation of voters in elections held periodically. For example, there is a good deal of analysis of alienation in relation to nonvoting in the United States (see for example Lipset and Schneider, 1983; Abramson and Aldrich, 1982; Shaffer, 1981; Piven and Cloward, 1988). This is quite understandable, given our hypothesis that the highly specialized orientations of academicians stem from a stratified worldview. Yet by so doing, current research loses the forest for the trees. If alienation in Marx's broad sense is indeed increasing as modernization proceeds, then we are faced with an invisible crisis in contemporary society. There is support for the existence of that increase, as illustrated by Kai Erikson's portrayal of automated procedures in the office as well as the factory (1986). To focus on patterns of voting while ignoring increasing alienation in the modern world is to fiddle while Rome is burning.

Although Marx's analysis was extremely broad, he did not take culture very seriously, as Pappenheim does. At least as important, he did not examine the metaphysical assumptions behind an industrial way of life with increasing alienation. This is not to fault Marx but rather to build on his work. His hypothesis of increasing problems in society parallels our own hypothesis of an increasing expectations-fulfillment gap. Yet his failure to see the importance of culture, and his failure to move to the level of metaphysical assumptions, prevented him from seeing any alternative to a violent political revolution as a means to address the problems he unearthed. Cultural and metaphysical changes are most difficult to achieve, yet they require no violent political revolution. Of course, we still know very little about how to achieve such fundamental changes in modern society.

## Simmel's "Metropolis and Mental Life"

Georg Simmel's orientation to the individual was no less broad than that of Marx, and he maintained his focus on the individual throughout his life, a focus that was and still is quite rare for a sociologist. If we look to figure I.1 and concentrate on the implications of that huge gap between aspirations or expectations and their fulfillment for the life of the individual, then we point ourselves in Simmel's direction. Along with other founders of sociology, Simmel was much concerned with the enormous changes in society that the industrial revolution was bringing about. His most well-known essay, "The Metropolis and Mental Life," centered on fundamental problems which such changes were posing for the city-dweller and, more generally, for the modern individual. His opening paragraph reads as follows:

> The deepest problems of modern life flow from the attempt of the individual to maintain the independence and individuality of his existence against the sovereign powers of society, against the weight of the historical heritage and the external culture and technique of life.... The eighteenth century may have called for liberation from all the ties which grew up historically in politics, in religion, in morality and in economics in order to permit the original natural virtue of man, which is equal in everyone, to develop without inhibition; the nineteenth century may have sought to promote, in addition to man's freedom, his individuality ... And his achievements which make him unique and indispensable (1903/1971:324).

Simmel manages to pack a great many ideas within his short essays, an ability based on his own emphasis on teaching as distinct from highly systematic, very well-documented and relatively narrow scientific papers or books. His essays are much like lectures one would give in a classroom, carrying ideas that are stimulating, covering very broad topics, and packing the emotional punch that metaphors can give to an argument. For example, his discussion in the above quote of the eighteenth and nineteenth centuries can help us to understand the revolution of rising expectations or aspirations—the top curve in figure I.1—that apparently followed the rise of science and technology in the seventeenth century. He points to intangible changes in our cultural values that center on the individual. The eighteenth century, associated with the American and French revolutions, yielded values emphasizing freedom, equality and democracy. The nineteenth century did not reject those values, and added on to them the cultural value of individuality or uniqueness. Although Simmel wrote those words a century ago, they remain most insightful as to the interests of the individual even now. Simmel's focus on intangibles such as cultural values contrasts with Marx's emphasis on hierarchies, such as between owners and workers. Yet we need both orientations for a fuller view of human behavior and human complexity.

In that same essay on the metropolis and mental life, Simmel described the impact of an urban way of life on the individual's emotional life, paralleling Marx's analysis of the emotional impact of work on the worker:

> [T]he essentially intellectualistic character of the mental life of the metropolis becomes intelligible as over against that of the small town which rests more on feelings and emotional relationships. These latter are rooted in the unconscious levels of the mind and develop most readily in the steady equilibrium of unbroken customs. Thus the metropolitan type—which naturally takes on a thousand individual modifications—creates a protective organ for itself against the profound disruption with which the fluctuations and discontinuities of the external milieu threaten it. Instead of reacting emotionally, the metropolitan type reacts primarily in a rational manner, thus creating a mental predominance through the intensification of consciousness....
>
> Money is concerned only with what is common to all, i.e., with the exchange value which reduces all quality and individuality to a purely quantitative level. All emotional relationships between persons rest on their individuality, whereas intellectual relationships deal with persons as with numbers.... It is in this very manner that the inhabitant of the metropolis reckons with his merchant, his customer, and with his servant, and frequently with the persons with whom he is thrown into obligatory association. These relationships stand in distinct contrast with the nature of the smaller circle in which the inevitable knowledge of individual characteristics produces, with an equal inevitability, an emotional tone in conduct, a sphere which is beyond the mere objective weighting of tasks performed and payments made (1903/1971: 325–327).

In the above quote we can understand more fully the differences between Marx and Simmel in Simmel's discussion of money, with his emphasis on the intangible impact of a money economy. Marx saw money in relation to the hierarchical relationship between owners and workers, or between the haves and the have-nots. He also saw money as part of an entire economic system that functions to strengthen that hierarchy and produce ever greater problems of poverty and alienation for the worker. Simmel saw the money economy as working to take away from people's individuality along with their ability to express themselves emotionally and develop close relationships with others. Simmel did not focus on the situation of the worker in the workplace, but was oriented to people's everyday lives throughout society. Both of them saw the money economy as linked to the entire way of life of contemporary society. Also, both of them were highly critical of the impact of a money economy on that way of life.

Later in that essay Simmel gives us a preview of a key idea he was to emphasize a few years later about a growing gap between "objective culture," following the usual definition of culture as widely shared interests and beliefs, and "subjective culture," having to do with the individual's unique personal life.

> This discrepancy is in essence the result of the success of the growing division of labor. For it is this which requires from the individual an ever more one-sided type of achievement which, at its highest point, often permits his personality as a whole to fall into neglect. In any case this overgrowth of objective culture has been less and less satisfactory for the individual.... [H]e is reduced to a negligible quantity. He becomes a single cog as over against the vast overwhelming organization of things and forces which gradually take out of his hands everything connected with progress, spirituality and value (1903/1971: 337).

Simmel elaborated on this distinction between "objective culture" and "subjective culture" in "Subjective Culture," an essay he published in 1908 (1908/1971: 227-234).

Simmel's emphasis on making the development of subjective culture central to contemporary society is linked to his desire to provide a basis for the development of individuality. Let us recall that he saw "the deepest problems of modern life" as linked to the attempt of the individual "to maintain ... independence and individuality." But does the threat to individuality lie simply in the sheer quantity of "objective culture," such as the millions of bits of information that computers send out, the millions of books in our libraries, and the thousands of hours we spend as audiences for film and television programs? Or does it lie in a worldview which, even in the past when far less "objective culture" existed, kept knowledge in isolated compartments? We hypothesize that it is the latter far more than the former. We also hypothesize that an interactive worldview would help the individual to pull together important knowledge and make that knowledge part of the individual's subjective culture no matter how large objective culture becomes. Simmel's many essays hint at his insights into the problems of contemporary society. Yet he remained unable to integrate those insights into a coherent and systematic theory of the forces which generated the scientific and industrial revolutions along with the problem of alienation in contemporary society.

## Horney's *The Neurotic Personality of Our Time*

Karen Horney's *The Neurotic Personality of Our Time* (1937)—along with the analyses of Marx and Simmel—points in a broad direction. She practiced psychoanalysis in Berlin before settling in New York, where she continued her practice and taught at the New School for Social Research. But her ideas emphasized the importance of culture and not just biology in the origins of neurosis, departing from some of Freud's basic principles, and she was expelled from the New York Psychoanalytic Institute. Here are some of her ideas about the impact of modern culture on all of us individuals:

> When we remember that in every neurosis there are contradictory tendencies which the neurotic is unable to reconcile, the question arises as to whether there are not likewise certain definite contradictions in our culture, which underlie the typical neurotic conflicts.
>
> The first contradiction to be mentioned is that between competition and success on the one hand, and brotherly love and humility on the other. On the one hand everything is done to spur us toward success, which means that we must be not only assertive but aggressive, able to push others out of the way. On the other hand we are deeply imbued with Christian ideals which declare that it is selfish to want anything for ourselves, that we should be humble, turn the other cheek, be yielding. For this contradiction there are only two solutions within the normal range: to take one of these strivings seriously and discard the other; or to take both seriously with the result that the individual is seriously inhibited in both directions.
>
> The second contradiction is that between the stimulation of our needs and our factual frustrations in satisfying them. For economic reasons needs are constantly being stimulated in our culture by such means as advertisements, "conspicuous consumption," the ideal of "keeping up with the Joneses." For the great majority, however, the actual fulfillment of these needs is closely restricted. The psychic consequence for the individual is a constant discrepancy between his desires and their fulfillment (287–288).

Let us begin with Horney's first contradiction, "between competition and success on the one hand, and brotherly love and humility on the other." We have here two opposing values or interests that Horney claimed exist within each of us. But how can she possibly make such a claim, since she saw relatively few patients in her psychoanalytic practice? Horney was well aware of the concept of culture. Although that concept has rarely been treated in a systematic way, there is a great deal of evidence that a people or the members of a society share many interests and beliefs. We can anticipate our discussion in chapter 7, "Anomie versus Cultural Value Fulfillment," by referring to two sets of cultural values which often oppose one another: work-related cultural values like "achievement and success," and people-oriented cultural values like "equality" and "individual personality."

We might recall Simmel's argument that the eighteenth century emphasized "equality" and "freedom," while the nineteenth century emphasized "individuality," suggesting the impact of cultural values.

Let us examine the implications of her first contradiction. With reference to figure I.1 she is discussing the top curve of widely shared aspirations or expectations, distinguishing between opposing aspirations. That top curve, then, is more complex than it appears to be in figure I.1. Beyond that complexity is the idea that an understanding of the components of culture can help us to understand ourselves along with every other individual within society. We need not do a psychoanalysis of ourselves or others in order to gain a great deal of understanding of people. An understanding of culture gives us a short-cut to understanding much of human behavior. Of course, people's interests do indeed vary to an extent. Not everyone has the same commitment to the cultural values of equality and success. Further, groups as well vary in their commitment to cultural values. Nevertheless, the idea of culture tells us that such variation is limited, and that all individuals in a given society share the same values to a certain extent. It is an idea that enables us to see what would otherwise remain invisible: that forces in society have shaped us, and that our deepest values and beliefs along with our personal problems are not simply the result of our own personal choices or of conformity to particular groups.

Horney's second contradiction, "between the stimulation of our needs and our factual frustrations in satisfying them," is much the same as the contradiction between the two curves of figure I.1: our revolution of rising expectations or aspirations, and our limited fulfillment of those aspirations. The result is the gap between what we expect and what we actually obtain, as depicted in figure I.1. Just as the idea of "culture" enables us to see that top curve as applying to all of us, so does the idea of "social stratification" enable us to see how that bottom curve applies to all of us. No other concept is backed up by as much research as is the existence of social stratification throughout society. It applies to every one of us, and it sharply limits our opportunities for fulfilling our cultural values or ideals. Let us recall John Berger's *Ways of Seeing* in chapter 2: "Publicity speaks in the future tense and yet the achievement of this future is endlessly deferred." Let us also recall Daniel Boorstin's analysis, presented along with the Berger example: "Yet never has a people felt more deceived and disappointed. For never has a people expected so much more than the world could offer."

As in the case of Horney's first contradiction, the implications of this second contradiction are substantial. For it speaks to other fundamental problems not only in contemporary society as a whole but also within each of us. It is no less invisible than are the contradictions within culture. Following Horney's argument, it is also a source of neurosis, deeply affecting our own well-being or satisfaction with life along with our ability to function effectively. Yet the forces shaping our problems are more complex than those of culture and social stratification alone, as illustrated by the chapter headings of this book. Robert Merton, who introduced us to the unanticipated consequences of purposive action in chapter 3, alerts us to some of those other forces in a footnote to one of the most well-known articles in sociology:

> Despite her consistent concern with "culture".... Horney does not explore differences in the impact of this culture upon farmer, worker and businessman, upon lower-, middle-, and upper-class individuals, upon members of various ethnic and racial groups, etc. As a result, the role of "inconsistencies in culture" is *not* located in its differential impact upon diversely situated groups. Culture becomes a kind of blanket covering all members of the society equally, apart from their idiosyncratic differences in life-history (1949: 379).

Merton is alerting us to the importance of the ideas in chapter 8, "Social Stratification versus Egalitarian Social Relationships." It is in that chapter that we take up the differences among groups to which sociologists have given a great deal of attention. When we couple those differences with what diverse groups share—such as culture, to be discussed in chapter 7—we open up to more of the complex forces shaping our behavior. Yet the spirit of Merton's footnote is one-sided, emphasizing the importance of group differences as against the impact of culture. For Merton, culture appears to be no more than some kind of blanket which distorts our true situation by covering us all equally. Given his emphasis on group differences, he fails to give culture its due and recognize its impact on every member of society, granting that this impact varies to some extent among different groups. More generally, he illustrates the spirit of specialization to be found throughout the social sciences. It is a spirit based on the idea that the specialized social scientist can go it alone, and that he or she need not pay that much attention to the other social sciences. It tends to separate those sociologists interested in culture—a rapidly growing number—and those interested in groups and social stratification. That same spirit of specialization would tend to take into account *either* the top or cultural curve of figure I.1 *or* the bottom curve emphasizing social stratification, thus missing out on an understanding of an absolutely central problem within contemporary society: the gap between the two curves.

Let us take note of Horney's concern with the time dimension. We might recall our emphasis on our residence in Flatland rather than Timeland in the discussion of Edwin Abbott's *Flatland* in chapter 1. That emphasis leads to our largely ignoring our personal past experiences or the long-term history of the human race, focusing instead on the present moment. Horney's interest in culture helped her to pay attention to history as well, since culture can and does change substantially over time. For example, figure I.1 portrays a dramatic increase in our expectations—nothing less than a revolution of rising expectations—over the past four centuries. It is commonly argued that every age has its problems, and that the older generation always looks nostalgically at the past when, supposedly, our modern problems are not unusually severe relative to earlier problems. Such an argument works in a direction opposite to the approach taken in this book: to bury awareness of deepening and extremely dangerous problems in contemporary society. But evidence from many sources may support an opposing hypothesis: that the gap in figure I.1 is widening.

Given the assumption that Horney's work is highly significant, the relative lack of attention to her work appears to be related to her breadth of orientation. For that violates the specialized orientations we have developed within a stratified worldview. She was oriented to the importance of culture, whereas Freud's followers had learned to see biology as central to understanding human behavior and ruled her out of the New York Psychoanalytic Institute. Also, that cultural orientation did not sit well with sociologists who emphasized groups, social stratification and bureaucracy. Neither did her interest in the individual endear her to the sociologists and anthropologists of her day. As if all this were not enough, she was a psychoanalyst who had a practice and was deeply concerned with solving problems. Just as in the case of the way physicists tend to see engineers, social scientists tend to see practitioners as limited in their ability to make genuine contributions to social science. By and large, then, Horney departed to an extent from the stratified worldview that appears to dominate social science.

In an effort to confront her first contradiction—"between competition and success on the one hand, and brotherly love and humility on the other"—Horney writes: "For this contradiction there are only two solutions within the normal range: to take one of these strivings seriously and discard the other; or to take both seriously with the result that the individual is seriously inhibited in both directions."

A third alternative, one which is outside of "the normal range," also can be applied to the second contradiction. It is to reject our stratified worldview and point toward an interactive worldview, which would also point toward dramatic changes in personality and social structures. Metaphorically, we can understand such a change as movement from a see-saw world to a stairway world, where our own success need not threaten others but rather might help them learn how to achieve their own success. The question of exactly what changes in society might lead to such a stairway world—where the contradictions between cultural values like those Horney cites are diminished—might be seen in relation to the Levin experiment. There we noted that even a limited orientation to an interactive worldview was associated with no increase in prejudice following frustration. This suggests the possibility of a lessening of competition without a lessening of the striving for success, a result that should also lessen a contradiction with brotherly love. But there would also have to be widening opportunities for economic success for all individuals, by contrast with a zero-sum situation where one individual's success would yield another's failure.

## Some Implications

The contrast between the breadth of orientation of these three figures and that of modern social scientists is striking. This is in itself evidence for an increasing gap between aspirations and their fulfillment, supporting hypothesis (1), at least with respect to the gap between scientific ideals and practices. Marx clearly supports hypothesis (1) with his emphasis on deepening problems for the worker in contemporary society. As for the sources of those problems, he supports (2) by seeing stratification between owners and workers as much of the basis for these problems. Simmel, too, supports (1), since he sees the individual's fundamental problems of attaining freedom and individuality as products of the eighteenth and nineteenth centuries. Simmel sees a negative impact on the individual of the growth of objective culture relative to the individual's subjective culture, for this reduces the individual to a "negligible quantity." In this way, he supports hypothesis (2). Horney's analysis of contemporary society finds very deep contradictions, pointing to a general failure to enable individuals to move toward achieving their basic goals, thus supporting hypothesis (1). Stratification, as illustrated by "conspicuous consumption," is for Horney a key culprit in that failure, suggesting support for (2).

Marx used metaphors with telling effect. Perhaps his most famous one comes from the last lines of the "Manifesto of the Communist Party," written jointly with Engels and published in 1848: "Let the ruling classes tremble at a Communistic revolution. The proletarians have nothing to lose but their chains. They have a world to win. WORKING MEN OF ALL COUNTRIES, UNITE!" (Marx and Engels, 1848/1972: 362). The metaphor invoked here is that the proletariat, which has every right to freedom, is in chains. As for Simmel, his images generally are not as powerful as those of Marx, but they are significant nevertheless. For example, he previews his later interest in subjective and objective culture in his "Metropolis and Mental Life" essay with these words: "In any case this overgrowth of objective culture has been less and less satisfactory for the individual.... [H]e is reduced to a negligible quantity. He becomes a single cog as over against the vast overwhelming organization of things and forces." The individual seen as "a negligible quantity," "a single cog," conveys a sense of the impact of contemporary society on the individual. Horney's metaphors, too, are somewhat deficient. Her most powerful one is the title of her book: *The Neurotic Personality of Our Time*. The concept "neurotic" has invaded popular culture, and Horney is letting us know that we are all neurotic to a degree.

Being neurotic has its positive aspects, granting the existence of negative ones. Ernest Becker has written about this:

> If man is the more normal, healthy and happy, the more he can ... successfully ... repress, displace, deny, rationalize, dramatize himself and deceive others, then it follows that the suffering of the neurotic comes ... from painful truth.... Spiritually the neurotic has been long since where psychoanalysis wants to bring him without being able to, namely at the point of seeing through the deception of the world of sense, the falsity of reality. He suffers, not from all the pathological mechanisms which are psychically necessary for living ... but in the refusal of these mechanisms which is just what robs him of the illusions important for living (1973: 176).

Following Becker, granting the suffering of the neurotic, he fails to take the easy path of repressing contradictions within contemporary society, and consequently he is able to see those contradictions as Horney does.

## CHAPTER 5

# "Hand"

## Addiction versus Pragmatism

THIS FINAL CHAPTER of part III, "Personality Structures," moves us from concerns with "head" and "heart" in chapters 3 and 4 to a focus on "hand" or behavior of the individual, which is much more visible. It is essential that we begin by clarifying "addiction" and "pragmatism," granting that the chapter as a whole will carry these initial remarks further. We can view these two concepts as very high up on language's ladder of abstraction. "Addiction" includes concrete repetitive behavior illustrating a physiological dependence on some substance, such as cigarettes, alcohol or drugs. But in addition we can include psychological dependence of all kinds, such as dependence on work ("workaholism"), watching television, working out, overeating, sexual experiences, or just about any other activity that comes to dominate much of one's way of life. All of those experiences can be most valuable in moderation, but it is an overriding dominance that narrows the range of one's possibilities to which "addiction" refers. We might have reference here to the many different twelve-step groups—following the lead of Alcoholics Anonymous—that have been organized to help the individual cope with psychological addictions, illustrating the scope of this problem. For example, there is Batterers Anonymous, Debtors Anonymous, Depressives Anonymous, Emotions Anonymous, Families Anonymous, Gamblers Anonymous, Molesters Anonymous, Sex Addicts Anonymous, Workaholics Anonymous, Shoplifters Anonymous, Spenders Anonymous and Women with Multiple Addictions. But these are no more than a small number of examples.

This approach to addiction is not simply that many of us go too far in that direction. Rather it is analogous to Horney's analysis in *The Neurotic Personality of Our Time.* Our hypothesis is that modern society itself fosters an addictive personality, and that we are all more or less addicted. We see addiction as the individual's subordination of individuality to dependence on external phenomena, as illustrated by this plethora of self-help groups. For further insight, we can refer to chapter 2's contrast between outward perception and inward-outward perception, although the emphasis there was on perception and here it is on action. Addiction is oriented outward, whereas an inward-outward orientation would place any external activity within a broad context and thus avoid the subordination of individuality. We might refer here to Simmel's analysis of the nineteenth century in chapter 4: "The nineteenth century may have sought to promote, in addition to man's freedom, his individuality ... and his achievements which make him unique and indispensable." Addiction creates a gap between this cultural value of individuality—perhaps even more fundamental in this century than in the nineteenth—and the individual's actual behavior involving an escape from concerns for developing individuality.

Addictive patterns of behavior appear to be linked closely to the other two key aspects of personality structures discussed in chapters 3 and 4: a stratified worldview and alienation. We hypothesize that with a stratified worldview the individual's narrow orientation to all aspects of life yields large and growing gaps between aspirations and their fulfillment, as illustrated in figure I.1. Those gaps in turn yield individual alienation, since the individual remains unable to fulfill ideals or values to a significant degree. One choice—given that one has no alternative worldview that can direct one toward closing those gaps—is to repress emotions, yielding continuing alienation or neuroticism in Horney's terms but allowing the individual to cope with everyday life. That repression in turn points one outward, away from the painful experience of looking inward. The individual adopts not only an emphasis on outward perception but also addictive behavior, which creates a structure or pattern of outward-oriented activities. As a result, "head," "heart" and "hand" all come together to support the individual's stratified worldview. Another choice, as suggested by Horney and Becker (chapter 4), is to remain conscious of the large gap between one's expectations and ability to fulfill them, yielding neurotic behavior along with difficulties in coping with everyday life. Here, the suffering of the individual, following Becker, is at least accompanied by a degree of realism about the nature of one's situation.

Another way of looking at addiction comes from the field of "behavioral economics," which has developed only over the past fifteen years (see for example Ainslie, 2001; Camerer, Loewenstein and Rabin, 2003; Ross, 2005). Behavioral economics is a subfield of economics, but it also opens up to aspects of psychology along with cognitive science, philosophy and rational choice theory in sociology. Its focus is on the choices individuals actually make in clearly defined and often experimental situations, yet it also includes attention to what individuals who act in perfectly rational ways would do. Thus, it encompasses aspects of both curves within figure I.1: the top curve with its focus on aspirations and the bottom curve with its focus on behavior, granting that those curves also point toward the aspirations and actions of groups and society as a whole. A key conclusion we might derive from this literature (especially the work of Ainslie) is that people in modern society generally act so as to maximize short-run utility, ignoring long-run consequences. This suggests a Spaceland versus Timeland orientation along with a stratified epistemological and metaphysical stance. It is addictive insofar as it subordinates the individual to dependence on a very limited range of external factors.

As for "pragmatism," it is the broad philosophy that serves as the best available framework for the scientific method. We might recall the Introduction to this book where we quoted from the work of Charles Peirce, the founder of pragmatism, as well as from William James, a key figure in its development, both of whom emphasized pragmatism's wide-ranging orientation. Addictive behavior, by contrast, places narrow blinders on the individual, ruling out such breadth. Abraham Kaplan, whose work we take up in this chapter, has claimed that the task for pragmatism in the modern world "is to assimilate the impact of science on human affairs" (1961: 26). We may, then, define pragmatism as a philosophy which aims to accomplish this task. More specifically, pragmatism aims "to provide a system of ideas that will make an integrated whole of our beliefs about the nature of the world and the values which we seek in the world in fulfillment of our human nature" (1961: 26). Here we see once again a stark contrast between the narrowness of an addictive personality structure and a personality structure oriented to the philosophy of pragmatism. Yet our focus here is on pragmatism as a *pattern of action* that follows the philosophy of pragmatism, rather than on pragmatism as a pattern of philosophical ideas that suggests a pattern of action. When we wish to emphasize pragmatist ideas we will refer to the philosophy of pragmatism.

It is essential that we move far away from how the philosophy of pragmatism has been stereotyped. It is widely viewed as the philosophy of the American businessman, that is, an anything-goes materialistic view of life that rejects abstract ideas or theory and centers on whatever is practical at the moment. This definition points away from a long-term or historical perspective and narrows attention to whatever is visible or material by contrast with ideals or cultural values like freedom, equality and the ultimate worth of the individual. In other words, it is a definition linking pragmatism with a Spaceland stance, whereas in fact it is a philosophy congenial to a Timeland perspective. Yet pragmatist philosophy, like the scientific method itself, calls for nothing less than a long-term perspective along with an extremely broad orientation that certainly includes ideals or cultural values. We have here a contrast between pragmatism's

Timeland orientation and the attempt to stereotype that philosophy as having a Spaceland orientation.

"Pragmatism" is a word that derives from a Greek root, *prak,* which yields such words as "practical," "practice" and "praxis." That root centers on making, doing or acting, and in this way it has much in common with our usage of "addiction" as emphasizing the "hand" by contrast with the "head" and the "heart." Similarly, the scientific method emphasizes not merely sitting back and thinking about the nature of the world but rather taking action to understand the world and solve problems. Yet that method is by no means limited to action, for we must begin by becoming aware of the nature of a problem, and we must follow that up with some idea or theory as to how to solve the problem. Thus, "heart" and "head" must precede "hand." Within a stratified worldview we separate "head," "heart" and "hand," and it is that separation which is the basis for the widely-held stereotype of pragmatism as a narrow materialistic approach that rejects ideals or values. But within an interactive worldview we can come to understand pragmatism's breadth as paralleling that of the scientific method.

Pragmatism brings philosophy out of the academy or university into the factory, the workshop and the home. Rather than a focus on ideas which philosophers continue to debate among themselves, the philosophy of pragmatism is a guide for everyone's ordinary life from one moment to the next. It is by no means simply a philosophy oriented to the scientific method as practiced in the academy. Seeing pragmatism in this way is much the same as seeing the scientific method itself as not only what professional scientists do but as what we all do as we go about our lives, following George Kelly's view of "man-the-scientist" (chapter 2). The breadth of pragmatism stands in contrast to the narrowness of addiction, which constricts life by making it subservient to dependence on something apart from the individual. By introducing pragmatism with its rich history in philosophical thought, we are able to become more thorough and systematic about the contrast between a stratified and an interactive metaphysics and epistemology. By so doing we also are emphasizing the importance of metaphysics and epistemology, just as William James saw philosophy as "the most practical and important thing about a man."

We will carry further this contrast between addiction and pragmatism by pursuing ideas developed by Herman Hesse, Abraham Kaplan and David Knottnerus. Hesse published *The Glass Bead Game* or *Magister Ludi* in 1943 in Switzerland during World War II, and this novel was largely the basis for the Nobel Prize he received in 1946. Hesse, just as C. P. Snow in his *The Two Cultures* (1959), centers on the splitting up of modern society into parts that fail to communicate with one another, and the resulting disasters that are waiting to occur. In Snow's case it is the split between scientists and literary intellectuals. In Hesse's case it is the split between those creating the many elements of culture—including philosophers, artists, composers and scientists—and the individuals throughout society attempting to cope with the devastating problems of our era. Prior to World War II Hesse idealized a world of culture set far apart from our everyday world full of unsolved problems, but it was in *The Glass Bead Game* that he demonstrated a radical change in his perspective. Culture is indeed important, but the artist and scientist must do their utmost to help society solve its urgent problems if they are to survive along with everyone else. Although Hesse came to be revered by the youth of the 1960s as an underground hero preaching active rebellion against the status quo, in fact he suggested not action alone but action guided by the vast cultural achievements illustrated by the elements of *The Glass Bead Game.*

Abraham Kaplan sees pragmatism as "giving us something to live by, a perspective in which a man can find meaning and value in existence." The emphasis of philosophy within England and America during the twentieth century has been on analytic philosophy, a much narrower orientation where philosophers communicate with one another but only rarely outside their own circle. We might even see analytic philosophers as generally "addicted" to a narrow emphasis on the "head"—or ideas, rationality and logic—by contrast with openness to the "head," "heart" and "hand." This contrasts with the pragmatic approach expressed by Kaplan, Peirce and James. We can make good use of Kaplan's pragmatist ideas to broaden our understanding of an interactive worldview. At the same time we can learn more about just what is involved in a philosophy that we can live by, taking us from an interactive scientific method to an interactive worldview. Yet the further development of pragmatism is closely tied to the further development of the social sciences. The social sciences apparently require the broad epistemological and metaphysical stance that pragmatism offers. And the philosophy of pragmatism apparently requires the understanding of human behavior that social science offers.

Knottnerus's studies of concentration camps and internment camps focuses on rituals in everyday life—a focus elaborated in his just published monograph (2007)—which may illustrate either a narrow addictive orientation or a broad pragmatist orientation. He examined the experiences of people who had been forced to live in concentration camps and internment camps between 1935 and 1955. Four different settings were involved: Germany, the Soviet Union, the United States, and Japan. Knottnerus saw such settings as severely disrupting the individual's accustomed ritualistic behavior, giving him an opportunity to explore the nature of such behavior in a variety of cultures. For example, are rituals examples of addictive behavior, or do they enable the individual to avoid the subordination of individuality to some external phenomenon? What enables an individual to develop meaningful rituals—avoiding that subordination—in an environment where he or she has very little control over that environment? What is the relationship between worldviews and rituals?

## Hesse's *The Glass Bead Game*

Herman Hesse's novel *The Glass Bead Game* (1943/1969) was a call to take action on the development of a broad approach to culture as well as on the social problems of modern society. The story takes place in the distant future, perhaps the twenty-fifth century, and the book is a biography of the life of Joseph Knecht, who was Magister Ludi or the master of the Glass Bead Game. Knecht had become the leader of an intellectual order, Castalia—much like Plato's Academy or a feudal monastery—devoted exclusively to the development of the mind and the imagination. The Glass Bead Game is a game played by members of Castalia in order to integrate and keep alive the wisdom of all ages, and it involves working with elements of all cultures derived from their philosophical, literary, dramatic, artistic, musical and scientific achievements. This is in fact what Hesse himself was attempting to do throughout most of his life: to keep alive elements of all cultures by means of his novels as well as by separating those cultural achievements from the pressing problems of the day.

But Hesse had a radical change of heart during World War II, when he came to see the isolation of an intellectual community from world problems as a threat to the future of humanity. His overall approach is illustrated in his very first paragraph, where we should be sensitive to both the style of writing adopted by the supposed biographer of Joseph Knecht as well as to what he has to say:

> It is our intention to preserve in these pages what scant biographical material we have been able to collect concerning Joseph Knecht, or Ludi Magister Josephus III, as he is called in the Archives of the Glass Bead Game. We are not unaware that this endeavor runs, or seems to run, somewhat counter to the prevailing laws and usages of our intellectual life. For, after all, obliteration of individuality, the maximum integration of the individual into the hierarchy of the educators and scholars, has ever been one of our ruling principles. And in the course of our long tradition this principle has been observed with such thoroughness that today it is exceedingly difficult, and in many cases completely impossible, to obtain biographical and psychological information on various persons who have served the hierarchy in exemplary fashion. In very many cases it is no longer even possible to determine their original names. The hierarchic organization cherishes the ideal of anonymity, and comes very close to the realization of that ideal. This fact remains

one of the abiding characteristics of intellectual life in our Province (1943/1969: 3).

Hesse demonstrates what he thinks of the isolated academic life by the style of this passage along with the style of this same supposed biographer throughout the novel: pedantic, unemotional, impersonal, prone to qualify any statement and take away its force, passive, heavy, self-important, humorless and repetitive. For example, why the impersonal nature and passivity of the first sentence which reads "It is our intention to preserve" instead of "I intend to preserve"? Why the double negative in the second sentence— "We are not unaware"—instead of a simple positive statement, "I am aware"? Why all the qualifications in the rest of that sentence—"that this endeavor runs, or seems to run, somewhat counter to"—instead of, say, "that this endeavor runs counter to"? Hesse is making fun of his fictional narrator, and he is hoping that the reader will catch on to what he is doing. The narrowness and lack of humor and perspective of the narrator is, for Hesse, a symptom of the fundamental problems not only of Castalia as well as the academic world, but also of modern society.

What about the content and not just the style of that first paragraph? The narrator refers to the "obliteration of individuality" as fundamental to life in Castalia, and much of the passage has to do with exactly this. He also makes several references to the hierarchy that prevails within Castalia: "the hierarchy of the educators and scholars," and "persons who have served the hierarchy in exemplary fashion." But this emphasis on hierarchy or stratification and the obliteration of individuality runs counter to fundamental cultural values that have been developing in recent centuries. We might recall here Simmel's analysis in chapter 4 of the eighteenth century as emphasizing individual freedom and the nineteenth century as stressing human individuality. We might also recall Marx's analysis of alienation, which has much in common with the obliteration of individuality along with anonymity. There is also Marx's emphasis on the evils of hierarchy within the workplace, where owners rule over the workers.

If we refer once again to figure I.1 we can understand Hesse's strategy more fully. Bearing in mind that Castalia represents his view of our contemporary academic world, he is telling the reader both stylistically and by means of his content that there is a huge gap between our ideals or cultural values and the way things actually work in academia. Instead of the ideal of equality, we have hierarchy or stratification there. Instead of the ideal of individuality, we have impersonality and anonymity there. More broadly, the entire way of life of the academic world departs very far from our ideals of the way that life should be.

Does Hesse give us any hint of what society might do about this gap? He does far more than hint. After reaching the pinnacle of achievement in

Castalia as master of the Glass Bead Game Joseph Knecht sends a letter to the ruling Board of his intellectual Order which includes the following:

> I have begun to doubt my ability to officiate satisfactorily because I consider the Glass Bead Game in a state of crisis.... Here I am sitting in the top story of our Castalian edifice ... And instinct tells me, my nose tells me, that down below something is burning, our whole structure is imperiled, and that my business now is not to analyze music or define rules of the Game, but to rush to where the smoke is....
>
> The history of societies shows a constant tendency toward the formation of a nobility as the apex and crown of any given society.... If, now, we regard our Order as a nobility and try to examine ourselves to see ... to what extent we have already been infected by the characteristic disease of nobility—*hubris*, conceit, class arrogance, self-righteousness, exploitativeness ... we may be seized by a good many doubts.... In brief, this Castalian culture of ours ... tends somewhat toward smugness and self-praise, toward the cultivation and elaboration of intellectual specialism.... Historically we are, I believe, ripe for dismantling. And there is no doubt that such will be our fate, not today or tomorrow, but the day after tomorrow.... Critical times are approaching; the omens can be sensed everywhere; the world is once again about to shift its center of gravity. Displacements of power are in the offing. They will not take place without war and violence....
>
> I herewith request the Board to relieve me of my office as Magister Ludi and entrust to me an ordinary school, large or small, outside in the country; to let me staff it with a group of youthful members of our Order (319, 321-2, 328-9, 335).

Knecht uses his letter of resignation as an effort to alert the rulers of Castalia to growing problems in the outside world which threaten to destroy their way of life through new wars which will impoverish their country and eliminate the luxury of their Order. Knecht is resigning from a Game that is a luxury that the world soon will no longer be able to afford, moving toward taking on responsibility for the fate of a world that is beginning to come apart.

Hesse was asking—from his position in Switzerland during World War II—all those in the academic world to take responsibility for a world situation which was rapidly deteriorating. He was doing much the same thing that C. Wright Mills did at the University of Wisconsin during World War II when he was appalled at the lack of commitment by his professors to apply sociological knowledge to the problems of the day. Mills expressed his horror at the failures of sociology to meet its responsibilities to society in a way that conformed to academic norms by analyzing some fifty textbooks on social problems in order to learn about "the style of reflection and the social-historical basis of American sociology" (1943). Mills concluded that those authors generally did not proceed scientifically, since they failed to build on key sociological concepts like social stratification, as developed by the work of Marx and Weber. Overall, they tended to hide from fundamental problems such as the way in which class structure works to prevent individuals from fulfilling the American ideal of rising in occupation status from the status of their parents, thus maintaining a stratified occupational system. Instead, those authors focused on the failure of the individual worker to "adjust" to a class situation that supposedly is fixed in concrete.

Yet the issue of the role of the academic in modern society is blurred by a widespread adherence to a stratified worldview along with a stratified epistemological stance. For example, much is made of a distinction between "facts" and "values," following a great deal of what has been claimed by analytic philosophers, a topic we shall take up further in chapter 6 with our contrast between the "scientistic" method and the scientific method. A key idea put forward within their widespread scientistic orientation is that research has to do only with facts, and that "values"—or what should be done about facts—is not a topic for scientists but rather should be considered by policy-makers or by individuals in their everyday lives. From our own perspective, such an orientation illustrates a stratified worldview and epistemological stance. There is a great deal of controversy on this point not only within sociology and other social sciences but also within philosophy, and we cannot possibly take up the details of that controversy in this book. However, a recent work that does take up such details, emphasizing issues within philosophy, can introduce the reader to this topic (Kincaid, Dupre and Wylie, 2006). Our own stance, following an interactive worldview and a pragmatist perspective, is that it is vital for the researcher to be concerned with the full range of phenomena that bear on any given problem, and that would certainly include both "facts" and "values." While it may be useful for some purposes to distinguish between "values" and other phenomena like ideas and actions, none of these categories should have priority over the others within any given investigation.

There is another major orientation to facts and values within the social science literature which also illustrates a stratified worldview and epistemological stance. Close to postmodernist thought, this orientation is equally unscientific in that it rejects the very idea of the scientific method as our major tool for developing an understanding of human behavior. It is a most pessimistic perspective. In our view, this stance stems largely from the failure of the social sciences to go very far in developing such an understanding. It amounts to giving up altogether on achieving scientific understanding of human behavior. What is thrown out as a result is the progress that has already been made within the social sciences. From our own perspective, there is much to criticize about the limitations of social science's achievements. Yet we believe that those limitations are not intrinsic to the nature of human behavior but rather are due to a general failure to follow scientific ideals along with a stratified worldview. These few ideas in this paragraph and the one above are inadequate for addressing the complexity of the many debates on the issue of facts and values. However, we hope that our own stance will continue to be clarified as we proceed in this chapter and in those to follow.

## Kaplan's *The New World of Philosophy*

The philosophy of pragmatism starts with this assumption stated by Kaplan: "There is no doubt that far and away the most significant development in Western culture in the past three or four centuries has been the rise of modern science and the transformation of civilization by the technology based on that science" (1961: 16). John Dewey, a key figure in the development of this philosophy, also states this idea. Although he believed in the importance and possibility of developing social science knowledge, he was concerned with its lack of development:

> The first step [of reconstructing philosophy] ... will be to recognize that ... the present human scene, for good and evil, for harm and benefit alike, is what it is because ... of the entry into everyday and common ... ways of living of what has its origin in physical inquiry. The methods and conclusions of "science" do not remain penned in within "science." ... The science that has so far found its way deeply and widely into the actual affairs of human life is partial and incomplete science: competent in respect to physical, and now increasingly to physiological, conditions (as is seen in the recent developments in medicine and public sanitation), but nonexistent with respect to matters of supreme significance to man—those which are distinctively of, for, and by, man (1920/1948: xxvii–xxix).

For both Kaplan and Dewey it is not just the task of pragmatism to assimilate the impact of science on human affairs: this is the task for modern philosophy in general, and this is why Dewey undertook his *Reconstruction in Philosophy*. But Dewey claimed that presently we are all making do with "a science which is still partial, incomplete, and of necessity one-sided in operation." Pragmatists center on the importance of social science because it is the human being who is the centerpiece of their concern and not the nature of the physical or biological universe. It is science which is our best guide to learning about the nature of the reality that the human being must face. But then the problem of reconstructing philosophy hinges around a problem that is yet to be solved: the understanding of human behavior. We can see, then, that pragmatism is about a metaphysics or worldview dependent on an epistemology, the scientific method, which in turn must produce an understanding of human behavior if that metaphysics is to help us learn how to live meaningful lives. Here again we must go up and down language's ladder of abstraction—from metaphysics down to epistemology and further down to theories of human behavior, and then back again up to epistemology and metaphysics—if pragmatism is to achieve its aims. The failure of this philosophy to maintain widespread influence in the modern world—granting some resurgence of interest—appears to be due largely to the failure of social science to integrate its knowledge so as to provide the basis for shuttling up and down language's ladder of abstraction.

Despite that failure, Kaplan argues that pragmatism can teach us a great deal. For example, there is the pragmatist's emphasis on method:

> Contrary to the popular reading of the word "pragmatic," his emphasis is not on results but on method. In his analysis, science turns out to be essentially a method of inquiry, democracy a method of arriving at public policy, morality a method of integrating impulse with intelligence, and even art and religion he conceives as methods of organizing and realizing potentialities of human value. If pragmatism is concerned always with bearings on action, it approaches action in terms, not of what we do, but of how we do it. The pragmatic philosophy itself is characterized by its *way* of philosophizing, not by a distinctive body of philosophic doctrine; William James' first book on pragmatism bore the subtitle "A New Name For Some Old Ways of Thinking" (Kaplan, 1961: 18).

It was the scientific method, and not the specific theories or findings of people like Newton, Einstein and Darwin, which was the basis for the scientific and technological revolutions of the past four centuries. That method guided thousands upon thousands of scientists in their efforts to achieve understanding of the physical and biological universe. It taught them to become committed to tackling almost any problem whatsoever, since experience had taught them to be optimistic about the power of the scientific method to help them solve problems. It also taught them to learn what had been discovered previously that related to their problems so that they could go beyond previous knowledge. And it taught them to be open up to a wide range of phenomena as they proceeded to investigate their problems. All of this was a far cry from what had been emphasized in previous centuries: conformity to the teachings of the Church with its truths established by proclamation and its ideas not requiring testing by observation or experiments. As a result, new knowledge developed, but that development depended on a method which created a path for scientists to develop that knowledge ever further. Other factors contributed as well, such as the invention of the printing press and the rise of the university. Such developments greatly widened the reach and depth of scholarship and knowledge, but it was the scientific method which enabled scientists to take advantage of those factors.

Although we normally don't think of the scientific method as fundamental to the fulfillment of democratic ideals, this may well be the case. Of course, the idea of democracy is that the people of a given society govern themselves directly or indirectly through elected representatives, by contrast with being governed by a hereditary ruler or by someone who seizes power. Yet if we are concerned with the democratic ideal that the people will as a result be able to act in their own interests, then they must be educated so as to be informed about how to advance those interests. They must learn to act intelligently so as to solve their problems. But if the scientific method itself is severely limited by a stratified worldview, the result will be what Dewey found: that the development of social science, which addresses the enormous complexities of human behavior, will also be severely limited. Given this situation, how can we expect the ordinary person—who must be educated to deal with those complexities according to democratic ideals—to have much chance of following the democratic ideal of intelligent action to solve problems? The failure of social science to develop may be equally a failure to fulfill democratic ideals.

The philosophy of pragmatism emphasizes the importance of democracy and education, for both are—like the scientific method—processes for fulfilling the goal of helping the individual to solve the problems that confront her. Like the scientific method, democracy and education are never-ending processes. The future is not closed but remains open as long as life continues. All of these processes require the active participation of the individual. This approach opposes rigidity, whether in science, politics or education. Instead, it is open to new possibilities. Behind it is the assumption that the human being has the capacity to continue to learn without limit, granting the existence of structures working against that capacity. Given that assumption, all of society's institutions must take it into account. Dewey made this clear: "Democracy has many meanings, but if it has a moral meaning, it is found in resolving that the supreme test of all political institutions and industrial arrangements shall be the contribution they make to the all-around growth of every member of society (Dewey, 1919/1948: 183–186)."

We shall have more to say about the philosophy of pragmatism in chapter 6, "Scientistic Method versus Scientific Method," where we take up the philosophy of Charles Peirce, the founder of pragmatism. We might note once again that for all of its strengths, the philosophy of pragmatism is limited by how far the social sciences themselves have developed. The failure of social scientists to integrate their understanding of the complexity of human behavior affects not only efforts to solve social problems but also our epistemological and metaphysical assumptions. The future of pragmatism thus apparently rests on the efforts of social scientists to demonstrate the fruitfulness of that philosophy. Equally, the future of social science apparently rests on the potential of the metaphysics and epistemology of pragmatism to point social scientists toward the fulfillment of their scientific ideals.

## Knottnerus on Concentration Camps

If we are interested in understanding patterns of action or rituals—as distinct from patterns of ideas like worldviews and patterns of feelings like alienation—then one approach is to examine situations illustrating the extreme disruption of those patterns. Our purpose in distinguishing between rituals, ideas and feelings is not at all to make an implicit assumption that these are quite different kinds of entities. Rather, it is to remind us to include all of them in any analysis of the behavior of the individual, just as the Web and Part/Whole Approach emphasizes that we should open up to a wide range of phenomena. David Knottnerus studied concentration camps between 1935 and 1955 in Germany, the Soviet Union, the United States and Japan as part of his series of studies of ritualistic behavior (2002: 85-106). Those studies are based on the assumption that ritualization—repetitive actions that have important meanings for the individual and the group, and are not just automatic habits—is a crucial component of human behavior. Those meanings link these patterns of actions with the "head" and the "heart." By contrast, automatic habits which have little or no meaning for the individual or group are not rituals. They may, instead, be examples of addictive behavior, where the individual subordinates individuality to dependence on external phenomena.

Knottnerus's study can help us to gain insight into the difference between genuine rituals which have important meanings for the individual or group, on the one hand, and automatic habits or repetitive behavior which may well illustrate the subordination of individuality to external phenomena, on the other hand. Although this study is no more than an exploratory one without any systematic analysis of a large number of cases, it can nevertheless help us to probe this question. By answering this question we are also gaining insight into everyone's ritualistic behavior in everyday life. If indeed we are an addictive society—where we all more or less subordinate our individuality to dependence on external phenomena—then how do we move away from such subordination? How can we learn to exchange such addictive behavior for rituals that have genuine meaning for us? A further question has to do with our potential for shifting from a stratified to an interactive worldview. Can we learn to move from rituals emphasizing the former to those emphasizing the latter?

Here is a statement by Janusz Bardach, who survived the severe conditions of the Soviet labor camps and later described his experiences in *Man Is Wolf to Man: Surviving the Gulag:*

> At four A.M. the ringing rail sounded for us to get up. Despite my fatigue and the cold, I kept the exercise routine I had followed at home and in the Red Army, washing my face and hands at the hand pump. I wanted to retain as much pride in myself as I could, separate myself from the many prisoners I had seen give up day by day. They'd stop caring first about their hygiene or appearance, then about their fellow prisoners, and finally about their own lives. If I had control over nothing else, I had control over this ritual, which I believed would keep me from degradation and certain death (1998: 130).

From this brief statement we can contrast a ritual with automatic behavior that has little meaning for the individual and might well be addictive: Bardach's ritual of washing his face and hands, and the repetitive behavior of many of the prisoners who had given up: "They'd stop caring first about their hygiene or appearance, then about their fellow prisoners, and finally about their own lives." Most significant is Bardach's statement: "If I had control over nothing else, I had control over this ritual, which I believed would keep me from degradation and certain death."

Bardach does not describe specifically the automatic behavior adopted by many of the prisoners, but limits himself to general remarks: "They'd stop caring first about their hygiene or appearance, then about their fellow prisoners, and finally about their own lives." Bardach had seen these other prisoners "give up day by day." Apparently, they came to define their situation as hopeless, with no possibility of getting out of the camp. From one moment to the next they were discouraged by their camp experiences. Such behavior appears to be addictive to the extent that it was repetitive and also largely unconnected to their past lives and future possibilities. It was narrow in its failure to connect with the wide range of their fundamental values.

This contrast between rituals and automatic or addictive behavior is further illustrated in a statement by Gustav Herling, who was also interned in a Soviet concentration camp. Herling described his own rituals, such as mending clothes, writing letters, or visiting friends in the barracks in the evening. He contrasts those rituals with the automatic behavior adopted by the majority of the prisoners, later recorded in *A World Apart*:

> All these activities had one quality in common—they imitated the normal occupations of a free life. Our behavior was a parody of the gestures, habits and responses of our former existence, observing the symbolic ritual of a dimly remembered routine.... The foregoing description, however, applies only to those few prisoners who made some effort to save themselves from complete demoralization. But the majority ... left their bunks during the evening only to fill up the hollowness of their stomachs with a pint or two of the inevitable hot water.... The majority of prisoners ... deluded themselves that this suicidal form of relaxation strengthened the organism of their bodies. In the camp the normal process was reversed: inertia and apathy hastened death, while any form of activity postponed it for an unforeseen period (1951: 143-144).

Herling is claiming that no more than a few prisoners engaged in the kinds of repetitive behavior which they had defined positively, that is, ritualistic behavior. Those rituals were similar to those they had engaged in prior to their lives at the camp, such as "mending clothes, writing letters, or visiting friends in the barracks in the evening." And that similarity helped them to define those rituals as helpful, yielding the expectation that they would eventually emerge from the camp. Most of the prisoners, however, engaged in suicidal automatic behavior, leading to their "complete demoralization." They stayed in their bunks all evening long, except for a brief period "to fill up the hollowness of their stomachs with a pint or two of the inevitable hot water." And the result was that this "inertia and apathy hastened death." Although superficially they maintained that their "relaxation strengthened the organism of their bodies," deep down they realized that their lack of movement was taking them rapidly toward death. Following our definition of addictive behavior, they were subordinating their individuality to dependence on what they had defined as a hopeless external situation. They were not able to develop patterns of behavior that had important meanings for their lives.

If we turn to an American camp for Japanese internees during World War II we find much the same contrast between two widely different kinds of behavior, as described by Kitagawa in *Issei and Nissei: The Internment Years*:

> Issei women thus unwittingly became the happiest people in the relocation center. They even began to look younger.... [T]he effect of life in the relocation center upon the Issei men was almost completely opposite

to that upon the women. The men looked as if they had suddenly aged ten years.... It was indeed pathetic to see such moral and psychic (if not spiritual) deterioration develop (1967: 90–92).

Those women had "become involved on a regular basis in a wide array of practices." By contrast, the men "became quite inactive and did not regularly participate in hardly any of the camp activities." Those older Japanese women, born in Japan, generally were not torn away from a place of employment: they had been homemakers who were also in charge of the family's social activities. As a result they were able to continue in the internment camp with the normal activities they had engaged in before they were interned. Not so for the men. Much like men who have retired without any hobbies or interests outside of a work setting, they found themselves with no meaningful activities, and generally they did not push themselves to find new activities that would be meaningful. Premature aging was the result. The women's activities had become genuine rituals in that they became quite meaningful patterns of behavior. By contrast, the men remained unable to develop ritualistic behavior in a setting so different from what they had previously experienced.

These brief excerpts describing the experiences of inmates in different concentration camps enable us to carry further the conclusions of the Levin experiment on prejudice in chapter 3. Levin set up an experimental microcosm oriented to retaining the basic features of the macrocosm of society as a whole. He created patterns of social stratification along with frustration as a result of failure on what the students believed to be an aptitude test for graduate school. The result was increased prejudice against members of a minority group, but only among those with a stratified worldview. They acted in see-saw fashion, and their pushing down Puerto Ricans with their prejudice was apparently a device—following their failing the test—for coming to feel better about themselves. We believe that those with the beginnings of an interactive worldview had nothing to gain by such see-saw behavior, since they saw themselves on a stairway. If they failed a test, then this information could become the basis for their learning how to improve on the next test.

However, as we've seen in Knottnerus's study of concentration camps, the individual need not take out frustrations on others but can also engage in addictive behavior where he or she is the enemy. Like the smoker who doesn't make a sufficient effort to abandon a habit or the drug addict who does the same, the prisoner in a concentration camp can also engage in suicidal behavior. Individuals can lie in their bunks passively and not attempt to find meaningful activities which strengthen their optimism about the possibility of surviving and leaving the camp. Instead of taking their frustrations out on others they can take them out on themselves. Such behavior becomes addictive when it involves repetitive actions oriented to the external environment that subordinate individuality.

It is not the physical act of lying in one's bunk which suggests addiction or suicidal behavior. It all depends on how the individual defines his situation, as we can see from this statement by David Matzner, interned in a Nazi camp:

> After the constant pressure and unbearable pushing of the kapos, the malicious watchfulness of the guards—after all this, the camp meant a temporary escape, something like home. I could crawl onto my board there.... When we marched out in the early morning I was already longing for the coming night so that I could once again stretch out on that little bit of space that, however dirty, cold, and overrun by lice, was mine. The chopped straw in the sack, the filthy blanket, two rusted tin cans, one twisted spoon, a broken fork, a few foul and stinking rags: these were my accessories, this was my "home." Each evening when we returned, my first step was to check my possessions, relieved to find everything intact (1994: 51–52).

Matzner, much like Bardach whose ritual of washing himself gave him some control over his life, had a sense of control over his life when he crawled onto his own board for a night's sleep. His own possessions, no matter how meager and worthless they appeared to be, were things that no one else controlled. His life was not simply one of conformity to the orders of his captors, and he could even daydream about what he controlled while he was obeying the orders of others. Those possessions did not enable him to reach out to great achievements. Nevertheless, they did enable him to retain his dream of some day leaving the camp. Relative to his horrible situation, they opened up the possibility of a better way of life. Here again we have an individual developing ritualistic behavior versus succumbing to meaningless automatic behavior and perhaps addiction.

These analyses of people surviving under extreme conditions nevertheless can be applied to the ordinary situations we all experience in everyday life, just as the Levin experiment can also be applied to our everyday behavior. We are presented with great differences between the impact of different kinds of repetitive behavior on the survival of the individual under such extreme conditions. For one thing, this study alerts us to the importance of how we define those many patterns of repetitive actions which make up a good portion of our lives. Do we see them simply as habits with no larger significance, as in the case of automatically washing our hands several times every day? Do we define those repetitive actions negatively, such as seeing our smoking a number of cigarettes as addictive behavior which not only speeds up our movement toward illness and death but also subordinates us to dependence on external phenomena?

Or do we define our repetitive actions positively, such as seeing exercise as a meaningful way to develop ourselves physically, a way that leads to a longer life with fewer health problems?

Is it our worldview which appears to largely influence what choices we make as we go from one pattern of action to another in our everyday lives? Just as most prisoners in the concentration camps adopted a passive view of their fate—and as a result hastened their exit from life—do we generally adopt a stratified worldview where our repetitive actions do little or nothing for our own long-term development? Do we generally see our repetitive actions as relatively trivial or negative, yet do they in fact have the potential for being important and positive? It appears to be awareness of the potential of our repetitive behavior which we generally lack, a lack that may well be associated with the narrow orientation of a stratified worldview. Would an interactive worldview, by contrast, help us to open up to the potential importance of every repetitive pattern of thought, feeling and action?

We hypothesize that just as Bardach used his ritual of washing his face and hands to define himself as someone with the ability to control his fate, so can we all learn to do this within more and more of our repetitive behavior. Just as Matzner learned to see his hovel as under his complete control, so can we all come to see our own patterns of behavior as under our own control. We are, fortunately, free from the extreme conditions of living in a concentration camp, but our stratified worldview points us away from seeing our own potential in our everyday patterns of behavior. We can understand reasons for the individual's sense of powerlessness and alienation in a concentration camp, but it is far more difficult to understand the powerful impact of a worldview that is invisible. But we may be able to learn to make our stratified worldview visible, granting the difficulty of doing so. We may learn to see those repetitive actions—such as watching our odometer and counting the miles we have driven without any thought given to our lives in general—as in fact subordinating our possibilities for personal development to dependence on external phenomena. Once we learn to make our worldview visible and come to see the loss of control and outward orientation which it fosters, we may be able to do something about it. For awareness of a fundamental problem—following the scientific method—appears to be a crucial step toward solving that problem.

There is at present little evidence from empirical research for these conclusions. Yet we can turn to theory emerging from the new field of behavioral economics—as outlined at the beginning of this chapter—for some support. If it is indeed the case that most inmates in concentration camps simply gave up their hope for a better future and succumbed to rituals supporting that definition of the situation, this would be supported by the work of Ainslie (2001). For Ainslie claimed the existence of a type of irrationality in modern society where we discount our long-range preferences in favor of short-term goals at the time when short-term choices must be made. This suggests, then, the irrationality of the modern individual, as illustrated by the gap in figure I.1 between expectations and their fulfillment. In other words, this is a Spaceland versus a Timeland perspective. We can add to these hypotheses others based on this epistemological and metaphysical contrast. For example, we can look to these patterns in groups and society as a whole, and not just to the behavior of the individual in relatively controlled or transparent situations. And we can also look to historical changes in this type of irrationality, such as the increasing gap between expectations and their fulfillment suggested by our hypothesis (1).

Knottnerus's preliminary analysis provides some hints for explaining why some inmates were able to develop meaningful rituals while others failed to do so. For example, the Issei women in the American camp were confronted with a familiar situation, by contrast with the Issei men. We also have—in the extreme situations of the Soviet and Nazi camps—those few who were able to construct rituals versus the many who could not. This raises questions for further research. Was a stratified worldview maintained by those many and the beginnings of an interactive worldview maintained by those few? Was this illustrated by the latter group's ability to engage in long-range thinking, including the possibility of leaving the camp, whereas the former group remained limited to short-term thought? Here again we can introduce Ainslie's hypothesis. Is it indeed the case that individuals in modern society generally tend to sacrifice long-term for short-term goals when they make decisions in a momentary situation?

There are very important possibilities for addressing serious problems of addiction in modern society to the extent that we come to understand the nature of addiction, and not just physiological addiction. For example, to the extent that we learn that addiction is indeed closely linked to a stratified epistemological and metaphysical stance, then we can focus on how we might learn to move to an alternative stance, such as an interactive one. Ainslie's work points in this direction. More specifically, he points toward the importance of devices which would help the individual to remain aware of long-term consequences while he or she is making short-term choices. Yet if patterns of addiction are near-universal and involve the full range of our behavior—paralleling Horney's theory of the neurotic personality of our time (chapter 4)—then it would appear that we require nothing less than a change of worldview to alter those patterns of addiction. For such a change, in the case of an interactive worldview, would appear to work toward closing the gap between aspirations and fulfillment, pointing us all toward more rational behavior. This might work to an extent even in the case of physiological addictions like patterns of smoking and drinking, since non-physiological forces would probably be operating there as well.

## Some Implications

Assuming an increasing gap between aspirations and their fulfillment, as depicted in figure I.1, it appears to be extraordinarily difficult to close that gap. This is illustrated by the failure of Hesse's Joseph Knecht to build on his extraordinary breadth of understanding and commitment on leaving Castalia so as to point a direction—based on his incredible cultural background—for helping to solve complex social problems. Yet we cannot decide on this basis that understanding and commitment are useless in the face of the complexity of human problems. Something was missing in Knecht's case, and the work of Kaplan, Knottnerus and students of behavioral economics can help us to discover what was missing.

What Kaplan brings to the table as a professional philosopher and a pragmatist is a breadth that exceeds that of almost all social scientists. He is able to take us far up the ladder of linguistic abstraction, even past epistemology or the scientific method, to the ethereal realm of metaphysics or worldviews. His analysis does not take up hypothesis (1) with its statement about the existence of an increasing gap within modern society. But we may see his very broad pragmatist approach, with its provision of a basis for the individual's finding meaning in modern society and coping effectively with the problem of living, as supporting hypothesis (2). That hypothesis, as stated in the Introduction, is: "To the degree that a worldview or metaphysical stance is stratified versus interactive, there will be a large gap between aspirations and their fulfillment." And, of course, the reverse is implied: an interactive orientation will tend to close the gap. Kaplan's pragmatism was deeply rooted, whereas Knecht was no more than a beginner in such behavior.

Knottnerus helps us to understand the importance for the individual of every momentary situation, granting that his work does not bear on hypothesis (1). The moment-to-moment addictive behavior that he describes apparently decided whether or not the victims of concentration camps lived or died. It was Janusz Bardach's exercise routine of washing his face and hands at the hand pump—rather than the routines of others who neglected caring about their hygiene, their fellow prisoners and even their own lives—which apparently saved him. It was such patterns of action from one moment to the next in their everyday lives, which evoked the prisoners' feelings that they had at least some control over their lives and apparently saved them, which constitutes evidence for hypothesis (2). It was a combination of "head," "heart" and "hand" which they apparently required.

Yet it is the questions that Knottnerus's research raises, questions requiring further research, which appear to be his most valuable product. Was it the beginnings of an interactive worldview or Timeland stance which was the basis for Bardach's achievement of rituals in the face of great adversity? Was it a stratified worldview or Spaceland stance which prevented the others from that achievement? In other words, was a lack of awareness of the impact of present choices on one's future possibilities—following the work of Ainslie in behavioral economics—associated with that Spaceland stance? Did the lack of understanding of the importance of an epistemological and metaphysical stance get in the way of Hesse along with Knecht?

As for images or metaphors, "the glass bead game"—Hesse's title—presents us with a way to view the academic world. It is too much of a game and too little of an enterprise that takes seriously the problems of the outside world. Knottnerus's most powerful image is simply the concentration camp, a situation that we can extend to aspects of our own everyday lives. Just as Marx called on workers to revolt because they have nothing to lose but their chains, Knottnerus is suggesting that all of us engage in automatic and meaningless behavior which may well be addictive and which constitutes a kind of concentration camp that we build around ourselves. He implicitly raises the question of whether or not we can learn to escape from that concentration camp by converting that automatic behavior into meaningful rituals. Following the work of behavioral economists like Ainslie, that conversion might well involve procedures for bringing future situations into the individual's momentary awareness. And following our own perspective, such a change in momentary awareness may well require a change from a Spaceland epistemological and metaphysical stance to a Timeland stance.

# PART IV

# Social Structures

Just as our analysis of personality structures in chapters 3, 4 and 5 had to do with thinking, feeling and action—or "head," "heart" and "hand"—so will this be true for our analysis of social structures. Chapters 6 and 7 emphasize "head" and "heart," respectively. But their focus is not on the ideas, beliefs, assumptions or opinions and the feelings, goals, ideals or motives of the individual. Rather, it is on "culture," namely, the widely shared and persisting beliefs and goals of the individuals in society. Granting the relative invisibility of such phenomena, the concept is a most powerful one. Once we have some understanding of the culture of a people or society, we have learned a great deal about the ideas or beliefs and the ideals or interests of any given individual in that society. Of course, there is a fair degree of individual variation from those widely shared beliefs and values. There is also a fair degree of variation from one group to another. Yet "culture" does succeed in giving us substantial insights into the thoughts and feelings of the individuals and the many groups to be found within society.

Chapters 6 and 7 do not take up culture as a whole. They are quite selective, centering on only some aspects of culture. Thus, although they are illustrative of the entire realm of culture, they take up only a tiny portion of that realm. They are focused on what can help us to understand the central problems of this book: (1) exploring the hypothesis of an increasing gap between aspirations or expectations and their fulfillment, as depicted by figure I.1, and (2) examining the impact of a stratified (versus an interactive) worldview on this gap. In chapter 6 we take up the nature of the scientific method, building on our discussions in previous chapters. Our focus there is on a contrast between the way that method is generally practiced and a scientific method that follows ideals for that method.

This is a contrast between "scientism" and "the scientific method." It is "the scientific method" and not "scientism" which enables us to construct figure I.1 and consider the evidence for and against it. Chapter 7, "Anomie versus Cultural Value Fulfillment," centers on the fundamental problem depicted in figure I.1: the hypothesized increasing gap between cultural values and patterns of action or interaction which limit their fulfillment. Although we have discussed this problem in all of the preceding chapters, it is in chapter 7 that we become more systematic, largely because we use the concept of cultural values.

Chapter 8 emphasizes not shared beliefs or ideas and motives or interests—as in the case of culture—but rather shared patterns of action or interaction that are elements of social organization. These patterns generally are more visible than those within culture. For example, social stratification has to do with persisting hierarchy or patterns of inequality within society. The concept of bureaucracy is another illustration of patterns of interaction and action. It includes both the idea of persisting hierarchy and the idea of specialization. Just as we cannot isolate the "head," "heart" and "hand" of the individual, we cannot isolate culture from social organization. For example, the scientific method—to be discussed in chapter 6—aims at deepening our understanding of phenomena, thus contributing to culture. But it is practiced by means of patterns of action and interaction. The problem of anomie to be taken up in chapter 7—and depicted in figure I.1—has to do with patterns of social stratification and bureaucracy which limit the fulfillment of cultural values.

Social structures—including both culture and social organization—might seem to be unreal, since we are accustomed to defining as real only what we can see, hear, feel, taste or smell as individuals. And social structures emphasize abstractions, such as what is widely shared among individuals. But the evidence for the impact of social structures is absolutely overwhelming, as illustrated by the many thousands of studies which have documented the impact of social stratification and cultural values on our lives. Figure I.1 can—in additiion to its impact on the individual—depict a key hypothesized impact of social structures on contemporary society, with its top curve emphasizing cultural values and its bottom curve emphasizing patterns like social stratification and bureaucracy that limit the fulfillment of those values. Yet phenomena like cultural values and social stratification cannot easily be seen by the individual.

We should note here our own departure in part IV from the widely accepted definition of social structure within sociology, namely, that social structure and social organization are synonyms. This excludes culture from being viewed as an aspect of social structure. We will elaborate on our own perspective in the introduction to chapter 8, but here we can at least outline our stance. We believe that by conceiving of culture as apart from social structure, sociologists learn to avoid attention to culture in their quest to understand social organization. And anthropologists equally are able to avoid attention to the phenomenon of social organization once they come to view culture as distinct from social structure. The result, from our perspective, is a widespread failure to pay attention to the links between social organization and culture. Such an orientation would exclude our own concern—as illustrated within figure I.1—with stratification's impact in limiting the fulfillment of cultural values. Our own alternative is, then, to define social structure as encompassing both culture and social organization. This is by no means a sociological effort to become more important than anthropology. Rather, it is an effort to help both sociologists and anthropologists pay attention to how social organization and culture interact with one another.

One way of developing a clearer view of the nature of social structure from a Timeland perspective is to have reference to the work of the contemporary sociologist Andrew Abbott (not to be confused with Edwin Abbott of chapter 1). His 1988 paper, "Transcending General Linear Reality," reprinted in his more recent *Time Matters* (2001), provides a view of reality emphasizing its sequential nature:

> The demographic model ... Allows entities to appear, disappear, move, merge, divide.... A sequence-based, central-subject/event approach ... Assumes, first of all, that the social world consists of fluctuating entities, accepting the demographic model just outlined. It deliberately makes order and sequence effects central. Moreover, it emphasizes the transformation of attributes into events. Thus, it interprets "Thirty percent of the cohort recruited by a certain occupation is retained after 20 years" not by comparing it to retention rates in other occupations, but by comparing it to previous and later rates in the same ... [occupation]; meaning is determined by story, not by scales that abstract across cases (2001: 61).

Abbott does not exclude cross-comparisons at a given time but rather emphasizes the importance of a sequential approach. Yet he does argue against an overemphasis on cross-comparisons to the general exclusion of a sequential or historical orientation. His approach opens up to the same complexity that Buckley addressed (chapter 1) in his presentation of "systems theory." Cross-comparisons are fine up to a point, but feedback relationships—as described by Buckley—are important as well, and they are almost completely omitted from current social science research. Further, one must take into account the past no less than the future, and different aspects of the present situation generally require different emphases on the past. Our Timeland metaphor helps us to see such complexity. It does not exclude the importance of examining relationships among phenomena at any given point in time, but it opens our eyes to the idea that phenomena which have occurred at a great many points in time back in history—as well as close to the present—can influence what is happening at the present moment. Overall, we come to see social structure as a process rather than as a fixed entity. We learn to look for the events that have yielded what we see today. The situation alters the structure, and the structure alters the situation, and in complex ways, following our interactive worldview. It is this attention to the detailed examination of phenomena which has been the hallmark of Thomas Scheff's Part/Whole methodological approach (chapter 9), and which is central to our Web and Part/Whole Approach to the scientific method.

As we proceed, let us remain aware of Herman Hesse's metaphor of "the glass bead game" (chapter 5). "This is not an intellectual game we are playing where we move concepts around in order to achieve some kind of beautiful or systematic result. If indeed a growing aspirations-fulfillment gap constitutes an invisible crisis in contemporary society, then in fact we are involved in a very serious enterprise. If our present stratified worldview fails to give us—following Kaplan—"the principles by which a man can live" in the modern world, then we must somehow learn to change that worldview. Our focus in these chapters and those to follow is, then, nothing less than an understanding of our worldview along with an alternative one which might indeed provide us with "the principles by which a man can live." Otherwise, following Knottnerus's metaphor, we will continue to construct a concentration camp around ourselves, waiting for the worst to happen.

## Chapter 6

# "Head"

## Scientistic versus Scientific Method

"SCIENTISM" IS THE IDEA that the specific techniques of the physical and biological sciences should be applied to all fields of inquiry, including the social sciences. The key problem here is that those techniques have severe limitations when it comes to the enormous complexity of human behavior. Granted that we can learn a great deal from them, they are guided by the stratified worldview that apparently dominates society as a whole. For example, instead of being open to the impact of all phenomena on the problem under investigation, they exclude a great deal in the interest of avoiding complexity. Thus, they generally exclude the intricacies of individual and social structures, and this includes the scientist's own impact on the research process. More generally, scientism tends to exclude the individual's own subjective experiences. As we learned from Kuhn's analysis of scientific revolutions in chapter 3, scientists are deeply affected by cultural traditions along with their own ingrained beliefs. Einstein had great difficulty in gaining acceptance for his special theory of relativity just because those traditions and beliefs ruled out any conflict with the laws of motion developed by Sir Isaac Newton. As a result, scientific revolutions are hindered by "scientism" or the "scientistic method," with its automatic acceptance of the limited approach to the scientific method of physical and biological science.

Another problem with scientism is its hierarchical separation of scientists from everyone else, thus creating an expert society. This does not work well for a society with the cultural value of democracy, where citizens must be well-informed about all issues if they are to be able to make intelligent decisions. For example, should the United States launch a long-term space program that will establish a permanent station on the moon and send people to Mars? This decision requires understanding, for example, of the costs and benefits of such a program. Will it divert funds from pressing social problems? More generally, will it widen a hypothesized gap between aspirations and their fulfillment, as depicted in figure I.1? What will be the result in knowledge gained from a manned program versus unmanned programs? What will be the impact on our economy? On our relations with other countries? Space scientists will be attempting to promote their own narrow agendas with little understanding of this range of problems. Not because they deliberately avoid such wider issues, but because, presumably, a stratified worldview has taught them to avoid such complexity in order to pursue narrow goals more effectively.

An illustration of the enormous danger of such narrow thinking appears to have been the recommendations by specialists within the armed forces to bomb Cuba during the Cuban missile crisis of October, 1962. Fortunately, President Kennedy had developed a perspective that was broad enough to anticipate that this might lead to a nuclear war between the United States and the Soviet Union.

In this chapter we begin with Charles Peirce's essays on the nature of the scientific method. Our focus here is on the scientific method as illustrating the widely shared beliefs or ideas to be found within culture as a whole. This discussion of Peirce, the founder of the philosophy of pragmatism, will carry further the discussion of pragmatism in chapter 5. And it will also help us to understand the nature of the scientific method, for Peirce focuses not on scientism but on the ideas that help us to follow scientific ideals. For example, how does the scientific method differ from other efforts to attain knowledge? How important is that first step of the scientific method, namely, gaining awareness of a problem? What is the significance of this idea which Peirce believed "deserves to be inscribed upon every wall of the city of philosophy": "Do not block the way of inquiry"? It has been a century since Peirce developed his ideas, which, unfortunately, did not gain a wide audience during his lifetime. Yet there is no one who can teach us more than he can about the nature of the scientific method.

We continue with Friedrich Nietzsche's *The Gay Science*, where he introduced an idea that shook the entire field of philosophy: the death of God. We can see "God" as a metaphor for the dogmas or fixed beliefs of all religions which call for conformity and thus get in the way of the scientific method. More generally, "the death of God" can serve as a metaphor for the end of any fixed belief whatsoever. It goes along with Peirce's most well-known idea: "Do not block the way of inquiry." Nietzsche used metaphor much as a novelist or poet uses figurative language, and this is the basis for much misunderstanding of his work. Yet it is also the basis for the power of his ideas, which have deeply influenced modern philosophy and much more. To illustrate, the idea of "gay science" opens up the question of how to bridge the divide between the scientist and the literary intellectual, the question raised by Snow in his *The Two Cultures* (1959). "That simple phrase also points toward a solution: the scientist might do well to open up—to a much greater extent than previously—to the breadth, humor and metaphors of the literary intellectual. In other words, the scientist might well learn to make much greater use of language's metaphorical or image-oriented potential, and the literary intellectual might well learn to make use of language's gradational potential. Of course, scientists presently use metaphors to some extent, but we suggest that such an image-oriented approach become no less than one leg of a tripod of the scientist's linguistic orientation: to dichotomy, gradation and images or metaphors.

C.Wright Mills's *The Sociological Imagination* was—based on a poll of members of the International Sociological Association in 1999—the second most influential book for sociologists published during the entire twentieth century. It is no accident that Mills's own doctoral dissertation, "Sociology and Pragmatism," gave recognition to the roots of the scientific method. It was there that he discussed the work of Charles Peirce, William James and John Dewey. It was in *The Sociological Imagination,* after experiences as an academic sociologist and as a very popular writer of books and magazine articles on both sociology and public issues, that he was able to build on and go beyond his early ideas on the nature of the scientific method. The title of *The Sociological Imagination* has much in common with Nietzsche's *The Gay Science,* for he invokes both the science of sociology as well as a concept—"imagination"—that is emphasized within literature and the arts, invoking language's potential for metaphor and imagery.

## Peirce on the Scientific Method

Charles Sanders Peirce's writing career began in 1867 and continued until just before his death in 1914. Like Thomas Kuhn—discussed in chapter 3—he was a student of both physical science and history, although he centered on the history of philosophy. His crowning achievement was the philosophy of pragmatism. But unlike Kuhn, it has taken a century before Peirce's powerful ideas have come to be appreciated by philosophers and social scientists. Nevertheless, he succeeded in deeply influencing a number of others who were able to advance pragmatist ideas much earlier, such as William James, John Dewey and George Herbert Mead. If we turn to Peirce's own words about his philosophy, we can gain a clearer idea of what he stood for:

> For years in the course of this ripening process, I used for myself to collect my ideas under the designation fallibilism; and indeed the first step toward finding out is to acknowledge that you do not satisfactorily know

already; so that no blight can so surely arrest all intellectual growth as the blight of cocksureness; and ninety-nine out of every hundred good heads are reduced to impotence by that malady—of whose inroads they are most strangely unaware.

Indeed, out of a contrite fallibilism, combined with a high faith in the reality of knowledge, and an intense desire to find things out, all my philosophy has always seemed to grow (1897/1955: 4).

If we take his emphasis on "fallibilism" together with the "intense desire to find things out," then we have a focus on the first and most important step of the scientific method: awareness or definition of a problem. Peirce drew his optimism about the scientist's ability "to find things out" from forty years of scientific work in physics, chemistry and mathematics, including scientific contributions to those fields. But let us not slide over his statement that "ninety-nine out of every hundred good heads are reduced to impotence by that malady [cocksureness]." Note that he does not refer to any collection of a hundred individuals but rather to "a hundred good heads." It is little wonder that someone with that belief was not able to find a regular position within the academic world. Yet that belief is similar to our own statement that we are all dominated by a stratified worldview, for that worldview inclines us all toward cocksureness. Such an emphasis on fallibilism is hard for any of us to accept, yet it appears to be an essential aspect of the scientific method: to become convinced that we do not know the answer to the problem that we pose.

Peirce's essay, "The Fixation of Belief" (1877/1955: 5–22), first appeared in *Popular Science Monthly,* and is one of his earliest public statements about the scientific method. The following selection expresses his idea of fallibilism:

> The irritation of doubt is the only immediate motive for the struggle to attain belief.... With the doubt, therefore, the struggle begins, and with the cessation of doubt it ends. Hence, the sole object of inquiry is the settlement of opinion ... as soon as a firm belief is reached we are entirely satisfied, whether the belief be true or false....
>
> That the settlement of opinion is the sole end of inquiry is a very important proposition. It sweeps away, at once, various vague and erroneous concepts of proof.... Some philosophers have imagined that to start an inquiry it was only necessary to utter a question whether orally or by setting it down upon paper, and have even recommended us to begin our studies with questioning everything! But the mere putting of a proposition into the interrogative form does not stimulate the mind to any struggle after belief. "There must be a real and living doubt, and without this all discussion is idle.... Some people seem to love to argue a point after all the world is fully convinced of it. But no further advance

can be made." When doubt ceases, mental action on the subject comes to an end; and, if it did go on, it would be without purpose (1877/1955: 10–11).

For Peirce, fallibilism implies not that everything must be doubted but rather that "the irritation of doubt" is fundamental to every inquiry or research project. It is such doubt which is basic to the first and most important step of the scientific method: awareness of a problem. Anything less than genuine doubt and genuine commitment simply will not carry the scientist very far on that journey. With this argument, Peirce moves away from a view of the scientific method as a cold procedure that has to do with only the "head" and not the "heart" as well. It is not just the artist who expresses emotions in her work: it is the scientist as well.

There is a relationship between Peirce's idea of "the irritation of doubt" as a motive for the scientist to eliminate that doubt and Festinger's social psychological studies of "cognitive dissonance" (1957) as a motive for any individual to act so as to eliminate that dissonance. "Dissonance" refers to an arousal brought about by one's inconsistent thoughts or actions or both, yielding tension that motivates the individual to relieve that tension. Festinger's theory has spawned a virtual cottage industry of contemporary research on cognitive dissonance (see for example Aronson, 1969, 1992; Bem, 1967; and Harmon-Jones, et al., 1996). Much of this later research centers on the importance of the involvement of an individual's self-concept within a situation of dissonance.

Later in his essay on the fixation of belief, Peirce contrasts the scientific method with three other methods for "fixing belief" or responding to a doubt that has been raised. The "method of tenacity" involves no more than adopting any answer that we fancy to the question and sticking to that answer indefinitely with no regard to any contrary evidence. The "method of authority," used by institutions such as the state or the church, involves their backing an idea with the full force of their power to compel obedience, even to the point of torturing or killing any who oppose them. And there is the "a priori method," illustrated by philosophers who stress "what is agreeable to reason" yet who avoid testing their ideas against observations. The scientific method differs from all of these methods of responding to doubt in that it yields conclusions that correspond to observed facts or evidence. If we choose this method, we should work and fight for it, and "not complain that there are blows to take," and "strive to be the worthy knight and champion" of that method, drawing inspiration and courage from the blaze of its splendors.

But what about learning to use the scientific method in everyday life, which is implied by Gouldner's advice to sociologists to be reflexive? In the 1870s knowledge had not yet moved into such specialized channels that ordinary individuals felt as far removed from it as they do now.

Peirce communicated those ideas in a non-professional and widely read magazine, *Popular Science Monthly*. The examples he used in his article included ordinary people trying to come to conclusions about some question or problem, and not just specialized scientists. His concern did not exclude those specialized scientists and philosophers, but it was also broad enough to include everyone else. We can see this in his arguments against the methods of tenacity and authority. Although those methods are used within the academic world all too often, they are characteristic of how most of us "fix belief." Peirce argues, then, for a drastic change throughout society as a whole, where we all learn to abandon our methods of tenacity and authority along with the a priori method and come to rely on the scientific method. He assumes that this will be difficult, yet he sees the potential of that method as so great that it is worth whatever hardships are involved in learning to use it.

Peirce's second essay for *Popular Science Monthly*, "How to Make Our Ideas Clear" (1878/1955), was published the following year. He continues with the importance of "the irritation of doubt" as fundamental to any learning, this time applying this first step of the scientific method to the most trivial of circumstances—such as deciding whether to pay with a nickel or to pay with five pennies—and not just to weighty problems. Here we have further evidence of Peirce's desire to develop a scientific method that can be used from moment to moment in one's ordinary daily experiences. It seems that as the sciences have developed further within modern times, they have simultaneously moved backward: further and further away from providing tools that ordinary folk can use in their everyday experiences. Yet Peirce does not water down any of his ideas in an effort to appeal to a wide public, for he has a great deal of faith in the human capacity to learn. And we can learn from his efforts by not oversimplifying the nature of the scientific method.

Peirce makes it clear that one cannot understand the "head" or belief without also taking into account "heart" and "hand," illustrating the broad approach of pragmatism as well as the interactive worldview. A belief "appeases the irritation of doubt": it is the result of the individual's motivation to question something, for the "heart" must be involved if the "head" is to develop. Yet beliefs are rules for action, bringing in the "hand," and they should be seen as no more than a temporary resting place. They are also a starting place for action. Thus, beliefs are a second step of the scientific method, for they are answers to the question raised in the first step associated with the irritation of doubt. A pendulum metaphor for the scientific method applies here. We may see belief and action as a swing of the scientific pendulum in one direction. This provides momentum for "further doubt and further thought," and the scientific pendulum swings further in the opposite direction. But there is no end to this back-and-forth process, just as there is no end to the achievements of the scientific method or of an interactive worldview. The first step of the scientific method leads to the second step, and that in turn leads back to the first step.

Peirce ranges even more widely in his effort to clarify the nature of ideas—beyond linking "head" to "heart" and "hand"—by bringing in the phenomenon of perception, as discussed in chapter 2:

> Our idea of anything is our idea of its sensible effects; and if we fancy that we have any other we deceive ourselves.... It is absurd to say that thought has any meaning unrelated to its only function.... It appears, then, that the rule for attaining ... clearness of apprehension is as follows: Consider what effects, that might conceivably have practical bearings, we conceive the object of our conception to have. Then, our conception of these effects is the whole of our conception of the object (1878/1955: 31).

"Sensible effects" have to do with what we perceive, and our perception is involved in everything that we think, feel and do. Here Peirce alerts us to understand thought not only in relation to feelings and action but also with respect to the perceptions that underlie "head," "heart" and "hand." As taken up in chapter 2, a stratified worldview—which is a system of beliefs—implies outward perception, whereas an interactive worldview implies inward-outward perception.

Peirce carries further his view of the scientific method as a process without any end, contrasting this idea with views that will end that process. In so doing he comes up with perhaps his most well-known statement:

> Upon this first, and in one sense this sole, rule of reason, that in order to learn you must desire to learn, and in so desiring not be satisfied with what you already incline to think, there follows one corollary which itself deserves to be inscribed upon every wall of the city of philosophy:
>
> *Do not block the way of inquiry* [italics added].
>
> ... [T]o set up a philosophy which barricades the road of further advance toward the truth is the one unpardonable offence in reasoning, as it is also the one to which metaphysicians have in all ages shown themselves the most addicted. Let me call your attention to four familiar shapes in which this venomous error assails our knowledge. The first is the shape of absolute assertion. That we can be sure of nothing in science is an ancient truth.... Yet science has been infested with overconfident assertion.... The second bar which philosophers often set up across the roadway of inquiry lies in maintaining that this, that, and the other never can be known.... The third philosophical stratagem for cutting off inquiry consists in maintaining that this, that, or the other element of science is basic, ultimate, independent of aught else, and utterly inexplicable.... The

last philosophical obstacle to the advance of knowledge ... is the holding that this or that law or truth has found its last and perfect formulation (1896/1955: 54–56).

The possibility for the continuing development of knowledge is not just an idea about the scientific method. True to the philosophy of pragmatism as well as an interactive worldview, it rests on the metaphysical assumption that the individual human being has infinite potential for development. Let us recall from chapter 5 John Dewey's view of how society itself should be constructed on the basis of this assumption: "Democracy has many meanings, but if it has a moral meaning, it is found in resolving that the supreme test of all political institutions and industrial arrangements shall be the contribution they make to the all-around growth of every member of society" (Dewey, 1919/1948: 183–186). Dewey's and Peirce's assumptions about the individual's possibilities return us to our emphasis on language's potential for enabling the individual to open up to those possibilities. And it is a scientific method that follows Peirce's ideals for that method which can help the individual move toward fulfilling that potential.

For Peirce, a fundamental problem holding back our ability to understand the scientific method—let alone use it in everyday life—is our metaphysical stance or worldview. He writes:

[T]here is one highly abstract science which is in a deplorably backward condition. I mean Metaphysics. There is and can be no doubt that this immature condition of Metaphysics has very greatly hampered the progress of ... psychology ... linguistics, anthropology, social science, etc. To my mind it is equally clear that defective and bad metaphysics has been almost as injurious to the physical sciences.... The common opinion has been that Metaphysics is backward because it is intrinsically beyond the reach of human cognition.... But metaphysics, even bad metaphysics, really rests on observations, whether consciously or not; and the only reason that this is not universally recognized is that it rests upon kinds of phenomena with which every man's experience is so saturated that he usually pays no particular attention to them (1898/1955: 310–311).

In our modern view we do not classify metaphysics as a science, as Peirce did. Rather, we see it as part of philosophy and involved with very general or abstract and fundamental assumptions about the nature of all reality. Yet those assumptions are tested indirectly by moving down the ladder of linguistic abstraction from the generality of metaphysics to epistemology, illustrated by the scientific method, and then even further down to scientific theories. Peirce argues that lack of progress in social science is largely based on what he calls the "immature condition of Metaphysics." This meshes with our own argument that a stratified metaphysical stance or worldview impedes our scientific progress, and that this can be reversed to the extent that we learn to shift to an interactive metaphysics or worldview as well as an interactive approach to the scientific method. But far more than scientific progress is at stake here, for we argue that the result of our stratified worldview is an invisible crisis in contemporary society.

## Nietzsche's *The Gay Science*

Friedrich Nietzsche was a child of the late nineteenth century; he was born in 1844 and he died in 1900, yet his work opens up questions yet to be resolved in the twenty-first century. He was a poet and musician as well as a philosopher, pointing—along with C.P. Snow—toward bridging the divide between art and science. The title of his *The Gay Science* (1887/1974) also suggests this bridge with its view of the scientist as linking "heart" with "head." He also communicated a profound sense of an incredible gap between the individual's infinite possibilities and the forces limiting their fulfillment. Like Georg Simmel (chapter 4), Nietzsche mainly wrote short essays and has been criticized for never integrating his ideas systematically. And his poetic style makes it all too easy to interpret him in widely different ways. Yet as we read more and more of Nietzsche we discover, just as we do with Simmel, that there is a great deal of unity in his writing.

Nietzsche helps us to go back in time to an era when science was beginning to flower, much the same time that Peirce developed his remarkable insights into the nature of the scientific method. He gives us a sense of what he felt when science finally emerged—with its power to yield understanding and solve problems—after mankind's many millennia of dwelling in relative darkness: He contrasts our situation with that of bygone ages with the metaphor of a shipwrecked man finally climbing ashore and standing on firm ground. Even without certainty about what scientists discover, we are in a completely different situation from those in bygone eras who had no method they could rely on that was at all comparable to the scientific method for bringing them ever closer to understanding and problem-solving. Yet let us not become too smug about this achievement, for we have yet to learn how to make the progress we desperately require on problems far more complex than those associated with space travel: problems of understanding human behavior. We should not forget Peirce's comment that the "blight of cocksureness" reduces "ninety-nine out of every hundred good heads" to impotence, evidence for our stratified worldview.

Nietzsche goes on to give us a clearer idea about the nature of scientific thinking, and in very few words he charts a course for how science might continue to develop:

So many things have to come together for scientific thinking to originate; and all these necessary strengths had to be invented, practiced, and cultivated separately. As long as they were still separate, however, they frequently had an altogether different effect than they do now that they are integrated into scientific thinking and hold each other in check. Their effect was that of poisons; for example that of the impulse to doubt, to negate, to wait, to collect, to dissolve. Many hecatombs of human beings were sacrificed before these impulses learned to comprehend their coexistence and so feel that they were all functions of one organizing force within one human being. And even now the time seems remote when artistic energies and the practical wisdom of life will join with scientific thinking to form a higher organic system in relation to which scholars, physicians, artists, and legislators—as we know them at present—would have to look like paltry relics of ancient times (1887/1974: 173).

Nietzsche's idea that a one-sided approach to science can function as a poison is most appropriate for understanding our modern situation. The failure of biological and physical science to open up to all relevant phenomena—human behavior in particular—has yielded an increasingly dangerous situation for all of us living in the modern world. In his last sentence Nietzsche suggests what a truly broad approach to the scientific method—by contrast with the science of his day and ours—would involve: integrating art and practical wisdom within the scientific method. His view of the present efforts of "scholars, physicians, artists, and legislators" without such an integration of knowledge is extremely critical. Compared to what they would be if such knowledge is integrated, they would look like "paltry relics of ancient times." In other words, the scientific method has failed to go very far just because it has separated art and practical wisdom from science. Here he takes a position similar to C. P. Snow's call for communication between the two cultures of science and literature. As for the union of the scientific method with practical wisdom, he points toward the idea of bringing science into everyday life.

Nietzsche carries further his vision of the union of art and science in his analysis of the relationship between the intellect and the emotions—or "head" and "heart"—in all of us:

In the great majority, the intellect is a clumsy, gloomy, creaking machine that is difficult to start. They call it "taking the matter *seriously*" when they want to work with this machine and think well. How burdensome they must find good thinking! The lovely human beast always seems to lose its good spirits when it thinks well; it becomes "serious." And "where laughter and gaiety are found, thinking does not amount to anything": that is the prejudice of this serious beast against all "gay science."—Well then, let us prove that this is a prejudice (1887/1974: 257).

This separation between the individual's intellectual and emotional life goes against the ideals of the scientific method. For example, how can scientists become deeply committed to pursuing investigations that might take years without bringing their emotions into their work? How can they gain satisfactions from their work over the years without feeling free to be emotional as well as intellectual? The pragmatists were much against separating phenomena that should remain in interaction. That separation also makes it difficult to apply the scientific method to the problems we all meet in our everyday lives. For few of us would argue that we should attempt to exclude our emotions as we go about the business of living.

Nietzsche's ideas about the nature of the scientific method strongly suggest an enormous gap within social science: between our present specialized approach with little communication among specialties and scientific ideals calling for openness to all phenomena relevant to a given problem. He saw clearly the gap between the scientist's "head" and "heart," our failure to integrate science with art, our failure to integrate science with wisdom, the importance of using the tools of literature and poetry—such as metaphor—to communicate scientific ideas in a powerful way, and the need to change science and the scientific method so as to solve its problems.

But Nietzsche is known far more for ideas which challenge not only the way science is conducted but the fundamental organization of society:

> Have you not heard of that madman who lit a lantern in the bright morning hours, ran to the market place, and cried incessantly: "I seek God! I seek God!"... The madman jumped into their midst and pierced them with his eyes. "Whither is God?" he cried; "I will tell you. We have killed him—you and I. All of us are his murderers. But how did we do this? How could we drink up the sea? Who gave us the sponge to wipe away the entire horizon? What were we doing when we unchained this earth from its sun? Whether is it moving now? Whither are we moving? Away from all suns? Are we not plunging continually? Backward, sideward, forward, in all directions? Is there still any up or down? ... Here the madman fell silent and looked again at his listeners; and they, too, were silent and stared at him in astonishment. At last he threw his lantern on the ground, and it broke into pieces and went out. "I have come too early," he said then; "My time is not yet. This tremendous event is still on its way, still wandering; it has not yet reached the ears of men. Lightning and thunder require time; the light of the stars requires time; deeds, though done, still require time to be seen and heard" (1887/1974: 181–182).

Given the universal existence of social stratification throughout the world and throughout history, Nietzsche's idea that God is dead—

interpreted metaphorically to include all kinds of persisting hierarchy—strikes a powerful blow at the fundamental structure of all societies. It is not only science which must be altered drastically but also society as a whole. Nietzsche was born just after the American and French revolutions, and he lived to see society change dramatically as a result of the continuing scientific and industrial revolutions. Like Marx and Simmel, he experienced firsthand the severe disruptions of life that accompanied the change from agricultural to industrial societies along with the alienation that accompanied it. "God is dead" can be interpreted in many ways, but one way is to understand it as meaning that cultural values emphasizing the importance of the individual have challenged the pattern of persisting hierarchy in a great many areas of life. A similar interpretation is that the world is experiencing a fundamental change from a metaphysics or worldview emphasizing outward perception—e.g., God, the nation, the expert, one's ethnic group, one's family—to an inward-outward worldview with far greater emphasis on the potential of every individual.

Yet if we follow Nietzsche's last sentences we receive a new message from him, conveyed by the words of the madman: "I have come too early," he said then; "my time is not yet. This tremendous event is still on its way, still wandering; it has not yet reached the ears of men." It is not that God is dead but rather that God is dying. It is not that social stratification has been eliminated, but rather that social stratification has received a death blow by events like the American and French revolutions along with the rise of science and technology. Nietzsche says much the same thing in another passage: "After Buddha was dead, his shadow was still shown for centuries in a cave—a tremendous, gruesome shadow. God is dead, but given the way of men, there may still be caves for thousands of years in which his shadow will be shown. And we—we still have to vanquish his shadow, too" (1887/1974: 167).

Of all the philosophers and social scientists who have ever put pen to paper, Nietzsche is in a class by himself with respect to the metaphorical power of his language. As in the case of C. P. Snow, Abraham Kaplan and Charles Peirce, he advocated the union of "head" and "heart." But he did far more than advocate this idea intellectually: he demonstrated the importance and power of that union with his poetic language. How can we forget his image of the madman who ran to the market place crying "I seek God!"? What prose can rival his description of the enormity of the death of God: "How could we drink up the sea? Who gave us the sponge to wipe away the entire horizon? What were we doing when we unchained this earth from its sun? ... Is there still any up or down?"

Unfortunately, Nietzsche's style of writing is a dinosaur among modern social scientists. Yet this may be due in large measure to our stratified worldview, and worldviews can be changed. Following Nietzsche's metaphors, the tremendous event of changing our worldview is still on its way.

The stratified worldview may still live, and we may still have to vanquish it. Social scientists generally learn to write in a truly deadly manner, boring readers just as Herman Hesse's narrator (chapter 5) succeeds in boring us. But exposure to Nietzsche may well help us to communicate more effectively to others as well as ourselves.

## Mills's *The Sociological Imagination*

C.Wright Mills's optimistic vision of the promise and possibilities of sociology has succeeded in motivating every generation of sociologists since his death in 1962 at forty-five. He moved from a journalistic career in Texas to taking up graduate work in sociology at the University of Wisconsin. There he analyzed some fifty textbooks on social problems—two written by the chair of his own department of sociology—in order to learn about "the style of reflection and the social-historical basis of American sociology." He was appalled at what he discovered:

> The level of abstraction which characterizes these texts is so low that often they seem to be empirically confused for lack of abstraction to knit them together. They display bodies of meagerly connected facts, ranging from rape in rural districts to public housing, and intellectually sanction this low level of abstraction.... Collecting and dealing in a fragmentary way with scattered problems and facts of milieux, these books are not focused on larger stratifications or upon structured wholes (1943: 168).

By failing to use general or abstract concepts from sociology—like social stratification, bureaucracy, cultural values and alienation—those textbooks failed to build on what sociologists had learned over many decades. Further, those authors—including his chair—turned out largely collections of relatively trivial isolated facts which could not be integrated to produce general and meaningful statements about important social problems. The result of this approach was a conservative stance on social problems. Sociological concepts like "social stratification" and "alienation" that point toward fundamental problems in modern society were ignored. To pay attention to them would involve considering "drastic shifts in the basic institutions" of society. Mills's criticism of his chair did not earn him a position at Wisconsin, but he went on to a career at Columbia and as a public intellectual with frequent magazine articles and a number of highly regarded books widely read both inside and outside of the academic world.

It was in *The Sociological Imagination* (1959), published only a few years before his death, that he expressed his ideas about a scientific method for sociology—and social science in general—in a more systematic and comprehensive way. He maintained that it is important for social scientists to shuttle far up and down language's ladder of abstraction.

To clarify his idea about shuttling up and down language's ladder of abstraction, Mills roundly criticized what he called "grand theory" and "abstracted empiricism." Grand theorists stay at a high level of abstraction and never move down to test their ideas in concrete and historical settings. Abstracted empiricists, by contrast, are much like those writers of textbooks on social problems. They stay at a low level of abstraction and produce as a result trivial works without any general significance. Mills states his own approach to the scientific method:

> One great lesson that we can learn from its systematic absence in the work of the grand theorists is that every self-conscious thinker must at all times be aware of—and hence be able to control—the levels of abstraction on which he is working. The capacity to shuttle between levels of abstraction, with ease and with clarity, is a signal mark of the imaginative and systematic thinker (1959: 34).

It is one thing to become aware of a problem, taking that first step of the scientific method. But it is quite another thing to be able to confront the enormous complexity of human behavior, taking that second step of the scientific method. By shuttling far up language's ladder of abstraction we are able to develop a broad understanding of a problem. That shuttling should take us up to epistemology or the nature of the scientific method that we are employing. It should even take us further: to our very metaphysical stance, or the worldview we are employing. Then by coming far down that ladder we can proceed to test those very general ideas—even our metaphysical ones—against the concrete facts within specific situations. Going far up that ladder does not imply that we do not go far down, as in the case of the grand theorists. And going far down that ladder does not imply that we do not go far up, as in the case of the abstracted empiricists. When we shuttle far up and down we are learning to use language in an interactive way, and we learn to move into an interactive worldview.

Yet this is easier said than done. When we proceed to move up the ladder of abstraction to general or abstract concepts like social stratification and alienation, we also move in a direction opposed to the highly specialized division of labor within social science. Let us recall that there are no less than forty-three distinct Sections of the American Sociological Association which generally fail to communicate with one another. And this high degree of specialization is no accident, since it conforms to our stratified worldview and approach to the scientific method, which is far from our ideals. However, with this gap between scientific ideals and practices in mind, we can move toward closing that gap by beginning to follow Mills's advice to shuttle up and down that ladder of abstraction. At least as important, in addition, would be efforts to shift to an interactive world-view which would in turn encourage such shuttling. Both efforts would be strengthened by Mills's powerful arguments about the importance of closing our gap between scientific ideals and practices.

But exactly what did Mills mean by his most well-known concept, "the sociological imagination"? What direction does it point to for social scientists? Mills explains himself:

> The sociological imagination enables us to grasp history and biography and the relations between the two within society. That is its task and its promise.... [T]hose who have been imaginatively aware of the promise of their work have consistently asked three sorts of questions: (1) What is the structure of this particular society as a whole? What are its essential components, and how are they related to one another? ... (2) Where does this society stand in human history? What are the mechanics by which it is changing? What is its place within and its meaning for the development of humanity as a whole? ... (3) What varieties of men and women now prevail in this society and in this period? And what varieties are coming to prevail? In what ways are they selected and formed, liberated and repressed, made sensitive and blunted? What kinds of "human nature" are revealed in the conduct and character we observe in this society in this period? ...
>
> Whether the point of interest is a great power state or a minor literary mood, a family, a prison, a creed—these are the kinds of questions the best social analysts have asked. They are the intellectual pivots of classic studies of man in society—and they are the questions inevitably raised by any mind possessing the sociological imagination (1959: 6-7).

Mills adopts a very broad approach to social science research, a breadth that is made possible by shuttling up the ladder of abstraction to general concepts and hypotheses. His is not another specialized approach. Rather, the student of human behavior must be prepared to investigate not only society as a whole, and not only the individual in society, but also the historical situation in which the individual and society find themselves. To achieve this the individual must develop an extremely broad intellectual orientation, a "sociological imagination." And it is that imagination which will enable him "to shift from one perspective to another—from the political to the psychological; from examination of a single family to comparative assessment of the national budgets of the world; from the theological school to the military establishment; from considerations of an oil industry to studies of contemporary poetry." Nothing less will enable to social scientist to confront the enormous complexity of human behavior.

Mills alerts us to the enormous potential of language for yielding an understanding of problems. By failing to move far up language's ladder of abstraction, we lose much of that potential power to understand the complexities of our own behavior, that of others, and the social problems all around us. For example, that failure makes it impossible to build on much of what social science has already discovered about human behavior. By contrast, learning abstract concepts from social science can enable us to build on the literally millions of studies buried deep within our libraries. The twenty-two concepts in the headings of these eleven chapters illustrate this approach. Beyond those concepts, we can learn to shuttle even further up language's ladder of abstraction to both epistemology and metaphysics, or more specifically to the scientific method and worldviews. There are good reasons why Mills found those textbooks on social problems departing far from scientific ideals. There are also good reasons why we appear to be experiencing accelerating social problems, as illustrated by figure I.1. We hypothesize that those reasons include both our failure to follow scientific ideals and our failure to adopt an interactive worldview.

There is much more that we can learn from Mills (see for example Phillips, 2004). There is his great optimism about our possibilities to penetrate the complexities of human behavior. There is his deep emotional commitment to knowledge along with his sense of humor, joining his "heart" with his "head." That emotional commitment also includes his belief in the existence of absolutely fundamental problems in modern society, as suggested by figure I.1. There is his commitment to learning how to solve our fundamental problems, adding "hand" as well. And there is his advice to his students which we can all adopt: "[T]he most admirable thinkers within the scholarly community you have chosen to join do not split their work from their lives. They seem to take both too seriously to allow such dissociation, and they want to use each for the enrichment of the other" (1959: 195). But now, half a century after Mills wrote *The Sociological Imagination*, we moderns find ourselves in what appears to be an increasingly threatening situation. At this time in history perhaps we can no longer afford the luxury of failing to develop a sociological imagination if indeed we ever expect to understand and confront our escalating problems.

## Some Implications

It appears that social scientists almost universally have been proceeding with their methods of research without taking into account their own metaphysical assumptions, assumptions which guide epistemology and thus shape those methods. The result of this ignorance of the worldview guiding research procedures may well be a fundamental basis for the failure of the social sciences to achieve rapid cumulative development. It may also help to explain the present limited ability of the social sciences to understand the complexities of human behavior, let alone provide tools for effective problem-solving procedures. Given this situation, an understanding of those assumptions is urgently needed. But if research efforts to uncover them are guided by those same assumptions, then there will be little chance of uncovering them.

Another implication of this chapter is the importance of building bridges connecting philosophy, history and literature with social science. Philosophical analysis can help social scientists make use of the most current conclusions of philosophers, thus avoiding what appears to have happened within quantitative sociology: an approach that does not build sufficiently on modern philosophy's openness to a very wide range of phenomena. Neither does a great deal of social science research open up to the importance of seeing hypotheses and propositions within a web of statements that include metaphysical and epistemological assumptions. As for literature, many of Nietzsche's insights provide an excellent illustration of the power of literary metaphors for uncovering the scientist's basic assumptions. Also, literature with its metaphorical emphasis may well help social scientists to communicate ideas to themselves as well as to others more effectively.

As for our two hypotheses, Peirce's analysis yields no direct implications for hypothesis (1), but that is not the case for (2). For he implied that the broad philosophy of pragmatism which he was developing would be most useful in yielding a meaningful approach to life, by contrast with a narrower philosophy. Turning to Nietzsche, he is most optimistic about changes in modern society, such as the death of God and increasing freedom for the individual, indicating his opposition to hypothesis (1). Yet at the same time he supports hypothesis (2) when he looks to a future world where all knowledge will be integrated with far more effective results than our present limited achievements. Mills's highly critical analysis of increasing failures of modern society yields support for hypothesis (1), and his own broad vision of the stratified forces producing those failures—such as "grand theory" and "abstracted empiricism"—provide support for (2). To illustrate increasing problems, Mills saw classical sociologists like Marx and Weber coming up with important ideas like that of social stratification, yet he also saw contemporary sociologists generally failing to build on those ideas or achieve the breadth of the classical sociologists.

As for images or metaphors, Peirce's "Do not block the way of inquiry" suggests that inquiry is a never-ending road that we travel, one not to be blocked by any rigidity or certainty whatsoever. He held that this statement "deserves to be inscribed upon every wall in the city of philosophy," extending the importance of his image. Let us recall his emphasis on the importance of "the irritation of doubt," which starts one on the way of inquiry, and his condemnation of almost all scientists for failing in this respect. With respect to Nietzsche, his most well-known metaphor is the death of God, which we can interpret to extend far beyond any theological meanings. It gets at the very core of our stratified worldview, opening up to the freedom of the individual to construct a new world and a new worldview. Mills's vision of "the sociological imagination" is somewhat abstract and difficult to see. Yet it has managed to capture the imagination of a great many sociologists and other social scientists. Perhaps this is because the phrase joins sociology with what is central to many in the humanities: the human imagination. For it is the liberation of our imagination which helps us open up to our possibilities as human beings.

# "Heart"

## Anomie versus Cultural Value Fulfillment

WHEREAS CHAPTER 6 EMPHASIZES THE "HEAD," chapter 7 stresses the "heart," and both chapters stress culture. In this chapter we will range over widely shared interests, ideals or goals—or cultural values—just as the top curve of figure I.1 is concerned with the revolution of rising aspirations or expectations in all areas of life. In chapter 8 we will also range over all areas of life, but we shall emphasize the bottom curve of figure I.1. There, our concern will be with social organization, or patterns of action and interaction such as social stratification and bureaucracy, which work to limit the fulfillment of cultural values, granting that such patterns have other impacts as well.

Yet let us be clear about the links between culture and social organization as we proceed to examine culture. Those links are crucial for an understanding of any given social structure. Indeed, it is in order to emphasize the importance of taking social organization into account in an analysis of culture that we have proceeded to define both as components of social structure. This approach differs from the more typical view of social structure as much the same as social organization. However, that typical view generally succeeds in undercutting the importance of culture for sociologists, who fail as a result to see culture as a central component of social structure.

Emile Durkheim's *Suicide* (1897/1951)—along with his own commitment to sociology's possibilities together with his organizational efforts in France—were central to the origin of sociology as an academic discipline throughout the world. He laboriously pulled together statistics on suicide, comparing rates in different countries, in different religious groups, in different time periods, and for people in different occupations and different marital situations. Among his conclusions was that economic development accompanying the Industrial Revolution is associated with increasing "anomie": "...greed is aroused without knowing where to find ultimate foothold. Nothing can calm it, since its goal is far beyond all it can attain...." He linked this gap between people's aspirations or expectations and their fulfillment with higher suicide rates. His remedy was that individuals should lower those aspirations so that they become more realistic, closing the gap depicted in figure I.1. By contrast with most contemporary social scientists, Durkheim saw the importance of understanding long-term historical changes and of focusing on fundamental problems in society, both of which are illustrated by the Industrial Revolution with the problems it produced.

Robin Williams's *American Society* (1970) helps us to understand the nature of the cultural values within modern society, thus giving us systematic guidance for understanding the top curve of figure I.1. It is that systematic orientation that can help us to take culture seriously despite its invisible nature. We may see those widely shared interests or ideals as falling into two broad categories: work-related values and people-oriented values. Both are closely associated with the continuing industrial revolution and process of modernization along with political revolutions, like those in the United States and France at the end of the eighteenth century. On the one hand we have cultural values like "achievement and success," "activity and work," "material comfort," "efficiency and practicality" and economic "progress." On the other hand we have cultural values like "equality," "freedom," "democracy" and "individual personality," or what Simmel referred to as "individuality" in chapter 4. It is a clash between work-related and people-oriented cultural values which Horney saw (chapter 4) as a key factor producing neurosis in modern society.

Amy Chua's *World on Fire* (2003) helps us to carry forward the implications of Levin's experiment on prejudice (chapter 3) for contemporary patterns of warfare, terrorism and violence. Levin saw a stratified worldview accompanied by the contradiction between egalitarian cultural values and patterns of social stratification as yielding prejudice against minority groups and aggression in general. Chua discovered much the same thing. She saw an emphasis on democracy—when associated with patterns of social stratification—as yielding warfare and terrorism. Although she did not assess the existence of a stratified worldview by contrast with Levin (chapter 3), we hypothesize its existence in modern society. Chua uses her analysis to explain widespread hatred and aggression directed against the United States at this time in history.

## Durkheim's *Suicide*

No one was more important in the founding of the discipline of sociology during the nineteenth century than Emile Durkheim. And no work of Durkheim's was more influential than his *Suicide,* published in 1897, which set the tone for the new discipline. Not only did he move far up language's ladder of abstraction to concepts like "anomie" but he also moved far down that ladder in order to locate anomie within particular settings as well as within history.

For Durkheim, "anomie" refers to the state of a society or a group where its norms or patterns of expectations are severely disrupted, patterns which he saw all around him in the late nineteenth century. He proceeded with an effort to explain its occurrence:

> If anomie never appeared except, as in the above instances, in intermittent spurts and acute crisis, it might cause the so-cial suicide-rate to vary from time to time, but it would not be a regular, constant factor. In one sphere of social life, however—the sphere of trade and industry—it is actually in a chronic state....
>
> Such is the source of the excitement predominating in this part of society, and which has thence extended to the other parts. There, the state of crisis and anomie is constant and, so to speak, normal. From top to bottom of the ladder, greed is aroused without knowing where to find ultimate foothold. Nothing can calm it, since its goal is far beyond all it can attain.... The wise man, knowing how to enjoy achieved results without having constantly to replace them with others, finds in them an attachment to life in the hour of difficulty. But the man who has always pinned all his hopes on the future and lived with his eyes fixed upon it, has nothing in the past as a comfort against the present's afflictions (1897/1951: 254-256).

Durkheim was able to back up this general argument with statistics that he had painstakingly gathered from published sources for rates of suicide in different groups. He focused on comparing suicide rates for those employed in trade or industry with rates for those employed in agriculture, since the contrast between those occupations reflected the changes associated with the industrial revolution. He found that suicide rates for those in trade were more than double for those in agriculture in seven different countries: France, Switzerland, Italy, Prussia, Bavaria, Belgium and Saxony. As for Italy, the rate for trade was no less than ten times that for agriculture, and in Bavaria the suicide rate for trade was triple that for agriculture. Shifting to industry, he found similar differences for those countries with the exception of Belgium, although the contrast was not quite as marked. And he concluded that anomie "is a regular and specific factor in suicide in our modern societies."

Durkheim's view that anomie is part and parcel of the nature of industrial or modern society is, like figure I.1, based on his linking together people's aspirations and the extent to which those aspirations are fulfilled. Since his time, other social scientists and students of human behavior have joined his assessment of the seriousness of this gap between expectations and their fulfillment. For example, in chapter 2 John Berger described the impact of advertising as creating dissatisfaction by teaching us to long for a lifestyle that we can only rarely come close to. In that same chapter, Daniel Boorstin argued that we moderns have learned to suffer from extravagant expectations, expecting "the contradictory and the impossible." Karen Horney (chapter 4) argued that modern society has created neurotic personalities produced in part by the contradiction "between the stimulation of our needs and our factual frustration in satisfying them." And Robert Merton, whose analysis of unanticipated consequences was discussed in chapter 3, believed that modern society produces "success goals for the population at large while the social structure rigorously restricts or completely closes access to approved modes of reaching those goals for a considerable part of the same population" (1949: 137).

It is useful to look at Durkheim's achievement in relation to the work of other founders of sociology discussed earlier: Marx and Simmel (chapter 4). All three looked to the enormous problems which the industrialization of Western society posed for the individual. Marx centered on social stratification, a topic to be taken up in more detail in chapter 8. For Marx, social stratification within the workplace between the bourgeoisie and the proletariat produces powerful forces leading to the alienation of the proletariat. But that impact cannot be understood without taking culture into account as well, something that Marx failed to do. For it is when social stratification is combined with the cultural value of equality that it yields the contradiction between expectations and fulfillment associated with the alienation of the individual. A high degree of alienation is a modern phenomenon, since an emphasis on the cultural value of equality is a modern phenomenon. By contrast, that cultural value was not stressed in preindustrial times. Although Marx did not see clearly the importance of culture, Durkheim did, along with modern social scientists. Apparently, it is when we combine the cultural value of equality with patterns of social stratification that we become sensitive to profound problems in modern society. These problems are no less fundamental than what Marx saw as a contradiction between the forces of production and the relations of production.

If we look to Simmel, the only founder of sociology who centered on the individual, we find that he emphasized the importance of culture along with Durkheim. Let us recall his discussion of cultural values in the eighteenth and nineteenth centuries from chapter 4:

> The eighteenth century may have called for liberation from all the ties which grew up historically in politics, in religion, in morality and in economics in order to permit the original natural virtue of man, which is equal in everyone, to develop without inhibition; the nineteenth century may have sought to promote, in addition to man's freedom,

his individuality ... and his achievements which make him unique and indispensable (1903/1971: 324).

Here we have further understanding of the changes in culture that, following Durkheim, led to anomie. For if the nineteenth century emphasized the cultural value of individuality, then we can more easily understand the clash between individuality and patterns of social stratification limiting individuality, resulting in anomie. Of course, individuality includes far more than simply the cultural value of materialism, which Durkheim emphasized in his analysis of anomie. Following Simmel, then, the case for the rise of anomie in modern society is much stronger because more of the individual's fundamental interests are thwarted with the development of contemporary society and its continuing patterns of social stratification and bureaucracy. If we refer back to Horney's analysis of modern culture in chapter 4, we can understand more fully the non-material basis for anomie. For example, she writes about the cultural value of "brotherly love," which is contradicted by an emphasis on patterns of competition and stratification in the marketplace. She also writes about the cultural value of individual freedom, which Simmel had suggested was so important not only in the eighteenth century but more generally in modern times. That value is closely associated with the value of equality.

To understand more fully the development of materialistic values along with the cultural values of freedom and individuality in the eighteenth and nineteenth centuries, it is necessary to uncover the forces behind the industrial revolution. For that revolution was coupled with a scientific revolution, as discussed in chapter 6. Neither should we forget the political revolutions of the eighteenth century, such as the American and French revolutions, which emphasized the cultural values of equality and democracy. But what is not widely understood as a force behind the industrial revolution is what Max Weber called "the Protestant ethic." Weber's *The Protestant Ethic and the Spirit of Capitalism* (1905/1958) viewed the Protestant ethic as focusing the individual on attaining religious salvation in an afterlife. Hard work along with the accumulation of wealth through saving rather than spending was an indication that one would be saved for an afterlife in heaven rather than eternal hell. Weber quotes Benjamin Franklin to describe the "spirit of capitalism," with Franklin's ideas that "time is money" and his focus on devoting one's everyday life to working (1905/1958: 48–49).

Yet there has been a great deal of debate about whether Protestantism also influenced the development of capitalism by providing individuals with an indication that they would be saved spiritually. For example, a recent study has pulled together much of this debate along with a good deal of evidence (Cohen, 2002). It has concluded that it was Protestantism's work ethic along with patterns of accumulating wealth far more than any other religious motives which accounts for Protestantism's impact on the development of capitalism.

Although we have focused on Durkheim's approach to anomie and its links to the work of classical sociologists, it is also useful to examine contemporary sociological research on anomie. There is Merton's highly influential article, "Social Structure and Anomie" (1949), which pointed anomie studies toward the analysis of deviant behavior and crime. There is, largely as a result, a great deal of attention to exactly how anomie and crime are related. Nikos Passas and Robert Agnew have reviewed this substantial literature, and we may note the continuing importance of the concept of anomie (1997). For example, there is "general strain theory," initially put forward by Agnew (1985), which emphasizes the pressure on adolescents to engage in delinquency. In more recent work Agnew differentiates among three kinds of strain: the failure to achieve positively valued goals, the removal of positively valued stimuli, and the presentation of negative stimuli (1992). Here we may note a broad approach to goals or values, by comparison with Merton's focus on economic goals.

While strain theory has focused on the individual, "institutional anomie theory," as developed by Messner and Rosenfeld (1994) along with others, emphasizes the macro level. To illustrate, Diane Vaughan has analyzed the forces producing the space shuttle Challenger disaster, focusing on organizational deviance (1997). She found the National Aeronautics and Space Administration (NASA) to be in competition with other governmental agencies over scarce resources, a situation yielding pressures for social stratification. Given this threat that NASA's goals might be defeated coupled with the ambiguous nature of norms guiding NASA's conduct, substantial pressures for organizational deviance developed. Although NASA did not have the economic resources that would be required to meet its flight schedule, it nevertheless proceeded to meet that schedule and consciously risked the safety of its flight crews. Further, it proceeded to cover up or "normalize" that deviance by developing a subculture that justified such behavior. Thus, we must look beyond the situation of the individual to culture or social structure in order to understand deviant behavior.

Such contemporary research extends our understanding of the implications of Durkheim's early work on anomie. Yet it also succeeds in narrowing our understanding of the possibilities of that early work for moving toward understanding the wide range of fundamental problems in modern society, as suggested by figure I.1's gap between aspirations and their fulfillment. Crime is indeed an important problem, but it is no more than one problem among many, and Durkheim's approach opens us up to a much wider range of problems. Further, contemporary research generally follows a Flatland perspective in its lack of concern for long-term history, by contrast with the work of the classical sociologists. A crucial exception is Rafalovich's "Assessing the Fallout of the Terrorist Movement: Anomie and the Factured American Weltanschauung" (2007).

By introducing the concept of cultural values we have been able to understand more fully relationships among the analyses of Marx, Durkheim, Weber, Simmel, Boorstin, Merton and Horney. We have also gained further insight into the origins and nature of anomie along with alienation and addiction. All this has been possible because that concept pulls together a great deal of knowledge developed by anthropologists and sociologists, and it is also systematically linked to other key sociological concepts like social stratification. Equally important, it is a concept that we can use to understand not only society and history but also the individual, for knowledge of culture translates into knowledge of each one of us. The sociologist most widely known for working with this concept of cultural values is Robin M. Williams, Jr.

## Williams's *American Society*

Williams was not attempting to analyze the nature of cultural values in modern society as a whole, but rather centered on the cultural values within American society. By so doing he was following the work of many anthropologists who had emphasized the differences among the cultures in different societies. Granting such differences, there are also great similarities based on the many forces involved in the continuing technological revolution throughout the world. For example, the mass media of communication, the computer, global economic forces and the near-universality of the English language have all worked together to yield a great deal of cultural uniformity throughout modern societies. The third edition of Williams's *American Society* appeared in 1970, when many of these trends were only beginning to be felt very strongly.

However, in the late twentieth and the twenty-first century we have experienced a great many ethnic conflicts worldwide, and the question easily arises as to whether the forces that make for commonalties or the sharing of cultural values are in fact effective. Given increasing ethnic conflicts throughout the world, doesn't such conflict yield evidence for the opposite of such sharing, which we would expect to bring people together? If we turn once again to figure I.1, we may note that it is not cultural values alone which create that gap but rather a combination of such values and the failure to fulfill them. Indeed, Chua argues in the last section of this chapter that it is the very spread of democratic values within countries that are highly stratified that fuels ethnic warfare. In other words, an understanding of ethnic conflict involves taking into account at least the two curves in figure I.1, and not merely the top curve. But we claim in this book that ethnic conflict along with other social problems is even much more complex than this. For example, the Levin experiment (chapter 3) provided evidence for the importance of one's worldview in the genesis of ethnic prejudice.

Let us build on the above analysis of anomie by separating two sets of cultural values which tend to conflict with one another and thus form a basis for anomie: work-related values associated with our continuing technological revolution, and people-oriented values, more closely associated with the American and French political revolutions. The following ten values were selected from Williams's list of fifteen because they apply most readily to contemporary society as a whole, granting that American society may emphasize many of them more than other societies. This analysis of the nature of modern cultural values oversimplifies by far the actual situation, where cultural values do change to some extent over time, granting that they generally persist. These two sets of cultural values are by no means in continual conflict. Further, each cultural value is not nearly as unitary as it might appear to be on the basis of our description of it. Further, some values are very closely linked to certain values and further removed from others. Also, this listing misses some fundamental cultural values that Williams probably assumed were characteristic of all modern societies, such as the importance of very close social relationships. Williams's analysis of "major value orientations" (1970: 452–500) was based on his reviewing a great many social science books and articles on the subject. Of course, it is vital that current research should update Williams's analysis, yet that analysis appears to be a substantial step forward in understanding the nature of contemporary cultural values.

## People-Oriented Cultural Values

*Equality.* At the level of explicit doctrine, intrinsic equality is widespread in American culture ... in the form of a specifically religious conception (the equality of souls before God ...).... At the level of overt interpersonal relations, adherence to a sense of intrinsic human value is discernible ... by an extraordinary informality, directness, and lack of status consciousness in person-to-person contacts.... A second major type of equality consists of specific formal rights and obligations ... from military service to voting, from public education to taxation—represent not only freedom but also equality....

*Freedom.* Always the demand was for freedom from some existing restraint ... a tendency to think of rights rather than duties ... a distrust of central government ... American spokesmen emphasize freedom of speech and assembly, a multiparty, representative political system, private enterprise, freedom to change residence and employment ... it has seemed to make a great difference whether the individual receives a certain income or has a certain type of occupation as a result of an apparently impersonal, anonymous, diffuse, competitive process, as against "being forced" to accept that employment or remuneration by law or by the command of a visible social authority....

*Democracy.* Along with majority rule, representative institutions, and the rejection of ... monarchical and aristocratic principles.... American democracy stressed the reservation of certain "inalienable rights" as unalterable by majority rule.... The new system was devised in such a way as to limit and check centralized governmental power and to establish an ordered pattern for agreeing to disagree.... Its ... fundamental assumption is the worth and dignity and creative capacity of the individual, so that the chief aim of government is the maximum of individual self-direction, the chief means to that end the minimum of compulsion by the state....

*Individual Personality.*... [W]e note a large number of important legal provisions [for] ... the protection of personal freedom or the physical or social integrity of the person ... illegality of slavery ... illegality of imprisonment for debt ... prohibitions against personal defamation (libel and slander); prohibition of "improper search and seizure;" prohibition of "cruel and unusual punishment;" right of habeas corpus.... The "value of individual personality" as impressionistically conceived represents ... uniqueness, self-direction, autonomy of choice, self-regulation, emotional independence, spontaneity, privacy, respect for other persons, defense of the self, and many others....

*Humanitarian Mores.* We shall use the term "humanitarianism," ... meaning by it emphasis upon any type of disinterested concern and helpfulness, including personal kindliness, aid and comfort, spontaneous aid in mass disasters, as well as the more impersonal patterns of organized philanthropy,... [for example] the commonplace United Fund, the "service club" activities, the public welfare agencies, the numerous private philanthropies....

## Work-Related Cultural Values

*Activity and Work.* America is the land of haste and bustle, of strenuous competition, of "ceaseless activity and agitation." In this culture the individual tends to "face outward"—to be interested in making things happen in the external world.... [H]e seeks to dominate the world of nature, to subdue and exploit the physical world around him.... In the American case the emphasis upon work as an end in itself represented ... a mutual reinforcement of self-interest, social recognition, and ethical and religious precepts....

*Efficiency and Practicality.* The Germans even coined the term Fordismus to refer to the standardization, mass production, and "streamlined" efficiency of American industrialism.... "Efficient" is a word of high praise in a society that has long emphasized adaptability, technological innovation, economic expansion, up-to-dateness, practicality, expediency, "getting things done." ... Emphasis on efficiency is ... related to the high place accorded science (especially as translated into technology)....

*Progress.* By the late nineteenth century ... [p]rogress could now become a slogan to defend the course of technological innovation and economic rationalization and concentration ... [p]rogress became identified with "free private enterprise," ... a belief in the positive value of ever-increasing quantities of goods and services, as illustrated in the dogma that ever increasing per capita gross national product is the touchstone of progress toward "abundance."....

*Material Comfort....* [A] certain kind of materialism may emerge in a society, even though it is not initially a primary criterion of desirability—in the sense that the sheer availability of creature comforts and the incessant advertising used to sell them creates a social pressure to concentrate effort and attention upon them.... [T]he objective opportunity to secure material comforts elicits, in the long run, a desire for them. Once a high standard of living has been enjoyed, ... it is extremely difficult to reduce the level of sensation....

*Science and Secular Rationality.* Applied science is highly esteemed as a tool for controlling nature. Significant here is the interest in order, control, and calculability—the passion for an engineering civilization.... But the prime quality of "science" is not in its applications but in its basic method of approaching problems—a way of thought and a set of procedures for interpreting experience.... Science is disciplined, rational, functional, active; it requires systematic diligence and honesty; it is congruent with the "means" emphasis of the culture—the focus of interest upon pragmatism and efficiency and the tendency to minimize absolutes (Williams, 1970:458-484, 487-489, 492-498).

We can understand a great deal about the development of these cultural values by returning to our earlier analysis of the work of Durkheim along with Marx, Simmel, Weber, Horney, Berger and Merton. They described—directly and indirectly—a scientific and industrial revolution fostering the cultural values of science and secular rationality, material comfort and economic progress. Let us also recall Weber's focus on the Protestant ethic and the spirit of capitalism with its associated orientation to activity and work. By contrast with these work-related cultural values, they also were much concerned with people-oriented cultural values that were being threatened by these revolutions. For example, Marx was concerned about equality and freedom, Simmel about individual personality, Durkheim about the very survival of the individual, Horney about mental problems, Berger about illusions, and Merton about unanticipated consequences.

Although Williams centered on American cultural values, those values generally reflect worldwide cultural values, as illustrated by the value of equality. The anthropological emphasis on differences among cultures tends to ignore what is widely shared across cultures. That emphasis emerges in particular whenever conflicts occur, as in the case of conflicts between Islamic and non-Islamic cultures. Yet if we look carefully for similarities without being swayed by stereotypes of cultural differences, we can locate them, as illustrated by this view of an Islamic scholar:

> It is often said that Islam is an egalitarian religion. There is much truth in this assertion.... The actions and utterances of the Prophet, the honored precedents of the early rulers of Islam as preserved by tradition, are overwhelmingly against privilege by descent, by birth, by status, by wealth, or even by race, and insist that rank and honor are determined only by piety and merit in Islam.... What is significant is that the emergence of elites ... happened in spite of Islam and not as part of it. Again and again through Islamic history the establishment of privilege was seen and denounced by both severely traditional conservatives and dubiously orthodox radicals as a non-Islamic or even an anti-Islamic innovation (Lewis, 2002: 82).

From Williams's presentation we can understand more clearly the implications of figure I.1. The people-oriented cultural values and the work-related cultural values give us better ideas about the elements within both curves. Overall, it makes good sense to break down that revolution of rising expectations or aspirations—the top curve—into both people-oriented and work-related cultural values, and also to specify the particular values that are listed. Those people-oriented cultural values all hang together, just as Simmel wrote about the emphasis on individuality in the nineteenth century as building on the emphasis on equality and freedom—and we should add democracy—in the eighteenth century. Those work-related cultural values also are integrated with one another and have become much of the basis for that top curve. It was the scientific method which opened up the industrial revolution, although coupled with other developments such as the Protestant ethic with its emphasis on activity and work, material progress and materialism. The resulting material successes in turn fostered people-oriented values, since they clearly demonstrated the possibilities of the individual human being. And those people-oriented values helped to make legitimate ever more economic development.

It also makes good sense to see the extent to which the fulfillment of each value has been limited as the industrial and technological revolutions continued, as indicated by the gap between the top and bottom curves of figure I.1. That limitation, emphasized by those early founders of sociology along with the other social scientists discussed, can be seen more clearly by looking to Williams's listing of cultural values. For example, science and secular rationality is most closely associated with the other work-related values: activity and work, economic progress, efficiency and practicality, and material comfort. These forces continue to propel one another ever further, often at the expense of people-oriented values. Material advantages once seen as luxuries become necessities and rights, and advertising—following Berger—continues to push us all ever further in a materialistic direction, often taking away from our ability to fulfill people-oriented values. The result, following Marx, Durkheim, Simmel and Horney, is loss of equality, freedom and individuality along with suicide and neuroticism. By contrast with the engine of physical and biological science along with their technologies, contemporary society has failed to invent an engine of social science which can work toward the fulfillment of its people-oriented cultural values, an engine which could move the bottom curve of figure I.1 closer to the top curve.

To understand more fully figure I.1 we must move beyond this analysis of the cultural values within its top and bottom curves and their relationships, moving up language's ladder of abstraction to metaphysics or worldviews. For example, progress has come to be interpreted as economic progress, and this narrow orientation that excludes people-oriented cultural values appears to be associated with a stratified worldview or metaphysical stance. Our engine of biophysical science and its technologies is oriented to the production of things rather than to achieving understanding of human behavior and enabling individuals to open up to their possibilities. Apparently, a stratified worldview is not broad enough to give us a framework for fulfilling the full range of our cultural values, and thus the development of the individual as a whole comes to be limited.

Despite the neglect among sociologists of the concept of cultural values relative to organizational concepts such as that of social stratification, there is nevertheless a body of contemporary social psychological research on the concept of cultural values. For example, there is the research of Milton Rokeach (1973) which we take up in chapter 11 in relation to the work of Greenstein. His focus is more psychological than cultural as he centers on such questions as the conditions under which values shape the behavior of the individual. He is best known for the Rokeach Value Survey (1967; see also Mayton, Ball-Rokeach, and Loges, 1994), an instrument widely used for the measurement of values. This is a questionnaire with two sets of eighteen items each, with subjects required to rank the items in each set according to their importance as guiding principles in their own lives, forcing them to commit to their own priorities. One set bears on "instrumental values," namely, those reflecting modes of conduct such as honesty, obedience and politeness. The other set has to do with "terminal values," such as freedom, equality, peace and salvation. Rokeach believed that the values involved are universal. This distinction between instrumental values and terminal values suggests the importance of the time dimension with its contrast between the present and the future. Also, the Rokeach tradition emphasizes the importance of seeing each value as related to all of the others, again suggesting the complexity of any understanding of values.

The literature on Rokeach's work comes almost completely from psychologists. For example, Rokeach argued that individuals attempt to maintain a consistent image or conception of themselves, following Festinger's theory of cognitive dissonance (chapter 6). As a result, they often change their rankings of values when confronted with contradictions experimentally introduced in "self-confrontation" studies, as illustrated by Greenstein's analysis of the Rokeach tradition (chapter 11). Building on Rokeach's work, Smith and Schwartz (1997)—also assuming that the values they measured were universal—developed cross-cultural studies of some 44,000 subjects in more than fifty countries, which quantitatively distinguished between individual and cultural values. The Schwartz Scale of Values includes fifty-six Rokeach-style value items, with each one ranked on a ten-point scale of personal importance. They found both cultural variation and individual variation in values, employing a variety of quantitative procedures. They found five cultural values promoting the welfare of others (universalism, benevolence, conformity, tradition, security) and five motivating the enhancement of persona interests even at the expense of others (power, achievement, hedonism, stimulation and self-direction). Smith and Schwartz argue, in common with the Rokeach tradition, that these values are dynamically related to one another, again suggesting the complexity of the phenomenon of values.

These studies contribute to our understanding of the significance of the top curve of aspirations or expectations in figure I.1 for the behavior of the individual. That curve should be understood as characterizing both the widely shared aspirations we associate with culture as well as the situational behavior of the individual. These studies within the Rokeach tradition also generally see the importance of distinguishing cultural values from the actual behavior of the individual, just as we have distinguished the top curve from the bottom curve of figure I.1. Given the complexity of understanding people's cultural values, we can well understand one conclusion suggested by these studies: the great difficulty in predicting the behavior of the individual on the basis of knowledge of the individual's cultural values and personal goals.

## Chua's *World on Fire*

Amy Chua, a professor at Yale Law School and a scholar of contemporary economic and political problems throughout the world, has written a sobering book that gives us a sense of immense and urgent problems with no clear direction for solving them. *World on Fire: How Exporting Free Market*

*Democracy Breeds Ethnic Hatred and Global Instability* (2003) was written after the 9/11 attacks on the World Trade Center and the Pentagon in 2001. Her basic idea is conveyed in her subtitle: the rapid development of free markets coupled with efforts to extend democracy have worked to create a "world on fire," yielding ethnic hatred and violence. Her thesis is well illustrated by the current situation in Iraq.

If we return to our analysis of cultural values, we can see the seeds of that violence in the conflicts between people-oriented cultural values and work-related cultural values, as discussed in the above section on Williams's *American Society*. Work-related cultural values are associated with a continuing industrial and technological revolution that has yielded worldwide globalization with its global market and multinational corporations. People-oriented cultural values are associated with democratic opposition to patterns of social stratification. Even within the United States we have a growing conflict or contradiction between these two sets of cultural values, as illustrated by Horney's analysis of the neurotic personality of our time (chapter 4) along with Berger's, Durkheim's and Boorstin's analyses of the gap between expectations and their fulfillment (chapters 2 and 7). But outside of the United States that conflict appears to be many times greater, yielding what Chua calls a "world on fire."

Chua summarizes her argument as follows:

> [T]he sobering thesis of this book is that the global spread of markets and democracy is a principal, aggravating cause of group hatred and ethnic violence throughout the non-Western world. In the numerous societies around the world that have a market-dominant minority, markets and democracy are not mutually reinforcing. Because markets and democracy benefit different ethnic groups in such societies, the pursuit of free market democracy produces highly unstable and combustible conditions. Markets concentrate enormous wealth in the hands of an "outsider" minority, fomenting ethnic envy and hatred among often chronically poor majorities. In absolute terms the majority may or may not be better off, ... but any sense of improvement is overwhelmed by their continuing poverty and the hated minority's extraordinary economic success. More humiliating still, market-dominant minorities along with their foreign-investor partners, invariably come to control the crown jewels of the economy, often symbolic of the nation's patrimony and identity—oil in Russia and Venezuela, diamonds in South Africa, silver and tin in Bolivia, jade, teak, and rubies in Burma.
>
> Introducing democracy in these circumstances does not transform voters into open-minded citizens in a national community. Rather, the competition for votes fosters the emergence of demagogues who scapegoat the resented minority and foment active ethnonationalist movements demanding that the country's wealth and identity be reclaimed

by the "true owners of the nation." As America celebrated the global spread of democracy in the 1990s, ethnicized political slogans proliferated: "Georgia for the Georgians," "Eritreans Out of Ethiopia," "Kenya for Kenyans," "Venezuela for Pardos," "Kazakhstan for Kazakhs," "Serbia for Serbs," "Croatia for Croats," "Hutu Power," "Assam for Assamese," "Jews Out of Russia" (2003: 9–10).

Chua is calling attention to powerful patterns of ethnic stratification in many countries of the world where an ethnic minority has taken control over a country's wealth. An emphasis on free markets, being brought about through economic globalization, serves to increase the concentration of wealth in the hands of that minority. And there is no numerous middle class that benefits to some extent from both free markets and democratization. Although economic globalization may benefit the ethnic majority in a given country to some extent, that improvement on an absolute scale is dwarfed by rising aspirations or expectations introduced by efforts at democratization. Instead, such efforts have encouraged ethnic warfare throughout the world, encouraging leaders of the poor majorities to lead violent attacks against the wealthy minorities. Our assumption that democratization is intrinsically a good thing under any circumstances does not take into account the differences between the West and the less developed countries of the world. Our economic and political institutions have been developing over centuries, creating mechanisms for avoiding violent conflicts and a powerful middle class that makes use of those mechanisms.

But the problem of ethnic warfare is even more serious than this. For a worldwide revolution of rising expectations or aspirations is propelled by global mass media and not just by political efforts at democratization. If we go back to figure I.1, we hypothesize that this revolution of rising expectations depicted by the top curve occurred over a span of centuries. During that time, as we can note from the rise of the bottom curve, there was substantial improvement in people's ability to fulfill their aspirations to a degree, based largely on the development of a middle class, granting that aspirations rose much faster than their fulfillment. But in countries throughout the world with ethnic minorities dominating the scene, the global mass media have fostered a worldwide revolution of rising expectations in a matter of mere decades. For example, we have Hollywood's picture of enormous wealth and the communication of facts about what appear to much of the world to be fabulous consumption patterns in the United States and the West. Yet there has been very little time for the fulfillment of aspirations to make much progress. Neither has there been much time for people-oriented cultural values to take hold and yield legal structures which hold in check an emphasis on violence.

Chua does not confine her analysis to countries with ethnic minorities in power. Rather, she extends it to the relationship between the United

States and the less developed countries of the world in an effort to explain the rise of hatred against America.

Chua is arguing not simply that market-dominating ethnic minorities within any given country spawn ethnic hatred by the majorities, and that rapid democratization fans the flames of that hatred. She is generalizing that argument to current international relations between the United States and the rest of the world. Just as ethnic minorities in many countries have come to dominate wealth and power, so has America, constituting a minority of the world's population, come to dominate the rest of the world. That domination has been accelerated as the result of economic globalization, increasing the wealth and power of those ethnic minorities in their own countries just as it has increased America's wealth and power in relation to the world as a whole. Further, just as democratic ideals and efforts at democratization have yielded violent confrontations between majorities and minorities in many of those countries, so do those same ideals stir up hatred of America throughout the world. For democratic ideals conflict with the incredible disparity between the wealth and power of America and the poverty and powerlessness of most of the people of the world.

The international problem of anti-American hatred is even more serious than Chua's analysis suggests, and for much the same reasons as apply to ethnic minorities. There appears to be a worldwide revolution of rising expectations or aspirations as a result of both the continuing industrial and technological revolution as well as the impact of mass media portraying the fulfillment of work-related and people-oriented cultural values in America. Very quickly, by contrast with the centuries that apparently yielded an aspirations-fulfillment gap for America along with the rise of a middle class, the gap between aspirations and fulfillment for most of the world may be widening, as suggested by our hypothesis (1). For example, economic growth rates in African countries are far below those of the main industrialized countries, and economic growth has generally been relatively slow in Latin America (Krugman and Obstfeld, 2003). More specifically, the per capita share of the Gross National Product in the poorest nations was $410 in the year 2000, by contrast with $25,730 in the richest nations, with the two differing by a factor of no less than 63 (666–667). To examine another measurement of well-being, life-expectancy in the low-income nations was 60 years compared with 78 years in the high-income nations (666–667). We believe that this situation is a most explosive one, threatening not just the rich nations but all countries of the world.

In her last chapter, "The Future of Free Market Democracy," Chua poses these questions: "So where does this leave us? What are the implications of market-dominant minorities for national and international policy making?" She takes up a number of possible policies, such as developing a very long-term perspective, backing off on democracy, backing off on free markets, education, giving the poor a stake in the market, redistributing income through policies of progressive taxation, giving the poor legal status and property rights, affirmative action programs, working against inequalities resulting from economic globalization, and increased foreign aid and philanthropy from rich nations and the rich to poor nations and the poor. But between the lines it is easy to read her own assessment of such efforts. They are all quite limited, and they all have drawbacks. By contrast, the problems presently existing throughout the world appear to be mammoth, urgent and accelerating. We no longer have the luxury of a long-range strategy that is based on the assumption that things will remain relatively stable while we are attempting to solve the problem of the increasing gap depicted in figure I.1. In other words, Chua is unable to come up with a clear solution to the problems which she has painstakingly unearthed.

This should be no surprise to readers of this book, for Chua has failed to move very far up language's ladder of abstraction to take into account both epistemology and metaphysics, choosing instead to stay at a more concrete level of abstraction. In her last chapter she did indeed cite many specific proposals for addressing the problems of violence and hatred she had analyzed. Although those proposals generally have something to offer, they do not build on the range of knowledge that social science has to offer. Chua is not to be blamed for this, since social scientists themselves have failed to integrate that knowledge. Given this situation, the best that Chua and others attempting to address fundamental international problems can do is to bring forward as many useful ideas as they can. But those ideas are inadequate when we take into account the scope and urgency of the problems which modern societies currently face.

To illustrate the limitations of such analyses, they do not take into account our understanding of the cultural values that peoples throughout the world have come to share as a result of the impact of the continuing industrial and technological revolutions over the past four centuries. They are summarized by Williams's analysis in this chapter, paying attention to both people-oriented and work-related cultural values. For example, understanding that those values were much of the basis for the continuing industrial and technological revolution in the West can give people in all societies insight into what is involved in order to achieve economic development. From this perspective, any rapid rush to achieve economic development or democratic institutions is naïve. By contrast, lowering expectations in the short run for fulfilling such goals becomes far more realistic. Yet an awareness of what appear to be the enormous gaps between those cultural values and their fulfillment in the West as well as in developing societies might help to motivate people to find ways to close those gaps. That in turn might make it more feasible, in the long run, to raise both aspirations and their fulfillment. Yet this approach remains limited to the extent that we fail to introduce epistemological and metaphysical considerations. For it is an effective scientific epistemology which can help us to penetrate these problems. And it is a metaphysics that points toward the basis for closing the aspirations-fulfillment gap that appears to be urgently required.

## Some Implications

If we pay close attention to the above presentation of works by Durkheim and Chua, then it appears that the modern world presently is facing a most grim situation. Looking at the growing aspirations-fulfillment gap from the perspective of the twenty-first century, it appears that those conflicts are on the rise. We have only to look at the above material on Durkheim and Chua to find evidence of growing threats to modern society with limited possibilities to meet those threats. For example, Durkheim tied suicide rates to the modernization process, a worldwide process which continues to roar ahead largely unchecked. The very title of Chua's book, *World on Fire,* speaks to her convictions as to the present state of the world, and her efforts to point toward effective solutions appear to carry limited credibility. As a result, we find that Durkheim and Chua support hypothesis (1) with its statement of an increasing gap between expectations and their fulfillment in modern society. Williams, however, gives no clear indication as to whether or not he believes that this gap is increasing in modern society.

As for (2), however, Williams joins Durkheim and Chua by indicating his support for that hypothesis. His treatment of a very wide range of cultural values without neglecting the importance of social organization suggests his belief in the importance of a broad approach to social structure. That breadth is enlarged when we realize that the understanding of cultural values that he conveys also gives us a crucial direction for understanding the nature of personality structures. He contrasts such breadth with the narrowness of an emphasis on nationalism and patriotism as well as ethnocentrism, which he sees as relatively destructive, and which we can see as illustrating patterns of social stratification. Durkheim's support for (2) stems from his view of the narrow avoidance of realistic considerations by those whose "greed is aroused without knowing where to find ultimate foothold." That narrowness points them in the direction of a stratified worldview as well as to the possibility of suicide. Chua sees stratification—implying a stratified worldview—as the enemy of democracy and as pointing toward violence when mixed rapidly with high aspirations. As a result, she also supports (2).

When we look to the images or metaphors of these writers, for Durkheim the most powerful image is the suicide of the individual. And we can extend that image to modern society just as Horney extended her image of the neurotic to the idea of a neurotic society. Do we moderns in fact live in a suicidal society? With respect to Chua, her image of a "world on fire" is indeed a powerful one. Her analysis is very well documented with a great many examples. She clearly depicts the inherent dangers of prematurely clamping the title "democracy" onto a group that lacks true freedom. In the absence of participatory and transparent governance and of an informed and interactive citizenry, the title alone often breeds little beyond ongoing poverty and malignant levels of social stratification and bureaucracy.

## CHAPTER 8

# "Hand"

## Social Stratification versus Egalitarian Social Relationships

IT IS HERE that we emphasize the bottom curve of figure I.1, looking to the forces which limit the fulfillment of cultural values and appear to be yielding an increasing gap between aspirations and their fulfillment. Social stratification with its hierarchical patterns points away from such cultural values as equality, freedom and individual personality or individuality. Yet it is both curves taken together which enables us to develop a historically based view of the impact of social stratification. This is also an argument for moving away from the specialization-with-limited-communication which is so prevalent throughout the social sciences. It will be in part V that we emphasize the situation and open up to momentary phenomena while at the same time build on what we have learned about structures.

The concept of social stratification is central to our understanding of the nature of a stratified worldview as well as a stratified epistemology, and this concept is also central to the literature of sociology. Consequently, let us step back to examine this concept in greater detail before plunging ahead in this chapter. Our definition of social stratification up to this point has been simply "persisting hierarchy or inequality." We may now extend that definition to "persisting hierarchy or inequality within a group or between groups." A group includes society as a whole, the context of most studies of social stratification. But it also includes small groups like the family and intermediate groups like organizations and communities. Thus, stratification encompasses the micro, the meso and the macro with respect to size. We can thus see, for example, the links between social stratification and the bureaucratic organization of groups, or "bureaucracies," a concept to which we have given little attention. Yet bureaucracies, following the literature of sociology, are groups that illustrate persisting hierarchy and inequality and thus are stratified. And we can see such bureaucratic organizations as joining with patterns of social stratification to limit the individual's fulfillment of expectations.

We would do well at this point to expand our overall approach to social structure, as presented in the introduction to part IV on Social Structures, given that it differs from a widespread orientation within sociology—and especially anthropology—that views culture apart from social structure. Within that orientation, social structure is viewed quite narrowly, perhaps in order to give equal attention to culture. Granting the importance of culture, a problem with that approach is that as a result we can no longer see the concept "structure" as an overarching one that includes cultural phenomena no less than personality, biological and physical phenomena. That definition would require us to see culture as somehow distinct from structure, but we have learned that culture does indeed include structures of all kinds, such as language, norms and values. Thus, that approach to culture would tend to exclude it from serious attention by sociologists, who would feel free to ignore it as they proceeded to examine social structure. By contrast, our own approach to culture includes it as a vital part of social structure, requiring any serious consideration of the latter to pay attention to the former. More specifically, we see social structure as including both culture, discussed in chapters 6 and 7, and social organization, discussed in this chapter. On the surface, this approach appears to be paradoxical, for how can we pay more attention to culture by making it no more than a part of social structure? Yet by so doing we must emphasize culture far more than sociologists presently do, since culture can no longer be ignored within any analysis of social structure. Further, our definition points the way for anthropologists to pay more attention to the structural aspects of culture, given a view of culture as a species of social structure. This overall approach was developed in detail by the senior author in a textbook written several decades ago (Phillips, 1979).

The early sociological literature on social stratification can yield insight into the specific nature of patterns of social stratification. For example, Marx (e.g., 1849/1964) emphasized economic stratification, involving such factors as the ownership of land, factories and liquid assets. Weber included in addition political and status stratification (Weber, 1946, 1964), involving such phenomena as authority within the workplace and government along with prestige within society and its groups. Following in the footsteps of Marx and Weber, a vast literature on social stratification has developed within sociology, modifying and extending their ideas. Our own approach to social stratification builds on insights from both Weber and Marx. On the one hand, Weber's interest in culture is central to that approach. On the other hand, we employ aspects of culture—a revolution of rising expectations—as a basis for emerging with fundamental and increasing contradictions within modern society. This parallels Marx's view of contradictions within the arena of social organization. Our own "forces of production" largely derive from the continuing scientific and technological revolutions with their accompanying cultural revolution of rising expectations. And our own "relations of production" have to do with existing and pervasive patterns of social stratification that limit the fulfillment of those cultural values. Thus, along with Marx we hypothesize increasing contradictions between the forces and relations of production, differing from Marx in our own view of the importance of culture, following Weber.

We also have seen many sociological studies of stratification with respect to gender, ethnic group, religion and age. Such studies have succeeded in expanding our understanding of the complexities involved in patterns of social stratification, moving us beyond the theories of Marx and Weber. And there are also many patterns of social stratification that have hardly been studied by sociologists yet nevertheless influence wide gaps between expectations and their fulfillment, such as hierarchies with respect to weight, height and what societies define as beauty. Apparently the lack of attention to such factors stems from their links to biological structures, an area which social scientists generally avoid. Overall, what we can understand from all of these insights is the pervasiveness of patterns of social stratification throughout almost every aspect of the individual's everyday life within contemporary societies. This strengthens our insight into the nature of social stratification in general as absolutely fundamental to modern social structures.

One additional link between our own approach to social stratification and that of the literature of sociology has to do with the causes of social stratification, with particular attention to whether or not social stratification is inevitable within human societies. The best-known effort to claim its inevitability was advanced by Davis and Moore (1945). They assumed the necessity of unequal rewards within society's occupational structure in order to motivate the most qualified individuals to fill society's most important positions. They were challenged by Wrong (1959), who found stratification systems so extreme as to exceed the requirements for a complex division of labor. And they were also challenged by Wesolowski (1962), who viewed systems of stratification based on hereditary criteria as having nothing to do with motivating the most qualified individuals to fill society's most important positions. Our own approach adds to this debate by introducing a factor that has been completely ignored: a society's metaphysical stance or worldview. From our perspective, it is indeed possible for a society to move ever further away from patterns of social stratification to the degree that there is a shift from a stratified to an interactive worldview or metaphysical stance. We have put forward Hypothesis (2) as a partial test of our approach, questioning whether such a shift is indeed tied to reducing the gap between aspirations and their fulfillment.

We turn now to the three publications to be examined in this chapter. George Orwell's *Nineteen Eighty-Four* (1949) is far more than a diatribe against the evils of totalitarianism in fictional form, for this dystopia probes deeply into language and culture along with patterns of social stratification. We may think of Big Brother and his telescreens which invaded everyone's privacy when we think of Orwell. But we would do well to think, in addition, of the language of Newspeak, which continued to constrict the language which the residents of Oceania were able to use. As a result, Big Brother worked both to lower people's bottom curve by means of extreme stratification and also lower people's top curve so as to destroy their ideals. But to what extent is this our own situation? Are the talking heads on CNN, Fox News and MSNBC also making it more difficult for us to think on our own, lowering our bottom curve as a result of our dependence on experts and neglect of our own human potential? Are we learning to accept our own inertia, perhaps waiting for the escalation of destruction by terrorists along with the erosion of our deepest cultural values?

Erving Goffman's *Asylums: Essays on the Social Situation of Mental Patients and Other Inmates* presents us, in his essay "On the Characteristics of Total Institutions" (1961), with a stark picture of patient degradation in the mental hospital. Not only do inmates generally experience "personal defacement that comes from being stripped of one's identity kit" and "mortification of the self" through treatment as grossly inferior beings and even punishment of inmate efforts to maintain a shred of human dignity. Mental hospitals share many of their characteristics with other total institutions like concentration camps, prisons, TB sanitaria, army barracks, harems, ships, boarding schools, monasteries and convents. Goffman's analysis helps us to understand the dehumanization that occurs in situations of extreme stratification with limited opportunities for egalitarian social relationships. In so doing, he also helps us to understand the implications of modern social stratification in general. To what extent are we all subject to personal degradation, the stripping of our identity kits and the mortification of the self? Yet the vernacular language he uses—while avoiding abstract social science concepts—yields a failure to build on the existing body of social science knowledge.

If a fringe of radical professionals point away from stratification by professionals and toward an extension of democracy, then Ivan Illich in his *Deschooling Society* (1972) carries this idea much further. He includes almost no references to the work of others, and this is illustrated by his neologism, "schooling," which is roughly equivalent to the concept of social stratification. By so doing he joins Goffman in a departure from the scientific method. As a result, the credibility of his work suffers. Yet he is able to achieve a powerful argument for the dehumanizing aspects of social stratification throughout the institutions of modern society. For Illich, schooling encourages dependency and helplessness with respect to learning, health, safety, national security, productive work and the improvement of community life. We learn to bow down to teachers, medical practitioners, police, the military, the business establishment and social workers. In Illich's words, "Everywhere not only education but society as a whole needs 'deschooling.'" Illich is able to open up fundamental problems tied to basic social structures of modern society without, however, developing a credible direction for how to solve them.

## Orwell's *Nineteen Eighty-Four*

We begin with the foreword to a book written just after 1984, Neil Postman's *Amusing Ourselves to Death: Public Discourse in the Age of Show Business* (1985). Postman compares Orwell's dystopia to another dystopia, Aldous Huxley's *Brave New World* (1939), and in the process helps to introduce us to *Nineteen Eighty-Four*:

> We were keeping our eye on 1984. When the year came and the prophecy didn't, thoughtful Americans sang softly in praise of themselves. The roots of liberal democracy had held. Wherever else the terror had happened, we, at least, had not been visited by Orwellian nightmares.
>
> But we had forgotten that alongside Orwell's dark vision, there was another—slightly older, slightly less well known, equally chilling: Aldous Huxley's *Brave New World*. Contrary to common belief even among the educated, Huxley and Orwell did not prophesy the same thing. Orwell warns that we will be overcome by an externally imposed oppression. But in Huxley's vision, no Big Brother is required to deprive people of their autonomy, maturity and history. As he saw it, people will come to love their oppression, to adore the technologies that undo their capacities to think.
>
> What Orwell feared were those who would ban books. What Huxley feared was that there would be no reason to ban a book, for there would be no one who wanted to read one. Orwell feared those who would deprive us of information. Huxley feared those who would give us so much that we would be reduced to passivity and egoism. Orwell feared that the truth would be concealed from us. Huxley feared the truth would be drowned in a sea of irrelevance. Orwell feared we would become a captive culture. Huxley feared we would become a trivial culture.... In short, Orwell feared that what we hate will ruin us. Huxley feared that what we love will ruin us. This book is about the possibility that Huxley, not Orwell, was right.

Postman sees Huxley as centering on culture and Orwell as focusing on social stratification, and he believes that it is changes in culture rather than in stratification which are the basis for our deepest contemporary problems. As a result, he concludes that it is Huxley and not Orwell who was prescient. Postman's emphasis on culture is well taken, as we might note from what has been going on in the social sciences over the past two decades. It certainly supports our own emphasis on the centrality of language for understanding human behavior in all of its complexity, including our own thought processes. Further, Postman's view of Huxley meshes with our focus on the revolution of rising expectations or aspirations along with our view of the importance of cultural values as a way to achieve a systematic approach to culture. Still further, Postman's approach supports contemporary research on the enormous influence of the mass media, as illustrated by Berger's analysis of advertising in chapter 2.

Yet if we examine *Brave New World* we find that Huxley by no means ignored patterns of social organization. Also, a reading of *Nineteen Eighty-Four* finds substantial evidence for Orwell's deep concern with culture. To illustrate, Huxley does indeed give us a view of a passive population of couch potatoes in the grip of mass media that yield continuing sensory gratification, where individual thought and deviant behavior become ever rarer. As a result, what we have is the continuation of a lowering of people's aspirations and, thus, of the top curve of figure I.1. But at the same time there are the Controllers who make the decisions as to how society is structured, with a focus on stability versus any hint of deviant behavior. It is the Controllers who use eugenics and drugs to construct a population that can be easily manipulated. Thus, along with a lowering of aspirations there is also a lowering of the bottom curve of a population's ability to fulfill cultural values. We can understand Postman's interest in culture and not social organization in relation to his own background as a psychologist oriented to the power of the mass media. We can also understand his conclusion on the basis of a worldview which orients him to pay little attention to sociologists' research demonstrating the importance of social organization. Within an interactive worldview, by contrast, it is essential that we pay close attention to both culture and social organization, just as we should pay close attention to the top and bottom curves of figure I.1 simultaneously.

As for Orwell, there is no doubt that it is Big Brother and his henchmen who rule Oceania, and who punish individuals who appear by their demeanor—as seen from two-way telescreens—to be unenthusiastic about his regime. There is also no doubt that he succeeds in turning relatively egalitarian social relationships between individuals like Winston Smith and Julia into hierarchical relationships. As a result we have the bottom curve of figure I.1 heading downward. But there is also the language of Newspeak, where humanistic concepts—along with the ideals that they represent—are continually being eliminated in new versions of the language. Orwell even goes on to present in an appendix "The Principles of Newspeak," where he proceeds to describe how the broad connotations of language can be eliminated and how language can become politicized to reflect conformity to Big Brother's three slogans: "War Is Peace, Freedom Is Slavery, Ignorance Is Strength." Thus, Orwell also gives us a vision of a top curve which is heading downward. With both curves moving downward, we have nothing less than what Goffman describes as "personal deface-ment," "degradation" and "mortification of the self."

Let us then approach Orwell's novel by examining *both* what he says about social organization *as well as* his argument about culture. To begin, we should not conceive the book narrowly as a diatribe against the Soviet Union under Stalin but rather as a way of gaining insight into all contemporary societies. Orwell's emphasis on social organization emerges in his focus on the relationship between Winston Smith and Julia. Somehow, amidst an impossibly tyrannical society, they manage to meet, communicate and come to love one another. They illustrate the romantic ideal implicit in cultural values like equality, freedom, individual personality and close personal relationships. That romantic ideal also calls for genuine reciprocity, illustrated by the couple when they manage to meet despite the watchful eyes and ears of Big Brother's Thought Police:

> Then, as though touching her waist had reminded her of something, she felt in the pocket of her overalls and produced a small slab of chocolate. She broke it in half and gave one of the pieces to Winston.... "You are very young," he said. "You are ten or fifteen years younger than I am. What could you see to attract you in a man like me?" "It was something in your face. I thought I'd take a chance. I'm good at spotting people who don't belong. As soon as I saw you I knew you were against *them*."...
>
> They had left the clearing and were wandering again through the checkered shade, with their arms round each other's waists whenever it was wide enough to walk two abreast.... He stopped thinking and merely felt. The girl's waist in the bend of his arm was soft and warm. He pulled her round so that they were breast to breast; her body seemed to melt into his. Wherever his hands moved it was all as yielding as water. Their mouths clung together; it was quite different from the hard kisses they had exchanged earlier. When they moved their faces apart again both of them sighed deeply....
>
> In the old days, he thought, a man looked at a girl's body and saw that it was desirable, and that was the end of the story. But you could not have pure love or pure lust nowadays. No emotion was pure, because everything was mixed up with fear and hatred. Their embrace had been a battle, the climax a victory. It was a blow struck against the Party. It was a political act (1949: 101–105).

But Big Brother's eyes and ears are everywhere, and the couple is caught and soon endures, separately, the torture of Room 101, which contains "the worst thing in the world." The worst thing is different for every individual, and for Winston it is rats. His head is placed inside a cage of ravenous rats eager to tear into his eyes, cheeks and tongue, separated from the rats only by a door which can be slid open easily. His fear knows no bounds as he shouts over and over, "Do it to Julia! Do it to Julia! Not me! Julia! I don't care what you do to her. Tear her face off, strip her to the bones. Not me! Julia! Not me!" (236).

Afterwards, Winston and Julia are released, since Big Brother has succeeded in removing whatever threat to his regime that they posed:

> "I betrayed you," she said baldly. "I betrayed you," he said. She gave him another quick look of dislike. "Sometimes," she said, "they threaten you with something—something you can't stand up to, can't even think about. And then you say, "Don't do it to me, do it to somebody else, do it to so-and-so." And perhaps you might pretend afterwards, that it was only a trick and that you just said it to make them stop and didn't really mean it. But that isn't true. At the time when it happens you do mean it. You think there's no other way of saving yourself and you're quite ready to save yourself that way. You *want* it to happen to the other person. You don't give a damn what they suffer. All you care about is yourself." "All you care about is yourself," he echoed. "And after that, you don't feel the same toward the other person any longer." "No," he said, "you don't feel the same." ...
>
> Winston, sitting in a blissful dream, paid no attention as his glass was filled up.... He gazed up at the enormous face. Forty years it had taken him to learn what kind of smile was hidden beneath the dark mustache. O cruel, needless misunderstanding! O stubborn, self-willed exile from the loving breast! Two gin-scented tears trickled down the sides of his nose. But it was all right, everything was all right, the struggle was finished. He had won the victory over himself. He loved Big Brother (240, 245).

Orwell's novel raises a serious question about contemporary society. Is modern society pushing all of us into Room 101, where we are learning to endure "the worst thing in the world"? For example, does our divorce rate suggest that we, along with Winston and Julia, are becoming less and less able to maintain close and egalitarian social relationships, which appear to be our central cultural value? Marx warned us about this as a phenomenon that our stratified experiences in the workplace is teaching us. Simmel also warned us about a similar phenomenon taking place in the metropolis, where close human relationships are being subverted in favor of an intellectualistic orientation and an orientation to the marketplace.

Contemporary sociologists like Thomas J. Scheff have also written about alienation taking place in modern society (2006). It would appear that the existence of a Big Brother is unnecessary in order to achieve such widespread alienation and high divorce rates. All that is necessary is a stratified worldview coupled with patterns of stratification in the face of cultural values which oppose hierarchies and point toward the ideal of close and egalitarian social relationships. Our heads are not being shoved into cages where hungry rats are waiting to chew us up alive, but the result still appears to be in the same direction, gradationally, as what happened to the relationship between Winston Smith and Julia.

We need not examine divorce rates or growth in the population of singles to locate substantial evidence for declines in efforts to achieve close relationships, as illustrated by Robert D. Putnam in his *Bowling Alone: The Collapse and Revival of American Community* (2000). He finds that voting among those eligible decreased from 63 percent in 1960 to 49 percent in 1996, that bowling with others has declined by over 40 percent in the last two decades while bowling alone has similarly increased, that regular church attendance has declined by about a third since 1960, and that there is a 20 percent decline since 1975 in attention given to public affairs, such as participating in political activites. Putnam sums up much of what he discovered:

> Evidence suggests that across a very wide range of activities, the last several decades have witnessed a striking diminution of regular contact with our friends and neighbors. We spend less time in conversation over meals, we exchange visits less often, we engage less often in leisure activites that encourage casual social interaction, we spend more time watching [television, and as spectators] and less time doing. We know our neighbors less well, and we see old friends less often. In short, it is not merely "do good" civic activities that engage us less, but also informal connecting (2000: 115).

Turning from social organization to culture, Winston's colleague in the Ministry of Truth, Syme, is one of the large group compiling the definitive edition of the Newspeak dictionary:

> You think, I dare say, that our chief job is inventing new words. But not a bit of it! We're destroying words—scores of them, hundreds of them every day....Do you know that Newspeak is the only language in the world whose vocabulary gets smaller every year? ... Don't you see that the whole aim of Newspeak is to narrow the range of thought? In the end we shall make thought crime literally impossible, because there will be no words in which to express it....Every year fewer and fewer words, and the range

of consciousness always a little smaller....By 2050—earlier, probably—all real knowledge of Oldspeak will have disappeared. The whole literature of the past will have been destroyed. Chaucer, Shakespeare, Milton, Byron—they'll exist only in Newspeak versions, not merely changed into something different, but actually changed into something contradictory of what they used to be. Even the literature of the Party will change. Even the slogans will change. How could you have a slogan like 'freedom is slavery' when the concept of freedom has been abolished? The whole climate of thought will be different. In fact there will be no thought, as we understand it now. Orthodoxy means not thinking—not needing to think. Orthodoxy is unconsciousness" (1949: 45–47).

Newspeak is an anti-educational device, pointing the individual ever further away from knowing how to think or understand and also away from cultural values like freedom, equality, the worth of every individual, and the importance of close and egalitarian personal relationships. Let us examine whether modern society is in fact doing the equivalent of learning to speak Newspeak just as it may be learning to move into Room 101. Neil Postman emphasizes such changes with his concern that a Huxleyan world poses a far greater danger for us than an Orwellian world. He gives us some insight into such changes in his discussion of television:

What Huxley teaches us is that ... [w]hen a population becomes distracted by trivia, when cultural life is redefined as a perpetual round of entertainments, when serious public conversation becomes a form of baby-talk, when, in short, a people becomes an audience and their public business a vaudeville act, then a nation finds itself at risk: culture-death is a clear possibility.... An Orwellian world is much easier to recognize, and to oppose, than a Huxleyan. Everything in our background has prepared us to know and resist a prison when the gates begin to close around us.... But what if there are no cries of anguish to be heard? Who is prepared to take arms against a sea of amusements? ...

Without a vote. Without polemics. Without guerrilla resistance. Here is ideology, pure if not serene. Here is ideology without words, and all the more powerful for their absence. All that is required to make it stick is a population that devoutly believes in the inevitability of progress (1985: 155–158).

Postman claims that our belief in the inevitability of "progress"—meaning our ever-developing biophysical science technologies—is yielding our ever deeper immersion into a Huxleyan world of amusement along with an abdication of our intellectual heritage and fundamental people-oriented cultural values. Our cultural enemy is relatively invisible, so that the problem it poses is that much more dangerous. Using Orwell's metaphor to convey Postman's argument, we are all learning Newspeak as we sit back and watch our news converted into entertainment, "amusing ourselves to death," and losing any ability to understand our problems and to take effective action on them. Following Postman, our only hope is a very slim one: to develop the kind of educational system where we learn to understand the media's impact on us. To see our situation as even worse, we can bring in our problem of social stratification together with this cultural problem: we appear to be entering room 101 at the same time that we are learning to speak Newspeak, yielding ignorance of ever-deepening and urgent problems. Thus, Postman is claiming much the same thing as the hypothesis of an increasing gap between expectations and their fulfillment, and that this phenomenon is largely invisible.

Yet by seeing our acceptance of the progress of biophysical science as creating our problem and by seeing education for awareness of this situation as the solution, Postman misses out to a degree on both the problem and a possible solution. Part of the problem appears to be the imbalance in the effectiveness of biophysical and social science technologies as well as the imbalance in our encouragement of and acceptance of those technologies. Behind that imbalance is a stratified worldview along with a stratified approach to the scientific method. What we appear to require is not simply education that helps us to question the impact of television on our lives, for much more is needed. We appear to need a scientific method that can follow scientific ideals that point toward the rapid cumulative development of social science knowledge and increasingly effective social technologies based on that knowledge. We also appear to need a worldview or metaphysical stance which not only encourages us to develop that knowledge and those technologies. Such a worldview might also enable us to question not just television's impact but the impact of every single one of our institutions on our lives. Blaming television is far too simplistic an analysis. Our complex problems in all areas of life appear to require nothing less than a direction for solutions that also impact all areas of our lives.

Orwell succeeds in giving us powerful metaphors such as Room 101 and Newspeak as a shorthand for our deepest problems. The impact of a novel, film or play appears to be based largely on its potential to give us powerful metaphors which we can bring to bear on complex problems. He achieves this by invoking the many different phenomena discussed in the chapters of this book and weaving them together into a story that has a measure of credibility for something that might have occurred or might happen in the future. Physical structures are involved (chapter 1), such as the cage placed over Winston's head as well as the huge picture of Big Brother with his enormous face and dark mustache. Biological structures (chapter 2) are illustrated by Winston's perception of Julia's soft, warm and yielding body. As for personality structures (chapters 3, 4 and 5), we have the huge change from Winston's earlier opposition to a totalitarian regime to his acceptance of it. Social structures (chapters 6, 7 and 8) are exemplified by the change from an egalitarian and warm relationship between Winston and Julia to a relationship of indifference and even dislike. They are also illustrated by the language of Newspeak. Situations (chapters 9, 10 and 11) are illustrated by Winston's experiencing the cage of rats in Room 101, and also by Syme's telling Winston about Newspeak. From this perspective, Orwell is making use of a Timeland or interactive worldview.

## Goffman's *Asylums*

An essay in Erving Goffman's *Asylums: Essays on the Social Situation of Mental Patients and Other Inmates* (1961), "On the Characteristics of Total Institutions," can be used to illustrate the impact of social structure as well as the situation on the inmates. A key device he uses is his definition of "total institution" so as to encompass a number of different kinds of organizations—such as mental hospitals, prisons, concentration camps and boarding schools—under the same label. For Goffman, within a total institution every aspect of life is conducted under the same authority and in the same place. Also, the individual is in the company of many other people who are being treated in the same way. In addition, the daily activities guided by official rules for what should and should not be done are tightly scheduled by those in authority, with one activity leading to the next. All of these enforced activities are supposedly designed to fulfill the organization's official aims. In this way, an individual's slightest infraction of the rules stands out easily, since it departs from the compliance of all the others. A small supervisory staff enforces the rules that apply to the large group of inmates. Communication between the staff and the inmates is severely restricted. All of this provides us with an example of extreme social stratification. Given the existence of social stratification throughout society, this can yield insights which would be difficult to obtain outside of total institutions. Throughout society stratification tends to be hidden because it contradicts fundamental cultural values like equality, freedom and individual personality.

As one illustration of Goffman's ability to bring to the surface within his analysis of extreme stratification what normally remains hidden in everyday social interaction, there is the phenomenon of what Goffman labels "looping":

> I have considered some of the more elementary and direct assaults upon the self.... I would now like to consider a source of mortification that is less direct in its effect.... The first disruption to consider here is "looping"; an agency that creates a defensive response on the part of

the inmate takes this very response as the target of its next attack; the individual finds that his protective response to an assault upon self is collapsed into the situation; he cannot defend himself in the usual way by establishing distance between the mortifying situation and himself (1961: 35-36).

We might have reference here to Orwell's description of telescreens, the Thought Police and enlisting a family's children as spies, all of which were used to detect the slightest lack of enthusiasm or conformity to Big Brother's regime. Any behavior deviating from complete enthusiasm and conformity became suspect. For example sullen conformity could lead to immediate "vaporization" of an individual. Big Brother required cheerful robots to do his bidding. We might wonder here as to the extent to which such "looping" occurs in modern society. For example, how much do employers generally employ and promote cheerful employees? To what extent does the authority figure in a given family negatively sanction sullen behavior on the part of other family members? "Looping" behavior gives us a window on the battle between the top and bottom curves of figure I.1. On the one hand, the inmate—or individual under the thumb of some authority figure outside of total institutions—is expressing a desire to pay at least lip service to fundamental cultural values like freedom, equality and individual personality. On the other hand, even such lip service is sanctioned negatively, so that the individual is dragged through the mud of having to face up to a huge gap between aspirations and their fulfillment. This is analogous to being shoved into Room 101.

Goffman brings forward many other illustrations of the impact of extreme stratification. One example is a requirement that an inmate ask permission for even fundamental bodily needs, such as going to the toilet, shaving, smoking, mailing letters or using the telephone. It is a most humiliating situation for a human being to have to plead for help about such desires yet to be frequently ignored. Goffman is intent on uncovering the specific or detailed social structures which are to be found within a total institution, granting that a total institution itself is a social structure. His approach is analyzed in some detail in a current monograph, which looks as well to his overall significance (Scheff, 2006).

Goffman's attention to detail, with his many examples of particular situations, not only helps him to understand the specifics of social structures. It also points him in the direction of situational analysis, an area which has become increasingly important for sociologists since Goffman wrote this essay. For example, an entire field of sociology—ethnomethodology—has developed which is much concerned with analyzing the complexity of any given momentary situation. Also, the field of symbolic interactionism has devoted more attention to the scene. This development helps sociologists to open up to the range of complexity involved in any given instance of human behavior. For example, it is difficult to understand how social change occurs without taking into account the momentary situation along with social structures. Ordinary language and literary language tend to pay considerable attention to the momentary situation, by contrast with the structural emphasis within the social sciences. This broader approach to human behavior within sociology builds bridges to the way people ordinarily think of human behavior. There can be traffic across those bridges in both directions, with non-academics learning structural concepts while academics apply their structural concepts to situations. As we might note from the headings of the chapters in part V, "The Situation," there are important sociological concepts which apply to the momentary scene, such as "labeling" and "reflexive behavior" (chapter 9) as well as "conforming behavior" and "praxis" (chapter 11). In addition, there are important concepts which psychologists have emphasized, such as "negative reinforcement" and "positive reinforcement" (chapter 10).

A key limitation of Goffman's approach is his avoidance of the concepts used within the literature of the social sciences. For example, "looping" has to do with the "feedback loops" which Buckley discusses in chapter 1 and which are the basis for causal-loop analysis. Goffman is attempting to avoid getting into technical social science concepts in his efforts to communicate to a wide audience of non-sociologists, and we can admire that effort. Yet at the same time his work fails to mesh easily with the literature of sociology and thus foster sociology's cumulative development. We might note much the same thing happening with David Riesman's *The Lonely Crowd* (1961), a book also addressed to a general audience, yet lacking in any focus on major concepts within the sociological literature. Howard Becker has defended such usage, exemplified by Goffman's neologism of "total institution," in the interest of being able to communicate widely by avoiding technical terminology (2002). Yet it is exactly technical terminology like "social stratification," "alienation" and "cultural values" which enables the social scientist to move far up language's ladder of abstraction and come down that ladder to unite diverse studies. That is what Mills was arguing in his *The Sociological Imagination* (chapter 6), and that is a basis for the approach taken in this book.

Yet it is unfair to single out Goffman or Riesman or Becker for failing to do what social scientists generally fail to do: move up language's ladder of abstraction so as to emphasize abstract concepts like those in the chapter headings of this book. Throughout the sociological literature there is almost no orientation to employing a system of abstract and interrelated concepts that are derived from that literature. One of the few efforts in that direction is the theoretical work of Talcott Parsons, but his theory has come under severe criticism for good reason. Generally, it is ahistorical along with a great deal of general theory throughout social science. It points toward an explanation of human behavior once and for all rather than tying theory to such phenomena as changing cultural values. Methodologically or epistemologically, it does not emphasize the importance of coming far down language's ladder of abstraction to the empirical research needed to assess the validity of its hypotheses. Further, its lack of reflexivity results in a failure to convey the conservative biases which are generally associated with a functional approach. Those biases suggest a metaphysical stance oriented to seeing a stratified and bureaucratized society—such as the United States—as a model society in evolutionary terms rather than as a society with fundamental problems requiring solutions.

However, criticism of Parsonian theory appears to have fostered criticism of any effort to develop a system of abstract and interrelated concepts derived from the literature of sociology. Any effort to build bridges connecting specialized areas, thus, can easily be seen to be a species of philosophy or Parsonianism *as opposed to sociology*. Similarly, criticism of Goffman's use of the vernacular, as well as his lack of emphasis on abstract sociological concepts, can come to be seen as anti-empirical. Yet such an approach to abstract sociological concepts appears to violate the history of the scientific method as it has been used throughout the physical and biological sciences. The stance taken here is that Goffman's insights and his emphasis on situational details are far too important to be left outside of the cumulative development of the social sciences. It is when his approach is wedded to abstract concepts that have withstood the test of time within the literature of the social sciences that we can build on them and thus do justice to them. In this way, for example, we can learn to pay far more attention to the specific social structures that go into making up larger social structures. We can also learn to focus much more attention on the complexities of any given human situation, but without abandoning concerns for social and personality structures.

## Illich's *Deschooling Society*

It was in Ivan Illich's *Deschooling Society* (1971) that he brought forward his revolutionary idea:

> Many students, especially those who are poor, intuitively know what the schools do for them. They school them to confuse process and substance. Once these become blurred, a new logic is assumed: the more treatment there is, the better are the results; or, escalation leads to success. The pupil is thereby "schooled" to confuse teaching with learning, grade advancement with education, a diploma with competence, and fluency with the ability to say something new. His imagination is "schooled" to accept service in place of value. Medical treatment is mistaken for health care,

social work for the improvement of community life, police protection for safety, the rat race for productive work. Health, learning, dignity, independence, and creative endeavor are defined as little more than the performance of the institutions which claim to serve these ends, and their improvement is made to depend on allocating more resources to the management of hospitals, schools, and other agencies in question.

In these essays, I will show that the institutionalization of values leads inevitably to physical pollution, social polarization, and psychological impotence: three dimensions in a process of global degradation and modernized misery. I will explain how this process of degradation is accelerated when nonmaterial needs are transformed into demands for commodities; when health, education, personal mobility, welfare or psychological healing are defined as the result of services or "treatments" (1971: 1–2).

Illich develops a profound critique of stratification between professionals and nonprofessionals, and he even begins to communicate a vision of how to develop such a society. He focuses not only on the institution of education but also on medicine, social work, the police, economic institutions and all of the other institutions constructed by society. He argues that although we have been taught or "schooled" to believe that such institutions in fact yield learning, health, independence, and a range of other cultural values, in fact they do not. In his words, we have learned to confuse the "process" of conformity to the demands of a given institution like the public school with "substance," or the actual fulfillment of cultural values. His argument is related to the analysis of people-oriented and work-related cultural values in the presentation of Williams's work (chapter 7). For example, he claims that "nonmaterial needs are transformed into demands for commodities," and that they are supposedly fulfilled by "services" or institutions like public schools. Thus, people-oriented cultural values are transformed into work-related cultural values. With reference to figure I.1, Illich is claiming that such institutions in fact fail to pull the bottom curve up to the top curve, fulfilling our cultural values, despite the claims of institutional proponents.

Illich labels those false claims of institutional proponents as "'the Myth of Unending Consumption' ... grounded in the belief that process inevitably produces something of value." He elaborates: "Once a man or woman has accepted the need for school, he or she is easy prey for other institutions. Once young people have allowed their imaginations to be formed by curricular instruction, they are conditioned to institutional planning of every sort. "Instruction" smothers the horizon of their imaginations" (1971: 55–56).

It is, then, this "Myth of Unending Consumption" which gives legitimacy to schools and other institutions. People have learned to substitute and accept as valid the mere existence of an institution producing services for the product which those services have been designed to produce. Efforts to point out that institutions are failing to deliver what they have promised to deliver are shunted aside. Illich attempts to explain how this state of affairs has come about:

> Since there is nothing desirable which has not been planned, the city child soon concludes that we will always be able to design an institution for our every want. He takes for granted the power of process to create value. Whether the goal is meeting a mate, integrating a neighborhood, or acquiring reading skills, it will be defined in such a way that its achievement can be engineered. The man who knows that nothing in demand is out of production soon expects that nothing produced can be out of demand. If a moon vehicle can be designed, so can the demand to go to the moon. Not to go where one can go would be subversive. It would unmask as folly the assumption that every satisfied demand entails the discovery of an even greater unsatisfied one. Such insight would stop progress. Not to produce what is possible would expose the law of "rising expectations" as a euphemism for a growing frustration gap, which is the motor of a society built on the coproduction of services and increased demand (1971: 156).

The "growing frustration gap" to which Illich refers is nothing less than the hypothesized increasing gap between expectations and their fulfillment depicted in figure I.1. His reference to "the law of 'rising expectations'" suggests that, since this law is actually "a euphemism," people generally believe that rising expectations will be accompanied by rising fulfillment of those expectations. It is that belief which Illich is challenging in this book. His statement that "such insight would stop progress" refers to the idea that his own insights challenge the assumption that the continuing development of materialistic technologies along with their goods and services are indeed generally progressive, that is, fulfilling the cultural value of progress.

Illich's analysis cuts across the usual political divides separating "fascist, democratic or socialist" states: they all create schooled societies. In other words, they are all organized around stratified and bureaucratic institutions, regardless of whether or not people are allowed to vote in elections. Within all of those states there is a "hidden curriculum" that "bureaucracies guided by scientific knowledge are efficient and benevolent." For Illich, the public schools along with educational institutions in general create a deep mentality—the impact of this "hidden curriculum" on the individual—which carries over to all other institutions. This idea parallels the idea of a stratified metaphysical stance or worldview. For such a worldview would also illustrate people's mentality and carry over to all of society's institutions. It would also be relatively invisible, just as is Illich's idea of a "hidden curriculum."

What is lacking in Illich's book is a clear and credible direction for reducing "schooling" or social stratification. Illich claims that any political program that fails to recognize the need for "deschooling" is in fact not revolutionary. He believes that reliance on the educational institution to solve the problems of society neglects the fact that the educational institution is the primary cause of the problems of society. When Illich wrote his book in the late 1960s, it was too early to learn just what would be the overall result of China's Cultural Revolution. He saw that revolution as, potentially, "the first successful attempt at deschooling the institutions of society." However that revolution resulted in devastating setbacks for China in cultural life as well as in the death and suffering of a great many innocent Chinese.

If all of our institutions are to be "deschooled," how is society to be organized? If the "hidden curriculum" teaches us all conforming behavior, what new curriculum is to replace it? If the "Myth of Unending Consumption" should be unmasked as a euphemism, just how is this to be accomplished? This is not to suggest that such questions cannot be answered but only that Illich himself has not taken them seriously, although he does make some suggestions. For example, he sees the library, where the individual is free to develop any curriculum whatsoever, as a substitute for compulsory schooling. But if attending school is no longer compulsory, does he actually expect young people to flock to libraries? Assuming that elections are still held in such a society, how informed would the electorate be? Would the schooling that he resents in the educational system still continue in the other institutions? If so, how would it be eliminated, and what would take its place?

For example, we know very little about just how stratification—or "schooling"—works within the diverse bureaucratic organizations which populate modern society. Half a century ago Stanley Udy suggested that the elements within bureaucracies which emphasize rationality and technical efficiency are negatively related to those elements emphasizing hierarchy (1959). His approach contrasts with that of Weber, who treated all such elements as contributing to bureaucratic efficiency (1946, 1964). In other words, we have a split between characteristics oriented to more egalitarian interaction and those opposed to such interaction. This raises the question of how organizations might be structured with less stratification, and to what extent that might in turn yield greater efficiency and, perhaps, some closing of the gap between expectations and their fulfillment. In the case of bureaucracies operating within the public sector, such as governmental agencies, there are additional questions having to do with their accountability and impartiality (see for example Wilson, 1989: 315-325). To illustrate, to what extent are governmental housing agencies impartial with respect to meeting the needs of minority groups? Do hierarchical or discriminatory patterns of race relations in society as a whole show up in such agencies, pointing away from egalitarian social relationships? Even without such discrimination, does the very existence of stratification or "schooling" within bureaucratic organizations in fact promote dependency and helplessness among those working within them?

Despite these unanswered questions, Illich carries forward the enormous optimism of the Enlightenment tradition into modern society. He is much concerned with the fate of the people-oriented cultural values that Williams discussed (chapter 7), such as equality, freedom and individual personality. And he is deeply critical of a materialistic and consumption-oriented society with a myth that present technologies are in fact fulfilling those cultural values. His idea of a "hidden curriculum" supporting "schooling" suggests, in vernacular terms, the existence of a stratified metaphysical stance or worldview that supports patterns of social stratification throughout society. Yet just as in the case of Goffman, his use of the vernacular ignores key ideas from the social science literature, limiting both his credibility and his impact on the cumulative development of social science knowledge. As a result, he does not work to close the gap between biophysical science and technology, on the one hand, and social science knowledge and technology, on the other hand. It is that gap which appears to be fundamental to the one-sided materialism of contemporary society. And to the extent that it is in fact increasing, it threatens all of us with an invisible crisis.

We might ask just what contemporary research has to say about the persistence of stratification in modern society, given its enormous impact on the fulfillment of expectations. A review of contemporary research comes up with these conclusions:

> In recent years, criticisms of the class-analytic framework have escalated, with many scholars arguing that the concept of class is "ceasing to do any useful work for sociology." ... This argument has not been subjected to convincing empirical tests and may prove to be premature. However, even if lifestyles and life chances are truly "decoupling" from economic class, this should not be misunderstood as a more general decline in stratification per se. The massive facts of economic, political, and honorific inequality will still be operative even if conventional models of class ultimately are found deficient in characterizing the postmodern condition. As is well known, some forms of inequality have increased in recent years (e.g., income inequality), while others show no signs of disappearing or withering away (e.g., political inequality).
>
> This persistence and in some cases deepening of inequality is coupled with the continuing diffusion of anti-stratification values and a correspondingly heightened sensitivity to all things unequal. As egalitarianism

spreads, the postmodern public becomes heavily involved in monitoring and exposing illegitimate (i.e., non-meritocratic) forms of stratification, and even small departures from equality are increasingly viewed as problematic and intolerable.... Moreover, because stratification systems are deeply institutionalized, there is good reason to anticipate that demands for egalitarian change will outpace actual changes in stratification practices. These dynamics imply that issues of stratification will continue to generate discord and conflict even in the unlikely event of a long-term trend toward diminishing inequality (Grusky, 2000: 2819–2820).

Following this reviewer, it is apparent that stratification not only still lives in modern society but is also a major source of conflict, given what he suggests are "the continuing diffusion of anti-stratification values and a correspondingly heightened sensitivity to all things unequal." This "spread of egalitarianism" coupled with the continuation of stratification is in large measure the basis for our focus on a gap between expectations and their fulfillment, as depicted in figure I.1. Given this situation, Illich's push toward "deschooling" or de-stratification will encounter massive resistance from fundamental patterns of stratification throughout modern society. Those patterns are in turn, we assume, bolstered by a stratified worldview or metaphysical stance. Even if Illich does not have a clear direction for achieving deschooling, he does succeed in raising the question of how to reduce stratification.

## Some Implications

Orwell sees an increasing aspirations-fulfillment gap—hypothesis (1)—as he proceeds to discuss the continuing development of Newspeak. The extreme stratification in Oceania is a fundamental cause of that gap, thus supporting (2) as well. Goffman unearths fundamental problems of the dehumanization of patients in mental hospitals, yielding a large expectations-fulfillment gap in the mental hospital. Yet since he does not compare this with the prior historical situation, this finding does not bear directly on hypothesis (1). However, he sees that gap as largely a product of patterns of stratification, supporting (2). Illich goes even further than these authors in finding that institutions throughout society are failing us with respect to the fulfillment of our people-oriented cultural values. His implication is that things are getting worse for the ordinary individual as a result of all this "schooling," implying support for (1). He supports (2) as well, since he sees social stratification—along with our worship of elites—as the key factor causing our basic problems in modern society.

As for images or metaphors, Orwell's vision of "Big Brother" as the epitome of the totalitarian ruler is a powerful one. Yet let us not forget that culture is involved in *1984* along with social organization, as illustrated by the language of Newspeak. Goffman's title, *Asylums,* can be used metaphorically to raise questions about modern society in general. Are we all living in an asylum, more or less, where the individual is dehumanized with respect to both patterns of social organization and culture? Illich's concept of "schooling" is a concrete way of looking at our abstract patterns of social stratification. It can evoke, for example, an image of a forest of hands of students—and the rest of us—desperately seeking to be recognized by their all-knowledgeable and all-powerful teacher, boss, elected official or celebrated guru.

# PART V

# The Situation

The momentary scene may well prove to be the "missing link" that socio-logicsts have largely ignored until recent decades with their focus on social structures. Yet we can see the foreshadowing of attention to the situation if we look back to past efforts by sociologists. For example, there is W. I. Thomas's idea that "Preliminary to any self-determined act of behavior there is always a stage of examination and deliberation which we may call "the definition of the situation" (1923). From chapter 1 we have Buckley's inclusion of the impact of the momentary scene within his analysis of any given social system, opening up to its complexity. From chapter 2 there is Gouldner's emphasis on the importance of a "reflexive sociology," with the sociologist applying sociology to his or her own momentary experiences. The Levin experiment in chapter 3 points up the impact of a given momentary experience like a poor test score accompanied by a feeling of relative deprivation. Simmel's analytic procedures, discussed in chapter 4, illustrate the importance of apparently trivial experiences, since he believed that "the most banal externalities are, in the last analysis, bound up with the final decisions concerning the meaning and style of life." From Knottnerus's analysis of concentration camps in chapter 5 we learn how specific actions taken by an inmate become the basis for rituals that work to protect him within incredibly difficult situations. Mills, discussed in chapter 6, anticipated Gouldner in his advice that sociologists should not split their work from their lives but, rather, use their personal experiences to advance their sociological understanding, and vice-versa. From Durkheim in chapter 7 we gain a sense of rapid changes in our historical situation as a result of the industrialization process and the increasing anomie that follows. And from Goffman in chapter 8 we have his sensitivity to the powerful impact on the mental patient of a situation where the patient's simple request to go to the bathroom is put off by the staff.

A great many contemporary sociologists have given us further insights into the situation, but citing their work is beyond the scope of this book. We might, instead, at least mention fields such as social psychology, ethnomethodology, symbolic interactionism, social exchange theory and expectations states theory as illustrative of further understanding of the complexities of the situation. The development of all of this literature in only a matter of several decades indicates the importance of the situation. What remains to be accomplished, however, is to integrate all of this knowledge so that it can be used within the analysis of any given situation.

If we now look to the analyses by non-sociologists in previous chapters, we can see much the same emphasis on the importance of the momentary situation. For example, Sommer's experiment described in chapter 1 where he arranged lecture chairs in a circle only to have students move them so that they all faced the instructor illustrates how a momentary scene can reveal the students' metaphysical stance or worldview. Kelly in chapter 2 stresses the importance of the individual's momentary process of perception and use of language. Horney, examined in chapter 4, is much concerned with the historical situation of modern society, where we have developed fundamental contradictions such as "between the alleged freedom of the individual and all his factual limitations." Kaplan's treatment of pragmatism in chapter 5 opens up to the importance of our momentary usage of language for solving fundamental problems. Peirce's analysis of the scientific method in chapter 6 stresses the importance of the investigator's feelings in initiating an inquiry—specifically, "the irritation of doubt," as central to the success of that method. And, in chapter 8, Orwell's invention of Newspeak is an eerie anticipation of most news on television, teaching us to think superficially by packaging complex issues in tiny segments. Such an orientation to the importance of the situation while not at the same time neglecting the importance of structures is characteristic of the breadth of an interactive by contrast with a stratified worldview.

By examining figure I.1 or graphs in general, we can see the importance of the momentary scene. For no curve can be drawn without deriving its points from the many points on the horizontal axis. Those points represent momentary situations, whereas the curves represent changing structures. Attention to the situation refers to the status of both curves at any given point along the horizontal axis, rather than vaguely describing those curves without specific awareness of exactly what is happening to those curves as we move from one point on that axis to the next point. The curves, by contrast, have to do with structures. The upper curve of figure I.1 centers on cultural values, and the lower curve emphasizes patterns of social organization like social stratification and bureaucracy. But personality structures are equally implied by those curves. For example, a growing gap between those curves implies the existence of individual alienation. Also, patterns of social stratification and bureaucracy imply a stratified worldview. Thus, attention to the situation *as well as* social and individual structures helps us to understand how a series of situations results in certain structures. Without attention to situations it becomes almost impossible to understand much about how structures change. Alternatively, once we know something about structures, then this helps us to understand the nature of given situations. For example, if we know that the gap between expectations and their fulfillment is increasing, then we also can look for a smaller gap in a preindustrial situation than in a modern situation, as illustrated by the difference between the chief and the grocer of Balgat and described in the introduction to this book.

To understand the importance of the situation we would do well to look to the behavior of other forms of life where language is not present or is only very rudimentary, and where we can understand more clearly the impact of momentary perception, as discussed in chapter 2. We humans share with other forms of life the importance of momentary perception. However, our development of language not only shapes the way we perceive but also apparently points us away from paying attention to the enormous power of perception. For our thinking and speaking processes tend to take us away from the fact that all the while that we are thinking and speaking we are also perceiving from one moment to the next. This movement away from understanding the power of perception apparently has been emphasized by the great change from oral to literate societies, where the printed word along with the vast stores of knowledge in libraries become crucial bases for our behavior. Yet we might note the dependence of ordinary or literary language on metaphors that invoke our perception. Such language moves us very quickly from abstractions to concreteness. We might also note in chapter 2's treatment of Berger's *Ways of Seeing* the hypothesized impact of advertising on television in shaping a large gap between aspirations and their fulfillment.

In Part V we will continue to emphasize within our three chapters the "head," "heart" and "hand," respectively. Chapter 9, Labeling versus Reflexive Behavior, looks to our momentary usage of language. When we give labels to phenomena we tend to fix our perception of such phenomena, but a reflexive orientation opens us up to changing the way in which we perceive and understand phenomena from one moment to the next. Chapter 10, "Negative versus Positive Reinforcement," takes up what psychologists have found to be vital for understanding the behavior of all organisms, and also what exchange theorists within sociology have also found to be fundamental for understanding human behavior. Chapter 11, Conforming Behavior versus Praxis, looks to momentary actions and interactions, by contrast with long-term patterns of interaction like social stratification and egalitarian social relationships. It is within all three of these chapters that we will come to grips with the missing link of situational analysis, taking into account the importance of perception in shaping whatever is done from one moment to the next.

## CHAPTER 9

# "Head"

## Labeling versus Reflexive Behavior

FOLLOWING MILTON'S PARADISE LOST, "The mind is its own place, and in itself can make a heaven of hell, a hell of heaven." If we choose hell, we can make no fundamental changes in sociology or society, and we will discover what we human beings are capable of unleashing on ourselves. Thus, we can choose, following Kelly, to classify constructs into "pre-emptive" ones, "which pre-empts its elements for membership in its own realm exclusively." Kelly is referring to "saying that if this man is a homosexual he is *nothing but* a homosexual." By contrast with a scientific orientation, "it is essentially a denial of the right of other people and ourselves to re-view, re-interpret and see in a fresh light some part of the world around us." Thus, labeling is analogous to prejudice, except that it provides us with a focus on language. We have seen such a focus on labeling in Levin's experiment on prejudice (chapter 3), which measured increased prejudice against Puerto Ricans following frustration for individuals with a stratified worldview. We have also seen labeling, without usage of the term, in Goffman's *Asylums* (chapter 8), where he details the many ways in which mental patients are humiliated. Scheff, whose work will be discussed in this chapter, developed "The Labelling Theory of Mental Illness" in an article (1974) as well as a monograph (1966). It is what he calls "a sensitizing theory," which alerts us to the power of language to categorize people so as to legitimize prejudice and discrimination. Although language gives us the potential to view phenomena dichotomously, gradationally and metaphorically, labeling emphasizes dichotomy to the exclusion of a gradational orientation and uses metaphor in support of that dichotomy.

Or we can make fuller use of these potentials within language, learning to continue to learn—with the aid of a broad scientific method—without any limit. For example, we can follow Kelly in coming to see ourselves as a "categorizing" animal who can classify constructs into "propositional" ones, thus behaving as a "scientist" in our everyday lives (chapter 2). Such learning is by no means limited to the head, but includes the heart and the hand as well. It is this which Mills had in mind when he advised the student of sociology that "the most admirable thinkers within the scholarly community you have chosen to join do not split their work from their lives" (chapter 6). It is also what Gouldner had in mind when he stated, "The historical mission of a Reflexive Sociology as I conceive it, however, would be to transform the sociologist, to penetrate deeply into his daily life and work, enriching them with new sensitivities, and to raise the sociologist's self-awareness to a new historical level" (chapter 2). We fish can thus learn to see the water of language and thought that we are all swimming in from one moment to the next. In this way we can learn to achieve what Korzybski called "consciousness of abstracting," or momentary awareness that one's concepts or verbal maps are not identical with the territory they supposedly portray, to be discussed in the piece on Van Vogt in chapter 10. Such reflexive behavior stands opposed to labeling.

Fred Hoyle's *The Black Cloud* (1957) is a science-fiction novel about a huge interstellar mass of matter that invades the solar system and parks itself in a position blotting out the sun's rays from the earth. Chris Kingsley, an astronomer at Cambridge University, manages to establish communication with the Cloud and discovers it to be a super-intelligent being much like a gigantic brain. Responding to Kingsley's questions about human intelligence, the Cloud reveals that our language is made up of simplistic "labels" which bear little relationship to the actual complexities of phenomena that they supposedly describe. Nevertheless, we humans are able to communicate with one another because we are like peas in a pod and thus can easily recognize the nature of others' experiences. Let us recall here Thomas Kuhn's closing question (chapter 3): "What must the world be like in order that man may know it?" Following Kingsley's interpretation of the Cloud, living beings "are constructed in accordance with the logic of the Universe." And the interactive nature of the Cloud—whose elements communicate with one another at the speed of light—along with the interactive nature of the human being suggest our existence within an interactive universe.

Thomas Scheff in his *Bloody Revenge: Emotions, Nationalism, and War* (1994) develops a theory of protracted conflict. He also develops his "Part/Whole" method that employs both micro and macro analysis. It is a method that has come to be integrated within the Web and Part/Whole Approach to the scientific method. He ranges widely over different kinds of protracted conflicts, emphasizing quarrel and impasse in a marriage, the origins of World War I and the origins of World War II. Scheff finds that unacknowledged shame or threats to the relationship set the stage for long-term conflict, whereas acknowledgment and reconciliation point toward the resolution of such conflicts. We can see the lack of acknowledgment of shame as linked to figure I.1 with its large gap between aspirations and their fulfillment in modern society. Assuming that such a gap generally exists, it would indeed be very difficult for any individual to give recognition to its existence, barring the availability of procedures for closing that gap. More recently, Scheff has employed the Web and Part/Whole Approach to an analysis of Goffman's contributions (2006).

Paulo Freire's *Pedagogy of the Oppressed* (1970), like Ivan Illich's *Deschooling Society* (chapter 8), places education at stage center in any effort to change society in fundamental ways. Just as Illich called for "deschooling" society in order to give genuine education of the individual a fighting chance in all institutions, Freire calls for the elimination of our "banking" concept of education so as to release the potential of every individual. Instead of an educational institution emphasizing that "the teacher knows everything and the students know nothing," a radically different educational institution is possible, one that can function to change society instead of functioning to continue its injustices by preserving the status quo. Teachers should also be students, and students should also be teachers, and this will release the creative power of both teachers and students. They both should focus attention on the enormous power of the words they use. Instead of using those words to program everyone into conforming behavior, Freire suggests that we must learn to use them to liberate ourselves from the tyranny of "the culture of silence." Those who are at the very bottom of society must learn to be able to say, "I now realize I am a man, an educated man."

## Hoyle's *The Black Cloud*

The Cloud's specific response to Kingsley's question on the nature of human intelligence argues that the human being communicates in such a way as to oversimplify complex phenomena:

> Your outstanding oddity is the great similarity of one individual to another. This allows you to use a very crude method of communication. You attach labels to your neurological states—anger, headache, embarrassed, happy, melancholy—these are all labels. If Mr. A. wishes to tell Mr. B. that he is suffering from a headache he makes no attempt to describe the neurological disruption in his head. Instead he displays his label. He says: "I have a headache."
>
> When Mr. B. hears this he takes the label "headache" and interprets it in accordance with his own experience. Thus Mr. A. is able to acquaint Mr. B. of his indisposition even though neither party may have the slightest idea what a "headache" really consists of. Such a highly singular method of communication is of course only possible between nearly identical individuals (1957: 150–151).

Kingsley then asks the Cloud whether this implies that no communication at all would be necessary between two identical individuals, since each would automatically understand the response of the other. Between nearly identical individuals, as the Cloud suggests is the case for human beings, a crude method of communication is sufficient. However, between two widely different individuals, a much more complex method of communication is essential. The Cloud responds, agreeing with Kingsley's analysis.

The Black Cloud is maintaining that our ordinary language fails to convey the complexity of any given individual's headache or emotional states like anger, embarrassment, happiness and sadness. Instead, we communicate with highly simplistic labels like "I have a headache," "I'm angry," "I'm embarrassed," "I'm happy" and "I'm sad." We might contrast such usages with technical communications with the aid of mathematics within the physical sciences, which can penetrate to a much greater extent the complexities of physical phenomena and which the Cloud would see as far superior. The Cloud, then, is indirectly referring to the failure of social science to explain non-physical phenomena as well as people's corresponding failure to incorporate social science knowledge into their everyday speech.

We might be reminded here of Gouldner's statement, in chapter 2, that "The pursuit of ... understanding, however, cannot promise that men as we now find them, with their everyday language and understanding, will always be capable of further understanding and of liberating themselves." Like the Cloud, Gouldner is claiming that ordinary language is limited. But he is centering on the language of social science, by contrast with the Cloud. Gouldner is also focusing on changing ordinary language to include the fruits of social science research so that it can fulfill more of what the Cloud is calling for: the ability to get into the complexity of phenomena like human emotions. This involves a two-step process, from the perspective of this book: (1) developing a direction for the rapid cumulative development of social science, including the integration of its bits and pieces of knowledge by means of a scientific method that follows the ideal of opening up to all relevant phenomena in relation to a given problem, and (2) communicating on a continuing basis the results of this more profound understanding of human behavior to the general public as effectively as possible. More specifically, our hypothesis is that accomplishing these two aims involves movement from a stratified to an interactive approach to the scientific method, and also movement from a stratified to an interactive worldview.

If we take up the Cloud's remarks about the close similarities among all human beings, there is indeed a good deal of evidence for this, despite the emphasis within Western society on the cultural value of individual personality, as discussed by Williams in chapter 7. For example, the very fact that this value—along with the other cultural values discussed by Williams—is widely shared speaks for similarities among human beings. We might add to such similarities our hypothesis of a shared worldview, which is linked in turn to such phenomena as outward perception, alienation, anomie and social stratification, as discussed in earlier chapters.

The Cloud is focusing on ordinary language and not the language of science. This is indeed important, since ordinary language appears to be the basis for thought and speech not only among lay people but also among scientists. We have argued that much in ordinary language illustrates our stratified worldview, and that we cannot expect social scientists to shift to the scientific ideal of openness to all relevant phenomena unless their worldview is changed to one that is more compatible with that scientific ideal. Following Gouldner's perspective, social scientists should work toward altering ordinary language so that it encompasses ever more of the important ideas of their fields. The Cloud, by contrast, is adopting a static position about human language, not taking into account the potential of the social sciences for altering our everyday usages so that they will deal ever more effectively with human complexity. The Cloud is assuming that the human race will remain unable to accomplish this and, with reference to figure I.1, will remain unable to penetrate the complexity of problems such as that gap between aspirations and their fulfillment. Just as social science remains invisible to the Cloud, so does it appear to remain invisible to Fred Hoyle, who is an astronomer when he is not writing science fiction.

We have emphasized throughout this book the importance of language's dichotomous, gradational and metaphorical or image-oriented potential. All three appear to be crucial both in science and in everyday life if we are to understand the complexity of human behavior and to address fundamental social problems. From this perspective, social scientists have much to teach everyone about crucial dichotomies, as illustrated by the dichotomies in the table of contents of this book. Biophysical scientists have much to teach everyone about the gradational capacities of language, again illustrated by the table of contents, once we envision movement from one pole of a dichotomy to the other. And literary intellectuals can teach everyone about metaphor and images, which are so essential for returning to our perceptions and our sensory experiences. Yet if our present worldview points toward the narrow usage of language by social scientists, biophysical scientists and literary intellectuals, then it becomes essential to alter that worldview to one which encourages utilizing the full range of language's capacities.

## Scheff's *Bloody Revenge: Emotions, Nationalism, and War*

Thomas Scheff dedicated his *Bloody Revenge* (1994) "To all innocent victims of humiliated fury," revealing his focus on the emotions of shame and anger and their disastrous repercussions both in two-person relationships and in conflicts between nations. The work is most unusual in several ways, departing very far from what we are accustomed to seeing in the literature of the social sciences. For one thing, he develops a highly systematic focus on emotions. Some other social scientists have examined emotions, as we've seen in Goffman's *Asylums* (chapter 8), but not in a systematic way. In addition, Scheff uses detailed dialogue to develop evidence for his arguments. It includes visual phenomena since it is based on videotapes, thus introducing the phenomenon of perception. Also, Scheff is tackling within the very same monograph protracted conflicts between two individuals as well as between nations, thus illustrating the kind of breadth that Mills called for in his *The Sociological Imagination* (chapter 6). Further, Scheff sees his book as illustrating a general approach to the scientific method—what he calls a "Part/Whole Approach"—which he has elaborated in other monographs (1990, 1997). That approach has been combined with the Web approach to the scientific method. And this combined orientation, now designated as the Web and Part/Whole Approach, is discussed in the Introduction and used in Scheff's new book (2006).

Scheff's analysis is based to a large extent on a case taken from a work by Suzanne Retzinger, *Violent Emotions: Shame and Rage in Marital Quarrels* (1991). Rosie and James—the fictitious names Retzinger used—had been married for eleven years, were in a trial separation and were considering divorce. The two were in their mid-thirties and were white, with James employed in the forestry service after completing four years of college and with Rosie enrolled in college. Much of their dispute centered on an airplane that James had purchased, with Rosie resenting James's spending much time with it. The plane was James's "pride and joy" although Rosie "hated" the plane, yet they had never actually had an argument about the plane even though it was a sore point between them. Rosie might occasionally express some irritation about it but would then quickly back down.

Here is a sequence of dialogue between Rosie and James taken from the videotape they had agreed to do where they have been asked to confront their conflict over the plane:

## Impasse

1. *R:* So what aspects of the plane do you want to talk
2. about?
3. *J:* Oh just airplanes in general it doesn't have to
4. be
5. *R:* Oh
6. *J:* Specifically the one we have now (laugh).

### Quarrel

7. *R:* No I wanna NARROW it RIGHT down TO that one!
8. *J:* Because I don't plan on it being the last the
9. end of the line.
10. *R:* NO! Well, I don't either—not for you.
11. *J:* Oh good!
12. *R:* No I wouldn't take your toy from you.
13. *J:* All right.
14. *R:* I ... I sacrificed a LOT for you to have toys.
15. [Both laugh tightly.]

### Impasse

16. *R:* But you didn't ask for it and I resented it later and
17. We're still going over it. OK?
18. *J:* Yeah, it (3) it uh goes back to another era (Scheff, 1994: 18-19).

Within this relatively small transcript taken together with the detailed audiovisual record of what happened, we can illustrate a great deal of Scheff's argument throughout the book. The words in all capital letters indicate loud speech, and in line 5 Rosie interrupts James, who then continues on line 6. Scheff divides the dialogue into three sections: impasse, quarrel, and impasse once again. The book is about "protracted conflict" and not conflict which is resolved at some point. Here we see an instance of conflict which is at first buried (initial impasse), then is asserted (quarrel) and then is buried once again (second impasse). The couple admitted that over the previous several years they had become increasingly tense and less affectionate with each other. Their normal mode of conflict was the silent impasse, and the above quarrel is a disruption of that normal mode.

Rosie's opening question (lines 1 and 2) was asked, following Scheff, "in an ingratiating, childlike manner," instead of her directly coming to grips with her own negative feelings about the plane and her wish to get rid of it. We may note (lines 3, 4, and 6) that James appears to interpret her meek question as indicating her desire to avoid a confrontation, permitting him to do likewise. But Rosie interrupts his response (line 5) with an "oh" that indicates surprise that James is avoiding the issue that upsets her.

It is at this point (line 7) that their conversation moves from an impasse to a quarrel, for Rosie is no longer willing to avoid a confrontation by contrast with her past behavior in the marriage. Throughout this quarrel phase, Rosie expresses anger in a number of ways. Her "NO" comes very quickly and loudly in response to James's statement, her speech is rapid, she leans forward in an apparently aggressive manner, her eyes narrow, and she lowers her eyebrows. Her statement on line 7 is a flat contradiction of James's previous statement, giving a loud intonation to a number of her words. James's verbal response (lines 8 and 9) to Rosie's angry statement indicates that the battle is joined, for his plans call for him to continue with having a plane despite his awareness of Rosie's negative attitude. Nonverbally, he shows his anger in more subtle ways than Rosie. For example, he reveals that he is somewhat flustered at Rosie's outburst by interrupting himself to change the ending of his sentence (lines 8 and 9). Also, he laughs at some of his words, and his fixed smile becomes slightly more tense.

Rosie then apparently escalates the battle (lines 10, 12, 14), continuing to lean forward with an expression of anger on her face. She begins by agreeing with him that this plane will not be his last one, but she drags out the last syllable—"you-ou"—with her face expressing contempt and even disgust, suggesting her own continued separation from James. In line 12 she calls the plane James's toy, implying her own contempt for his childish behavior. She repeats this reference to the plane as James's toy in line 14, also referring to her own sacrifices for James, which she apparently regrets. As for James, after his confrontational statement (lines 8, 9) his responses (lines 11, 13) are only two words long and relatively quiet. He appears to be withdrawing emotionally from the conversation, with signs that he is sinking into his seat.

By line 16, however, it appears that Rosie has swallowed her anger and has returned to a non-confrontational dialogue. Perhaps she has noticed James's withdrawal and is afraid that he will break off the discussion completely if she continues with her angry responses. In this way she shifts from the quarrel phase of the dialogue back to an impasse stage, where they both bury once again their deep feelings, returning to the status quo. Rosie admits (line 16) that James did not ask her to make any sacrifices for him, and she recognizes her own feelings of resentment, ending with "OK," a different ending from her endings in the quarrel phase. For his part, James is stammering and mumbling in his response (line 18), but his long response indicates that he has come out of his withdrawal.

Retzinger held a debriefing session several weeks afterwards where Rosie and James saw the videotape of their conversation. As a result, they both became more aware of the emotions that they had expressed. Rosie looked at her own image, when the tape was paused at a moment of her high emotion, saying, "*That* is one angry woman." And James turned to Rosie at one point, saying, "*That's* the expression on my face that you have been telling me about." He was referring at the time to his state of withdrawal, when he had a tense look on his face which he called his "hurt" look. Apparently, both of them were relatively unaware of their emotions at the time of the quarrel. Although the normal debriefing session lasted one hour, the couple extended it to three hours. By contrast with the usual perfunctory participation of couples in such sessions, Rosie and James reacted very strongly to what they saw and heard. In a follow-up three years later when the two were living together, Rosie told the interviewer that their lives had been changed by that debriefing session. James still had his plane but it was no longer a bone of contention, and their participation in the study had changed their relationship for the better.

Scheff interprets what has occurred throughout this conversation between Rosie and James as illustrating a "shame-anger loop," suggesting a continuing recurrence of shame and anger in their relationship without any fundamental change. He sees that continuation as based on the fact that their mutual shame remains hidden from their eyes, and that anger is the only way that they have learned to react to that shame. This is an illustration of what he calls "a feeling trap," where negative emotions work together in a never-ending feedback relationship so as to produce behavior which threatens the kind of relationship that is generally valued, and where the emotions expressed are largely hidden from those who are involved. The complexity of human behavior and feedback relationships in particular was discussed by Buckley (chapter 2) in his *Sociology and Modern System Theory,* and that complexity has been exemplified throughout the above chapters.

More specifically, Scheff sees shame in both Rosie and James in the initial impasse section of their conversation, as both show false smiles, talk in low voices and avoid the central issue that they have been asked to discuss. During the quarrel phase of their encounter both show anger, and James shows shame as well. Afterwards, during their second impasse, Rosie shows shame by becoming soft-spoken, by mumbling and by jumbling part of her response (lines 16, 17), and James continues to reveal shame. James shows anger during the quarrel phase, probably because Rosie is so angry and is treating him with contempt, and he then proceeds to withdraw and reveal shame. Scheff sees anger as not only a reaction to someone who insults us but also as a way of avoiding negative feelings of pain, that is, as a defense against becoming aware of painful emotions. But the result, as in Rosie's case, may be further shame because of our anger. Thus, anger can be directed against oneself as well as against others, creating an internal shame-anger loop that supports our external shame-anger loop. This makes the situation of individuals even more complicated and reinforces their inability to maintain a positive relationship.

In our own interpretation of this marital conflict along with Scheff's analysis, we see a situation that is far more complex than even Scheff suggests, and also a situation which has fundamental similarities to social relationships throughout modern society. We can most easily uncover that complexity by making use of the key sociological concepts within our chapter headings, concepts referring to additional phenomena which Rosie and James are unaware of just as in the case of their shame and anger. For example, we may note here the phenomenon of social stratification in general and gender stratification in particular. From the above brief excerpts we know very little about long-term patterns of hierarchy—or patterns of social stratification—within Rosie's relationship with James. Yet those excerpts do indicate that each one is attempting to dominate the other with respect to James' ability to be involved with the plane. Those attempts lead each of them to denigrate the other, violating "cultural values" such as the worth of the individual, and this adds fuel to the fire. What we have then is an illustration of the curves depicted in figure I.1: a pattern of social stratification which limits abilities to fulfill cultural values. Yet we must bear in mind that we are making inferences about a long-term relationship on the basis of very little evidence.

Employing our own basic concepts, Rosie and James appear to be "labeling" one another, with Rosie labeling James with such epithets as selfish and James labeling Rosie with such terms as a nag and a mental abuser, although Rosie a bit later becomes somewhat "reflexive" so as to move away from the quarrel phase. That movement appears to have been influenced by her adherence to "cultural values" such as equality along with a recognition that her previous "social interaction" with James had illustrated a pattern of "social stratification." Such a contradiction between cultural values and patterns of social stratification apparently results from "conforming behavior" to a "stratified worldview." By making such a shift she was able to move from "negative reinforcement" to some "positive reinforcement," although she still feels shame or negative reinforcement. That shift apparently was based in large part on her "outward percep-tion" of James's withdrawal from the situation as a result of her angry behavior. As for James, he is able to "conform" to Rosie's expectations in the new impasse situation, also based on his "outward perception" of the changed situation. Like Rosie, he feels shame or "negative reinforcement" in that situation. Like Rosie, he continues to be committed to contemporary "cultural values" like equality, and he continues to conform to a "stratified worldview." That worldview, with its ties to forces within social struc-tures, individual structures, and the situation, appears to be much of the basis for the "feeling trap" which Scheff describes.

It is most interesting to note the great impact of the debriefing session on Rosie and James which, according to Rosie when she was interviewed three years later, changed their lives for the better. Apparently they had learned to move in directions which were taking them away from the stratified worldview that was working to generate their "feeling trap." We might assume, for one thing, that the session helped them to learn to become aware of their own emotions, by contrast with their continually hiding them from themselves, thus moving in a reflexive direction. We can see the beginnings of this in Rosie's surprise, on viewing the videotape, at how angry she was, and also in James' recognition of his own "hurt look." The fact that they were living together in a better relationship rather than continuing to remain separated speaks worlds about the possibility of their having learned to achieve more of an egalitarian social relationship than they had in the past, implying greater fulfillment of their cultural values and a degree of abandonment of their former stratified relationship. Yet we should not jump to conclusions, given the lack of data on this possibility. Although we have no direct evidence about their behavior to one another within particular situations, we might infer the possibility of a corresponding shift toward more interactive situational behavior, given Rosie's statement of an improved social relationship.

Scheff applies his theory and methodology to large-scale problems like the causes of World War I, with a particular focus on Adolph Hitler and his relationship to the German people. He concludes his review of social science literature on Hitler's life by finding consistent and substantial evidence for Hitler's having developed a great deal of hidden shame and for his becoming prone to continuing shame-rage cycles. Although space does not permit us to examine that evidence, we can at least look to a quotation from *Mein Kampf* (1943). Hitler refers here to the Treaty of Versailles after having described it as an instrument of "abject humiliation":

> How could every single one of these points have been burned into the brain and emotion of this people, until finally in sixty million heads, in men and women, a common sense of shame and a common hatred would have become a single fiery sear of flame, from whose heat a will as hard as steel would have risen and a cry burst forth: *Give us arms again!* ... If at the beginning of the War and during the War twelve or fifteen thousand of these Hebrew corrupters of the people had been held under poison gas, as happened to hundreds of thousands of our very best German workers in the field, the sacrifice of millions at the front would not have been in vain. On the contrary: twelve thousand scoundrels eliminated in time might have saved the lives of a million real Germans, valuable for the future (1943: 632, 679).

Scheff uses the literature of social science to refer to the "anomie" which the German people were experiencing after the Treaty of Versailles: Large portions of German territory were transferred to other nations, Germany was excluded from the League of Nations as an "unworthy" state and was required to pay large sums of reparations for the war, and Germany was required to confess sole responsibility for having caused World War I. In other words—following the nature of anomie—the Treaty appears to have enforced a large gap between widespread aspirations or cultural values and their fulfillment, a gap that Hitler translated into a sense of national shame and a rationale for national hatred. But even before World War I, according to one author, Germany was experiencing a great deal of anomie because its industrialization process had come quite late by comparison with England, France and the United States, and that process had to proceed very rapidly to give Germany a chance to compete effectively (Dahrendorf, 1967). The above passage from *Mein Kampf* refers to Germany's situation as one of intense shame, seeking to legitimate enormous hatred because of that shame, and thus it illustrates Scheff's analysis of shame-rage cycles on a national level. That rage is well exemplified in the final sentences where Jews become the targets of Hitler's rage.

We might think here of the Levin experiment (chapter 3), where those Boston University students with a stratified worldview increase their prejudice against Puerto Ricans when they come to experience frustration of their needs, a sense of deprivation relative to others. That worldview suggests the enormous complexity of the forces that were involved in that increase in prejudice of the Boston University students, just as it suggests the great complexity of the forces involved in Hitler's rise to power. Scheff's analysis helps us to understand the similarity of the forces operating in small-group situations, such as between Rosie and James, and in entire nations. Thus, he illustrates the possibility of moving far beyond the narrow specialization with limited communication among specialists which dominates the social sciences. His Part/Whole methodology, with its emphasis on exploring the enormous complexity of any given situation, is now combined with the Web orientation, with its focus on a systematic approach to the abstract concepts and propositions of the social sciences. Together, they constitute the Web and Part/Whole Approach.

## Freire's *Pedagogy of the Oppressed*

Paulo Freire in his *Pedagogy of the Oppressed* (1970) describes his "life-affirming" and "humanizing" pedagogy by contrasting it with what he calls a "banking" concept of education, which mirrors "oppressive society as a whole," as illustrated by these attitudes and practices:

a. The teacher teaches and the students are taught.
b. The teacher knows everything and the students know nothing.
c. The teacher thinks and the students are thought about.
d. The teacher talks and the students listen—meekly.
e. The teacher disciplines and the students are disciplined.
f. The teacher chooses and enforces his choice, and the students comply.
g. The teacher acts and the students have the illusion of acting through the action of the teacher.
h. The teacher chooses the program content, and the students (who were not consulted) adapt to it.

    i. The teacher confuses the authority of knowledge with his own professional authority, which he sets in opposition to the freedom of the students.

    j. The teacher is the Subject of the learning process, while the pupils are mere objects (1970: 59; see also Freire, 1973).

These ideas all illustrate patterns of social stratification between teachers and students, as suggested by their implication of persisting hierarchy and inequality. For example, (a), (b) and (c) state and imply that the teacher has a monopoly of the knowledge and thought present in the classroom, and that the students have nothing whatsoever to contribute to understanding the phenomena under discussion. As for (d), (e), (f), (g) and (h), we have students conforming to the actions of the teacher rather than exercising any initiative whatsoever. And the hierarchy of the teacher over the students is further illustrated by the teacher's equating his own professional authority with the authority of knowledge, and also by his treatment of students as nothing more than objects. Of course, we might well assume that the teacher has substantially more knowledge of the subject at hand than any given student. But that is not the same as the teacher's viewing the students as having no knowledge whatsoever and treating them accordingly.

Who was this man who had these ideas? Here is a brief biography from the *Britannica Concise Encyclopedia*:

*Freire, Paulo* (1921–1997) Brazilian educator. His ideas developed from his experience teaching literacy to Brazil's peasants. His interactive methods, which encouraged students to question the teacher, often led to literacy in as little as 30 hours of instruction. In 1963 he was appointed director of the Brazilian National Literacy Program, but he was jailed following a military coup in 1964. He went into exile, returning in 1979 to help found the Workers Party. His seminal work was *Pedagogy of the Oppressed* (Pappas, 2002: 695–696).

Here we see Freire not only as an educator but also as a non-violent revolutionary, someone who threatened the military regime sufficiently to be thrown in jail. We also see him as an individual who focused not on literate middle-class students but on illiterate peasants as well as on workers. We see him as a highly effective educator in his efforts to teach literacy, someone whose effectiveness was recognized by Brazilian authorities, who appointed him director of the Brazilian National Literacy Program just prior to the coup. Freire was born to a middle-class family in northern Brazil, but they became impoverished by the economic crash of 1929, and he vowed to struggle against the hunger he shared with many others.

Freire's overall approach to human behavior is broad and interactive, just as the above biography cites his "interactive methods," meshing with an interactive worldview or metaphysical stance. He states this orientation as follows:

> To deny the importance of subjectivity in the process of transforming the world and history is naive and simplistic. It is to admit the impossible: a world without men. This objectivistic position is as ingenuous as that of subjectivism, which postulates men without a world. World and men do not exist apart from each other, they exist in constant interaction. Marx does not espouse such a dichotomy, nor does any other critical, realistic thinker. What Marx criticized and scientifically destroyed was not subjectivity, but subjectivism and psychologism. Just as objective social reality exists not by chance, but as the product of human action, so it is not transformed by chance. If men produce social reality (which in the "inversion of the praxis" turns back upon them and conditions them), then transforming that reality is an historical task, a task for men (1970: 35–36).

We may note Freire's breadth in his view of *both* subjectivity *and* objectivity as important, whereas subjectivism and objectivism are equally one-sided. For example, we might think of subjectivity as emphasizing the behavior of the individual, as emphasized in parts III (Personality Structures) and V (The Situation), with objectivity emphasizing the behavior of the group or society as a whole, as in part IV (Social Structures). Part II (Physical and Biological Structures), especially chapter 2 with its focus on individual perception, also emphasizes subjectivity. Thus, Freire ranges widely over the material in this book. As we can see from his critique of the one-sided nature of "banking" education as well as this quoted passage, his approach is most interactive. Students and teachers should both be learning from one another. Freire's activist orientation to transforming an oppressive society is similar to Illich's focus on deschooling society (chapter 8). They both were exiles from Latin America, with Illich being a defrocked priest, and they influenced one another during their exiles. And they both called for fundamental changes in both social and personality structures.

Freire has much to say about the dangers involved in liberating the oppressed masses from their oppressors, for he sees them as all too easily changing roles and becoming oppressors themselves. If they have no vision of what freedom in fact involves, they will escape from freedom on being liberated and turn on their former oppressors, thus continuing the existence of an oppressive society. Freire's analysis seems to apply to Chua's analysis (chapter 7) of the impact of attempts to insert democratic or egalitarian cultural values, but without a precedent of widespread liberty and justice. This can very rapidly yield societies where a minority dominates a majority. From our own perspective, we might understand such behavior as a reversal of former patterns of social stratification, where stratification is continued but those who were on bottom formerly rise to the top of the hierarchy, and vice-versa. Such a continuation of social stratification appears to be in turn a product of a stratified worldview or metaphysical stance, where no alternative worldview—such as an interactive one—is available. From Freire's alternative perspective, the oppressors require liberation along with the oppressed, just as teachers who open up to learning from their students are able to move beyond the static nature of their own understanding. He would see Marx's idea of a temporary "dictatorship of the proletariat" as dehumanizing the proletariat by treating them as things that can be manipulated rather than as fellow human beings. In Freire's view, the oppressed must continue to experience a pedagogy helping them to develop consciousness if indeed they are to be truly and authentically liberated, a development that would precede the construction of a genuine democracy.

Freire's techniques were practiced by a group of educators who entered a given agricultural area and took notes on the key words that the peasants were using, such as "slum," "profession," "government," "Afro-Brazilian dancing," "land," "food," "rain," "plow," "wealth," "work," and "sugar mill" (1973: 82–84). Such words along with their associated images were then discussed within "culture circles" that included both peasants and educators. They were linked to a given theme that involved a fundamental contradiction within society, such as "domination" versus "liberation" within what Freire calls a "critical dialogue." Such dialogues apparently involved genuine egalitarian interaction, and not any imposition by educators on peasants, and vice-versa. As such dialogues continued, both peasants and educators learned to link that contradiction within society to the words that they were using, and those words took on new meaning. For example, they might come to see their previous approach to work as shaping their previous fatalistic and conformist orientation to life, thus making possible their being dominated. The new meaning they might then give to "work" coupled with a new approach to their work might then, following Freire, point toward their own liberation by expanding their understanding of themselves and their world with its problems along with directions for solutions.

Thus, when peasants learned to speak the word "work," they were "saying their own word," "naming the world" and "transforming the world." They were linking their many ideas in a way that pointed them toward understanding both their problems and directions they could take toward solving them. A key direction was lifting themselves out of alienation, fatalism and hopelessness, and toward hope, intellectual development and emotional development. They became transformed into actors on the world stage.

Following Freire, they were changed from illiterate peasants inhabiting a "culture of silence" into individuals who could say, "I now realize I am a man, an educated man." Thus, when they learned to speak a true word they were learning to transform themselves and the world. They were learning to say, "I work, and working I transform the world." "Before this, words meant nothing to me; now they speak to me and I can make them speak." "Now we will no longer be a dead weight on the cooperative farm."

Freire uses the word "praxis" to refer to the combination of thought and action:

> But men's activity consists of action and reflection: it is praxis; it is transformation of the world. And as praxis, it requires theory to illuminate it. Men's activity is theory and practice; it is reflection and action. It cannot ... be reduced to either verbalism or activism.... [A] revolution is achieved with neither verbalism nor activism, but rather with praxis, that is, with *reflection* and *action* directed at the structures to be transformed. The revolutionary effort to transform these structures radically cannot designate its leaders as its *thinkers* and the oppressed as mere *doers* (1970: 119–120).

A key question we might pose is whether or not Freire's educational work with peasants in less developed countries has relevance for people in contemporary modernized societies. Further, Freire wrote in the late 1960s, at a time when young people in the Western world were attempting a cultural revolution which they believed would transform society but which in fact failed to go beyond a certain point. Richard Shaull, who wrote the introduction to Freire's book, attempts to make the case for its broad relevance for modern societies. Yet there appear to be fundamental gaps in Freire's approach that largely ignore the complexities of both less developed and modern societies. As we saw in the widespread efforts of students in the United States to develop a cultural revolution in the late 1960s that would transform the fundamental structures of modern society, severe limitations accompanied their achievements. For example, by focusing on the negative aspects of the educational system—as well as modern society in general—they failed to build on the enormous achievements of that institution, such as whatever progress had been made in understanding the complexities of human behavior. As a result, they had little understanding of their own limitations along with the strengths of modern society. More generally, that ignorance prevented them from moving beyond a stratified approach to the scientific method and a stratified worldview: for all their efforts at change, they failed to develop a systematic direction for changing the epistemology and metaphysics of contemporary society.

This failure appears to be Freire's problem no less than the student revolutionaries of the late 1960s. His general vision about human possibilities, his view of the enormous damage wrought by patterns of social stratification and his own commitment and achievements with respect to educating illiterate peasants are all most inspiring. Yet his whole approach appears to throw out the baby with the bath, just as the student revolutionaries of the 1960s generally did the same. He and his educators in dialogue with peasants had limited understanding of their own situation, much less the enormously complex situation of their society. They tried to invent a new kind of society on their own, instead of building on the thousands of years of earlier efforts. Such building involves the question of learning from one's oppressors, and not only attempting to liberate them. By turning to the work of Marx, Lenin, Mao, Castro and Che Guevera, Freire signaled his desire for a rapid revolution which would turn society upside down. Yet granting the enormous problems within less developed and modern societies, solutions are not achieved easily. Those attempting to change society might do well to learn their own limitations, and they might also learn the strengths of whatever they are attempting to change. Freire's slogans are most inspiring, but slogans have their limitations: they oversimplify what is in fact enormously complex. Nevertheless, we have much to learn from Freire's vision.

## Some Implications

Given Hoyle's concern with the nuclear capabilities of some contemporary societies, we might assume that he supports the idea of a growing gap, specified by hypothesis (1). And we might also assume that he supports hypothesis (2), given his interest in the incredible breadth of perspective of the Black Cloud by contrast with the narrowness of national leaders who attempted to destroy the Cloud. Scheff strongly supports hypothesis (1) with an analysis suggesting increasing hidden shame in modern societies, with one result being the rage that is illustrated by Rosie and James. Such repression is for Scheff an instance of a narrow approach to human behavior, contributing to such phenomena as World War II, and thus he also supports (2). As for Paolo Freire, his support for (1) is quite strong, given his view as to the negative impact of the "banking" education that he saw as prevalent throughout less developed as well as modern societies. That kind of education was, in his view, strongly stratified, depriving students of the kind of education they needed, supporting (2).

Yet we must avoid oversimplifying the complexity of human behavior along with the problems of achieving fundamental changes in modern society, for that mistake of Freire and other revolutionaries can have drastic consequences. We should take note of the tragedies that we have seen in Stalinist Russia along with Mao Tse Tung's China. We should also take note of the failures of the student revolutionaries of the late 1960s. For example, Marx's idea of praxis—also central to Freire's efforts—is indeed an extremely important concept, for it links the momentary thoughts and actions of the individual with the very transformation of society as a whole. Yet in order to make that journey we may well need an epistemology and a metaphysics that opens up to the complexity of all the phenomena that we will meet along the way. Such an epistemology might teach us to remain open to learning from all the phenomena we will meet along the path of that journey, following Peirce's pragmatic maxim: "Do not block the path of inquiry."

As for images or metaphors, Hoyle's "Black Cloud" with its ability to communicate at the speed of light and the enormity of its brain offers us a vision of a being's potential for interaction. Our contemporary internet exemplifies that potential for rapid communication and depth of communication. But without a clear direction for how to integrate information as a basis for solving problems, which neither the Cloud nor the internet provides and which is certainly not provided by a stratified worldview, all of that potential can come to naught. With respect to Scheff, his Part/Whole Approach to methods provides us with an image of integrating phenomena in a momentary scene with phenomena in society as a whole. The slash indicates that the two types of phenomena are equally important, an approach that is very far from what social scientists generally practice. Freire's concept of the "culture of silence" depicts the situation of the illiterate peasants whom he taught: they were oppressed, and their ignorance kept them in that state. But as they became literate they learned to "say their own word," to "name the world," and to "transform the world" as a result. As one peasant said, "I now realize I am a man, an educated man."

## CHAPTER 10

# "Heart"

## Negative versus Positive Reinforcement

IF INDEED A MISSING LINK to our understanding of human behavior resides in the complexity of the situation, then human emotions—with all of their transitory nature, invisibility and power—are central to that link. Scheff's analysis of shame at the micro and macro level (chapter 9), building on the work of Retzinger and many others, alerts us to the centrality of emotions in human conduct. It also alerts us to the importance of perception in detecting and interpreting fleeting yet highly significant feelings. We have of course already been introduced to that significance in preceding chapters. Indeed, our focus throughout this book has been on a gap—between aspirations and their fulfillment—which may become highly motivating. Metaphorically, following Orwell in his *Nineteen Eighty-Four,* we can view the march of technological development in modern society as pushing us all into Room 101, where we are being confronted by our deepest fears. Yet, following Berger's *Ways of Seeing* (chapter 2), advertising succeeds in creating a "thicket of unreality" that smothers us in illusions and prevents us from seeing our situation. That analysis is much the same as Boorstin's conclusion in *The Image* (discussed in chapter 2) that pseudo-events in the mass media teach us to avoid reality. Thus, as we move into Room 101 we fail to see what is in fact happening to us and what will shortly happen to us.

We begin with A. E. van Vogt's *The Players of Null-A* (1948), his science-fiction sequel to *The World of Null-A* (1945). Both books are based on Alfred Korzybski's theory of "general semantics." It is rare for an author of fiction to base his work on non-fiction, yet it indicates his breadth of perspective. Gilbert Gosseyn—pronounced "go-sane"—is attempting in a future world to teach Prince Ashargin, who had been humiliated throughout his life, to re-examine those scenes of humiliation from a much broader perspective. Following Scheff's and Retzinger's ideas as to the destructive impact of unacknowledged shame (chapter 9), Prince Ashargin learns to acknowledge his shame along with other emotions and comes to interpret his own past behavior in a far more positive fashion. As a result he gains inner strength, and he continues to build on that strength through his subsequent decisive and perceptive actions. We can see van Vogt's analysis as giving us a fuller understanding of Scheff's and Retzinger's thesis. Also, since van Vogt focuses on Ashargin's reviewing specific scenes from his past, he emphasizes the importance of perception as well as the momentary situation. But there is much more to this work, which is full of powerful metaphors.

If our immersion in illusions and pseudo-events—following Berger and Boorstin—has taught us to avoid seeing our movement toward Room 101, then Vidich and Bensman succeed in teaching us other procedures of avoidance in their *Small Town in Mass Society* (1960). The Springdalers, who live in a small town in upper New York State, have unfulfilled goals, just like the rest of us, and their techniques of avoidance appear to be much the same as everyone else's. There is "the technique of particularization," which teaches us to avoid our perception of inequalities through a narrow focus on relatively trivial phenomena. There is also "the falsification of memory," where we learn to focus on the present rather than on our long-term aspirations. For example, the Springdalers bury themselves in specialized work and avoid thinking about their failure to fulfill their aspirations. Such techniques might be applied equally to our own avoidance to take seriously the long-term increasing gap between expectations and their fulfillment which is hypothesized in figure I.1.

Lawrence Busch's "A Tentative Guide to Constructing the Future" (1976), based on his doctoral dissertation, provides us with a general approach to fundamental social change that centers on the importance of people's image of the future, thus following a situational orientation. Its orientation to change foreshadows our emphasis on praxis in chapter 11. In addition, we can gain understanding of just how negative and positive reinforcements come together with images as well as change. For example, Busch builds on the work of Thomas Kuhn (chapter 3), extending his ideas about scientific revolutions to society as a whole. He also builds on the work of Fred Polak, a Dutch sociologist whose *The Image of the Future* (1973) suggested that such images are perhaps the most powerful force in society that can work to produce fundamental change. Busch's approach achieves its strength through the systematic integration of a number of important approaches to change within the literatures of social science and philosophy. As a result, he achieves the kind of breadth that meshes with the Web and Part/Whole Approach to the scientific method.

## Van Vogt's *The Players of Null-A*

A. E. van Vogt's sequel to *The Worlds of Null-A* (1945)—*The Players of Null-A* (1948)—carries to a conclusion the struggle of Gilbert Gosseyn to discover his identity, to combat the forces in the galaxy led by Enro the Red attempting to achieve totalitarian control, and to create a direction for the next stage in the development of all human beings. In a most unusual introduction to a science fiction novel, van Vogt tells us in a 1970 revised edition of *Worlds*—originally printed as a serial in *Astounding Science Fiction*—about the impact of the book. In addition to numerous awards and translations, it stimulated great interest in the field of General Semantics, with students eager to study under Alfred Korzybski at the Institute of General Semantics in Lakewood, Connecticut, and with courses in the field developing in many universities. Van Vogt summarizes his approach in this way:

> Because of the limitations of his nervous system, Man can only see part of truth, never the whole of it. In describing the limitation, Korzybski coined the term "ladder of abstraction." Abstraction, as he used it, did not have a lofty or symbolical thought connection. It meant, "to abstract from," that is to take from something a part of the whole. His assumption: in observing a process of nature, one can only abstract—i.e. perceive—a portion of it.... In *World,* we have the Null-A (non-Aristotelian) man, who thinks gradational scale, not black and white—without, however, becoming a rebel or a cynic, or a conspirator, in any current meaning of the term. A little bit of this in the Communist hierarchies, Asia and Africa in general, and our own Wall Street and Deep South, and in other either-or thinking areas ... And we'd soon have a more progressive planet (1945/1970: 10).

Use of Korzybski's concept of the "ladder of abstraction" is fundamental to our own understanding of a Web and Part/Whole Approach to the scientific method that is able to follow the scientific ideal of openness to all phenomena relevant to a given problem. Korzybski's stress on the importance of gradational thought, which is emphasized within the scientific method, is most understandable, given the dichotomous emphasis within our everyday way of thinking and speaking. We can see the dangers of a purely dichotomous mode of thinking following his illustrations of stereotyped or prejudiced thought applied within "Communist hierarchies" as well as "our own Wall Street." But what he appears to object to is not any use of dichotomies whatsoever—for we would not be able to think or speak without them—but rather dichotomies not accompanied by gradational thought as well. Thus, we can have a clear either-or definition of communism, but then we can see any one of us on a gradational scale with reference to our adherence to that set of beliefs. We might add that Van Vogt's effort to convey Korzybski's ideas in novels illustrates a third aspect of language: its capacity to convey images or metaphors. Korzybski himself did not discuss this, but we have seen the importance of this capacity in our own earlier chapters.

Neither van Vogt nor Korzybski see human language as isolated from the rest of human behavior. Just as chapters 9, 10 and 11 focus not only on the "head"—including language—but also on the "heart" and the "hand," respectively, so do van Vogt and Korzybski emphasize the importance of human emotions and actions in relation to language. They focus on language because there is so little understanding of its complex nature. But they fully recognize that it is tied closely to our emotions, and that it is also a tool for generating important questions and solving problems. They see the implications of penetrating the complexities of language as vast. For van Vogt and Korzybski, it is a "Null-A" or non-Aristotelian approach to linguistic complexity which holds unbelievable promise for the future of the human race. By this they mean an approach that is not exclusively dichotomous or static. In Kelly's terms (chapter 2), it is an approach that is "propositional" versus "pre-emptive" or "constellatory," and thus it carries a scientific approach into everyday language. Van Vogt suggests this idea in the last chapter of *Players*:

> *Possibly, the most important requirement of our civilization is the development of a Null-A oriented political economy. It can be stated categorically that no such system has yet been developed. The field is wide open for bold and imaginative men and women to create a system that will free mankind of war, poverty and tension* (1948: 186).

We begin by referring to key episodes from van Vogt's *The Worlds of Null-A* in order to set the stage for a more detailed presentation of his *The Players of Null-A*. The action begins with Gilbert Gosseyn's identity being questioned by Nordegg, a store-owner from Cress Village, Florida, on an Earth existing some five centuries from now. They are in a large hotel room along with many others, located not far from the Games Machine, which would be conducting a thirty-day competition beginning the following day to assess the degree to which the competitors had successfully achieved training in null-A thinking. Such thinking had become a growing part of Earth's mental environment for several hundred years. No less than twenty-one games would be involved, and passing all of them would insure a competitor a passage to Venus, where a genuine null-A society—by contrast with Earth's A society—existed. Gosseyn had studied long and hard for this day, including a careful analysis of all of the records of the games over the last twenty years. He saw himself not only as six feet one inch tall, age thirty-four and weight one hundred eighty-five, but also as a long-time resident of Cress Village. But Nordegg, who knows everyone in that town, challenges Gosseyn's identity, a lie detector confirms his suspicions, and Gosseyn is evicted from the hotel with the realization that he has no idea of who he is.

The focus of *Worlds* is on Gosseyn's strenuous efforts to foil a plot by Enro the Red, ruler of the Galactic Empire, to extend his empire over the entire galaxy and, in the process, destroy Venus and subjugate Earth. Although Gosseyn is not able to enter the Games, he has succeeded in developing null-A abilities, and he also has an enlarged cortex which he must somehow learn to use if he is to save the solar system. More specifically, he begins to learn how to link his thalamus, the seat of emotions, to his enlarged cortex, and as a result gains incredible power to move instantaneously between two points in space, to move other objects as well, and also to harness and deliver enormous energy for destructive purposes through a systematic use of his mind. Gosseyn is unable, however, to prevent Venus from being invaded by an army of millions from the Galactic Empire. Although the null-A Venusians suffer heavy losses, they succeed in overcoming the forces of the Empire as a result of their own ability to link emotions with intellect and achieve both intellectual superiority as well as enormous emotional commitment to achieving victory. Their approach is similar to the techniques used by Gandhi and his supporters in freeing India from British rule, to be discussed in chapter 11.

It is in *The Players of Null-A* that Gosseyn learns to move across the galaxy and confront not only Enro the Red on his home planet of Gorgzid but also the Follower, who is also the High Priest of Gorgzid. Both of them have unusual abilities. However, they ultimately prove to be no match for a null-A individual with an enlarged cortex, especially when that cortex has been integrated with the thalamus. Enro can see and hear what is going on in other places, and the Follower is a member of a race of Predictors who are able to see into the future to an extent. Working together, they initiate a battle with the Galactic League for supremacy over the galaxy, and they are close to succeeding with Predictors manning their warships and anticipating the movements of the League. Gosseyn's mind is transported into the body of Prince Ashargin, heir to the throne of Gorgzid, whose parents along with their retinue had been murdered by Enro when he seized Gorgzid. That transportation is achieved by an unseen player who finally reveals himself at the close of *Players* as an individual who had escaped from another galaxy which was self-destructing, and he had to maneuver Gosseyn into a certain position in order to reveal the history of that vast migration. Gosseyn trains Ashargin in null-A principles, giving him the strength to aid in opposing Enro, who once again is threatening to destroy Venus. Gosseyn manages to reach Venus and help the null-A Venusians develop effective defenses against the invading army of the Galactic Empire. Enro is defeated, and Gosseyn is able to confront and vanquish the Follower with his own Sleeping God, whom Gosseyn awakens to rise up, accuse the Follower of being a traitor and demand his death.

The significance of *Players* for our purposes is in its many powerful metaphors along with the details of the action. For example, the question of Gosseyn's true identity suggests the same question for every human being: Are we far more, potentially, than the relatively insignificant creatures—within the world scheme of things—that we appear to be? Although we don't have Gosseyn's enlarged cortex, have we somehow failed to learn how to educate our minds in such a way that each of us can actually move toward our vast potential? Prince Ashargin has led a life of abject humiliation enforced by Enro for years, a life that may not be so different from the lives that so many of us led when we were young, yet can Gosseyn teach him to make use of his potential? Van Vogt gives us a glimpse of Ashargin's earlier experiences:

> Another mind had once controlled this body—the mind of Ashargin. It had been an unintegrated, insecure mind, dominated by fears and uncontrollable emotions that were imprinted on the nervous system and muscles of the body. The deadly part of that domination was that the living flesh of Ashargin would react to all that internal imbalance on the unconscious level. Even Gilbert Gosseyn, knowing what was wrong, would have scarcely any influence over those violent physical compulsions—until he could train the body of Ashargin to the cortical-thalamic sanity of Null-A (1948: 24).

Gosseyn imparts a basic approach to the Prince: "Prince, every time you take a positive action on the basis of a high-level consideration, you establish certainties of courage, self-assurance and skills" (1948:100). Such general ideas were followed by more specific procedures:

> In the bedroom Gosseyn rigged up a wall recorder to repeat a three-minute relaxation pattern. Then he lay down. During the hour that followed he never quite went to sleep.... Lying there, he allowed his mind to idle around the harsher memories of Ashargin's prison years. Each time he came to an incident that had made a profound impression he talked silently to the younger Ashargin.... From his greater height of understanding, he asssured the younger individual that the affective incident must be looked at from a different angle than that of a frightened youth. Assured him that fear of pain and fear of death were emotions that could be overcome, and that in short the shock incident which had

once affected him so profoundly no longer had any meaning for him. More than that, in future he would have better understanding of such moments, and he would never again be affected in an adverse fashion (1948: 115–116).

A crucial technique within Null-A training is the "cortical-thalamic pause," which is analogous to the idea of reflexive behavior (chapter 9). That pause is especially important when an individual is under severe threat and is tempted to act solely on the basis of emotions like fear or shame rather than to make good use of intellectual capacities. Under enormous pressures, Gosseyn-Ashargin responds:

> I am now relaxing ... And all stimuli are making the full circuit of my ner-vous system, along my spinal cord, to the thalamus, *through* the thalamus and up to the cortex, and *through* the cortex, and then, and only then, back through the thalamus and down into the nervous system. Always, I am consciously aware of the stimulus moving up to and through the cortex.
>
> That was the key. That was the difference between the Null-A super-man and the animal man of the galaxy. The thalamus—the seat of emo-tions—and the cortex—the seat of discrimination—integrated, balanced in a warm and wonderful relationship. Emotions, not done away with, but made richer and more relaxed by the association with that part of the mind—the cortex—that could savor unnumbered subtle differences in the flow of feeling. All through the palace, men would be struggling in a developing panic against the powerful force that had struck at them. Once that panic began it would not stop short of hysteria.... Yet all that the individual had to do was to stop for an instant, and think: *The stimu-lus is now going through my cortex. I'm thinking and feeling, not just feeling* (1948: 177–178).

Throughout these two novels Gosseyn undergoes one major threat to his life after another, and these are also threats to the population of Venus with its many millions. In addition, they are threats to the outcome of the entire history of the human race, with Null-A education offering hope for mankind's emergence from its wars, poverty and other funda-mental social problems. We might see Gosseyn's sense of urgency as a metaphor for the urgency within the situation of modern society. In the case of *Worlds* and *Players* the threats are both visible and relatively invis-ible. For example, there are visible threats such as Gosseyn's being faced personally by a blaster or Venus being invaded by battleships with armed men. A relatively invisible threat is the persistence of Aristotelian modes of thinking which are the basis, following van Vogt, for war as well as most other social problems.

In these novels Van Vogt creates a number of metaphors that succeed in communicating many of the complexities of Korzybski's elaborate theories and, in the process, help us to understand the nature of an interactive worldview. By providing these metaphors, he demonstrates the importance of literature in general and perception in particular in conveying abstract ideas. He also succeeds in issuing a challenge to educators and social scientists to investigate the possibilities for delivering on humanistic ideals. For example, there is John Dewey's ideal—which Van Vogt would certainly support—that "the supreme test of all political institutions and industrial arrangements shall be the contribution they make to the all-around growth of every member of society" (1920/1948: 186). Van Vogt's metaphors, seen within the framework of an interactive worldview, point a direction for helping the individual to change from negative to positive reinforcements. For example, Gosseyn trained Ashargin to reinterpret his past negative experiences, helping him to raise them to the surface and acknowledge them—following the emphasis of Scheff and Retzinger (chapter 9)—and eliminate their function as negative reinforcements. By Gosseyn suggesting that "in the future he would have better understanding of such moments" as a result of this analysis, Van Vogt shapes that analysis into a positive reinforcement. We see this also in the "cortical-thalamic pause," which enables the individual to escape from an endless cycle of negative reinforcements by introducing an intellectual understanding of any situation from a broad perspective.

A key problem with Van Vogt's novels, viewed not from the perspective of their effectiveness as science fiction but rather from the perspective of their insights into human behavior, is their focus on the work of Korzybski to the exclusion of the full range of knowledge that social scientists have developed. This is more the fault of social scientists than of Van Vogt, for they generally have failed to integrate their specialized studies so as to create a platform of knowledge on which Van Vogt and others wishing to apply social science knowledge can stand. Without far more specific ideas on how to achieve, for example, the "cortical thalamic pause" and a Null-A education, we have little to go by. We have much less to go by when it comes to the possibility of constructing an entire Null-A society. Van Vogt's and Korzybski's ideas and ideals are visionary in the best sense of the word. But we have yet to learn how to proceed, one step at a time, so as to convert such visions into reality.

## Vidich's and Bensman's *Small Town in Mass Society*

Arthur J. Vidich and Joseph Bensman collaborated on a study in the late 1950s of "Springdale," a town in upper New York State, publishing their results as *Small Town in Mass Society: Class, Power and Religion in a*

*Rural Community* (1960). Springdale township had a population of only about 3,000 when Vidich and Bensman did their study. Economically, the central village—with a population of about 1,000—serves as a farm trading center, with retail establishments having farm merchandise and with the presence of a milk collecting plant. Lumber is the chief economic resource of the community, with a commercial sawmill operated by two families. Vidich and Bensman saw their study as "an attempt to explore the foundations of social life in a community which lacks the power to control the institutions that regulate and determine its existence" (1960: x). More specifically, they explored the divergence between the way the community saw itself and institutional realities, and they examined how individuals managed to adjust to that divergence.

Springdalers generally hold negative stereotypes of metropolitan life, such as seeing their existence as a breeding ground for corruption, as an unwholesome environment, as a hotbed of un-American sentiment, and as opposed to rural ways. Supposedly, Washington, DC, is full of parasites who live off hard-working country folk, industrial workers are overpaid, labor leaders foment trouble, and universities along with big city churches are full of atheists.

Since modern society is becoming more and more urbanized, and since the proportion of the population engaged in farming has been becoming ever smaller, we can begin to understand such prejudices as foreshadowing fundamental problems for the Springdalers. Just as the Springdalers are stereotyping urbanized life as evil, they are also stereotyping themselves as good, and this sets them up for a fall. How do Springdalers manage to cope with their failure to fulfill their goals? One overall hypothesis in this book is that there exists an increasing gap within modern society between aspirations or expectations and their fulfillment. It is that problem which, in our view, is the basis for an invisible crisis in modern society. To the extent that a large gap generally exists for the Springdalers, how are they able to function with such a gap? This problem, according to our hypothesis, affects all of us moderns. To the extent that we are aware of such a gap for our own personal history, that generally will constitute a negative reinforcement for us. But, following this chapter's title, if we have procedures for removing any such awareness from our momentary experiences, then we may be able to avoid any such negative reinforcements. We might recall here the analysis of Berger (chapter 2) on illusions fostered by advertising which divert us from reality. Vidich and Bensman help us to fill out this picture of avoidance. These are ways of reducing negative reinforcements in the short run. But in the long run they appear to have disastrous consequences.

Vidich and Bensman focus in their last chapter on four phenomena, all of which illustrate a gap between aspirations or expectations and their fulfillment (1970: 291–292):

(1) The small-town resident assumes the role of the warm, friendly, sociable, helpful good neighbor and friend. However, the forms of social competition and the struggle for individual success ... [tend] to devalue his neighbors' success....

(2) The goal of success as a major value and meaning in life stands in contrast to the inaccessibility of the means to achieving success ... [which] are not equally available to all groups....

(3) The illusion of democratic control over his own affairs given by the formal structure of government stands in sharp contrast to the actual basis of local politics.... Most of the professionals, the old aristocrats, workers, traditional farmers and all of the shack people stand entirely outside the decision making process....

(4) The belief and illusion of local independence and self-determination prevent a recognition of the central place of national and state institutions in local affairs. The reality of outside institutional dominance ... is given only subliminal, pragmatic recognition.

Given such fundamental gaps between aspirations and their fulfillment, how do Springdalers manage to cope with them? We noted in our discussion of Orwell's *Nineteen Eighty-Four* (chapter 8) two major metaphors: being pushed into Room 101 and learning to speak Newspeak, both of which lead to a betrayal of one's deepest cultural values and thus temporarily reduce one's gap between expectations and their fulfillment. Do the Springdalers also somehow manage to reduce that gap? If so, how do they achieve this, and does this yield insight into how the rest of us manage to do the same?

Vidich and Bensman analyze the "major modes of adjustment" to those four gaps described above under six headings, emphasizing three in particular: (1) the repression of inconvenient facts, (2) the falsification of memory and the substitution of goals, and (6) the externalization of the self. We can best understand these modes of adjustment in relation to figure I.1. They all work, in one way or another, to reduce the gap between the top curve of expectations and the bottom curve of the fulfillment of expectations.

## (1) The Repression of Inconvenient Facts

All these explicit mentions of community dependence are made in the context of highly specific detailed cases. No generalization sums up these detailed statements, so that individuals are not explicitly aware of the total amount of their dependence. Particularizations prevent the realization of the total impression. The technique of particularization is one of the most pervasive ways of avoiding reality. It operates to make possible not only the failure to recognize dependence but also the avoidance of the realities of social class and inequalities. The Springdaler is able to maintain his equalitarian ideology because he avoids generalizing about class differences. The attributes of class are seen only in terms of the particular behavior of particular persons (1970: 299).

This "technique of particularization" apparently was also used by the authors of textbooks on social problems whom Mills criticized (chapter 6): "The level of abstraction which characterizes these texts is so low that often they seem to be empirically confused for lack of abstraction to knit them together. They display bodies of meagerly connected facts, ranging from rape in rural districts to public housing, and intellectually sanction this low level of abstraction." By staying at a low level on the ladder of abstraction, they violate a fundamental aspect of the scientific method of shuttling up and down that ladder. As a result, they are able to avoid defining a general and important problem, which has to do, for example, with the contradiction between the cultural value of equality and the Springdalers' own failure to fulfill that value. There is also the same failure of those at the top of the social hierarchy. As another example, they fail to see the contradiction between their own cultural value of freedom and the actuality of the community's limited power relative to external forces.

## (2) The Falsification of Memory and the Substitution of Goals

The realization of lack of fulfillment of aspiration and ambition might pose an unsolvable personal problem if the falsification of memory did not occur, and if the hopes and ambitions of a past decade or two remained salient in the present perspective. But the individual, as he passes through time, does not live in spans of decades or years. Rather, he lives in terms of seasons, days and hours and the focus of his attention is turned to immediate pressures, pleasures and events.... As they [hopes and aspirations] are in process of disappearing, other thoughts of a more concrete and specific nature occupy the individual's attention, and new goals are unconsciously substituted for those that are being abandoned.... As a consequence, his present self, instead of entertaining the youthful dream of a 500–acre farm, entertains the plan to buy a home freezer by the fall (1970: 303).

The technique of particularization and the falsification of memory both involve movement down language's ladder of abstraction, with the former staying with the present and the latter erasing the past. What is happening in the case of both techniques is much the same as an abandonment of the potential for understanding that language offers to all of us. Metaphorically, this is like learning to think and speak Newspeak, as explained by Orwell (chapter 8): "Don't you see that the whole aim of Newspeak is to narrow the range of thought? In the end we shall make thoughtcrime literally impossible, because there will be no words in which to express it." By abandoning abstract concept in favor of concrete ones, the Springdalers are abandoning the very tool which, more than any other, makes them human. By resorting to the technique of particularization and the falsification of memory, they are learning to speak Newspeak. No Big Brother is needed to alter the Springdaler's language, since they learn to alter it themselves. Further, this alteration also enables them to escape from Room 101, where they would have to face up to the destruction of their most fundamental ideals or values.

## (6) The Externalization of the Self

> The greatest dangers to a system of illusions which is threatened by an uncompromising reality are introspection and thought.... [H]e must falsify ... facts in order to live in the present. In order to succeed in avoiding the reality of the situation, he must give a major portion of the life span to developing forms and techniques of self-avoidance.... The major technique of self-avoidance is work.... Religious activities such as suppers, choirs and fund raising involve a great deal of physical and social effort and support the process of continuous externalization.... But the people of Springdale are unwilling to recognize the defeat of their values, their personal impotence in the face of larger events and any failure in their way of life. By techniques of self-avoidance and self-deception, they strive to avoid facing issues which, if recognized, would threaten the total fabric of their personal and social existence.... Because they do not recognize their defeat, they are not defeated. The compromises, the self-deception and the self-avoidance are mechanisms which work; for, in operating on the basis of contradictory, illogical and conflicting assumptions, they are able to cope in their day-to-day lives with their immediate problems in a way that permits some degree of satisfaction, recognition and achievement (1970: 311–320).

It appears that Vidich and Bensman succeed—to a fair degree—in describing not just the lives of the Springdalers in the late 1960s, and not just the lives of contemporary sociologists, but also the lives of all of us living today in contemporary societies. Figure I.1 is indeed a very bare indication of the nature of our lives. But when it is accompanied by Vidich's and Bensman's analysis, that figure springs to life. They are able to succeed with their "major modes of adjustment" much like Simmel (chapter 4) in leaping up from the very concrete to the very abstract. In this way Vidich and Bensman are able to achieve what Mills called for in his advice that we shuttle up and down language's levels of abstraction (chapter 6). Instead of presenting us with "bodies of meagerly connected facts," they are able to connect the dots. Instead of using techniques of particularization, the falsification of memory, and the externalization of self, they refuse to particularize, falsify, and externalize in such ways and refuse to enter a realm of illusion. Their understanding of Springdalers, because it penetrates nothing less than the Springdalers' worldview, is also an understanding of modern society.

Yet that minority of Springdalers who had some genuine understanding of their situation were unable to communicate that understanding to the townspeople in general because it would challenge the very fabric of their existence with no clear direction for solving their problems. Analogously, Vidich and Bensman are unable to communicate their insights about the illusions of sociologists and the rest of the inhabitants of modern society. For their understanding, at least as indicated in *Small Town in Mass Society*, provides no clear direction for abandoning our illusions and solving our fundamental problems. The focus of our own book also aims at the uncovering of at least some of the illusions of sociologists and modern society in general, namely, our hypothesized increasing gap between aspirations or expectations and their fulfillment. In addition, however, we aim to offer a direction for solving our problems, as illustrated by our second hypothesis on the role of a stratified worldview and the possibilities of an interactive worldview. Further, we require an alternative epistemological stance or approach to the scientific method to help us move toward that worldview.

## Busch's "A Tentative Guide to Constructing the Future"

If the late 1960s gave rise to enthusiasm about the possibilities of changing modern society by means of a cultural revolution, then the 1970s inaugurated critical assessments of what went wrong and how those ideals can in fact be brought to fruition. Of course, there was also a good deal of pessimism and cynicism, but Lawrence Busch shows neither of those traits. His "A Tentative Guide to Constructing the Future: Self-Conscious Millenarianism" (1976) was based on his recently completed doctoral dissertation, "Macrosocial Change in Historical Perspective: An Analysis of Epochs" (1974). Fundamental historical changes in Western society—for example, "a Protestant-capitalist world-view was able to supplant the decaying world-view of the Medieval church"—were not planned on the basis of social science knowledge. Yet it may indeed be possible, on the basis of such knowledge of historical failures and successes in achieving such changes, to come up with a list of what appears to be required for the achievement of basic social change throughout modern society. Busch does not claim that his list of seven factors is complete, considering it rather as no more than a useful step in the right direction, and we may thus view it as an extended hypothesis.

There are two centerpieces of Busch's approach. One is a work by the Dutch sociologist Fred Polak, *The Image of the Future,* which initially appeared in two volumes (1961) and was later combined into a single volume (1973). Polak reviewed the history of Western religion, coming up with this overall conclusion: "The more powerful the *image* of the future is, the more powerfully it acts in determining the actual future" (1961, II: 341). Yet the question remains open as to the nature of those images of the future—along with the historical situations in which they were originated—which proved to be successful. The second centerpiece of Busch's analysis is Thomas Kuhn's *The Structure of Scientific Revolutions* (1962), discussed in chapter 3. Kuhn centered on fundamental changes in science, but he also makes the connection between scientific and political revolutions. It is that connection which Busch uses and which is also the basis for our own discussion of Kuhn's book. For example, in order for a new scientific "paradigm" (or a new cultural paradigm, by extension) to be successful, it must promise to resolve the contradictions or problems within the old scientific paradigm.

Busch states a precondition for a successful image of the future: "a crisis must be widely perceived in the existing order," for the crisis is the felt problem that an alternative image of the future is put forward to solve, just as the scientific method starts with a problem and then is oriented to solving it. Here, then, is Busch's list of his hypothesized seven characteristics of a successful image of the future:

> 1. *An image of the future must be holistic if it is to achieve widespread acceptance....* [T]he image must provide a grand panoramic view of an achievable future state.... It must hold the promise of resolving the immediate problems of the day as well as explaining all that the old order explained. It must offer a new epistemological base upon which to construct knowledge itself. It cannot restrict itself to a particular problem but must forthrightly address *all* the problems plaguing the present....
>
> 2. *A successful image of the future must provide the promise of the resolution of the anomalies and contradictions of the existing order....* Like scientific paradigms, images of the future are historically specific.... The problems of a decaying Roman Empire were vastly different from those that confront us now.... On a societal level, a new image of the future must soon include the promise of solving in concert the problems of environmental decay, maldistribution of food and resources, overly powerful military machines, authoritarianism in the workplace, sexism, and racism....

*3. The future must be constructed in the present, not the future.* The personal commitment of individuals to a new image of the future changes the context in which the present is interpreted. The future does not begin after the present but has its groundwork laid in the present. The future we envision is only directly relevant to us now, in the present, and not to the people of some future present....

*4. A successful image of the future must provide an escape from the existing order, but it must find that escape within the existing order itself.* It is impossible to provide an alternative image of the future that captures the imagination and loyalty of the entire society by retreating to a place spatially remote from the rest of society. While such places may serve as testing grounds for experimental organizational forms, it is only by active involvement in everyday life within the larger society that a new image of the future becomes a meaningful alternative. Most nineteenth-century utopian communities and the present day retreat communes ... share this major flaw....

*5. A successful image of the future must provide an operationaliz-able methodology for the individual....* This is not to say that everyone should go off and "do their own thing." ... The choice, though made by individuals on a conscious level, nevertheless remains within strict limits that are unique to each situation ... nor by methodology do we mean the creation of a highly disciplined, clandestine organization with an elaborate hierarchical structure.... What is meant by an *individual* methodology is a set of rules and examples that provide the individual with a modus operandi similar to the rules of a game (Huizinga, 1950). They make clear what needs to be done without the necessity for an order from some higher authority. The early Christians had no need to consult with a priest before acting as Christians....

*6. All successful images of the future are structured....* The shape and form of the structure will vary from image to image, stressing one portion or another of human life. Hence our present-day image, originating in the Protestant Reformation, has tended to stress economic life. The ancient Greek image apparently stressed the political.... There is a tendency on the part of many who are concerned with replacing the existing structure to expend a great deal of time and energy combating the existing order and to devote almost no time to the structure of the alternative they propose.... It may be that the lack of a clear image was Marx's greatest failing.... By comparison, we may examine the activities of America's founding fathers, who felt that their image of the future had to have its structure defined in writing....

*7. A meaningful image of the future must involve the mundane.* Its proponents must be concerned about details of everyday life, for it is the collapse of the routine of everyday life that directly affects everyone.... When money ceases to have value, when essential goods are nowhere to be found, when essential services cannot be delivered, when laws are enforced erratically, when tomorrow appears completely uncertain, then the routine of everyday life collapses along with the legitimacy of the existing order. The challenge to a new image of the future is to be ready to re-establish the routine of everyday life in a new way (1976: 29–36).

Busch's focus is on specifying the conditions under which fundamental changes in the structure of society will occur, by contrast with our own focus on hypotheses (1) and (2). However, these two goals are interrelated. If indeed we have obtained substantial evidence as to the existence of an increasing gap in modern society—in relation to hypothesis (1)—then that will constitute what Busch sees as a precondition for a successful image of the future: "a crisis must be widely perceived in the existing order." For such an increasing gap involving the fulfillment of a wide range of our work-related and people-oriented cultural values will indeed indicate a threatening crisis of broad scope. Further, if we found that a stratified worldview is indeed contributing to that gap—following hypothesis (2)—then that also would contribute to a crisis that would be a precondition for a successful image of the future that might address such a crisis. Of course, following Busch's statement, such a crisis must come to be "widely perceived in the existing order," and that perception has by no means yet occurred.

Given our focus on negative and positive reinforcement in this chapter—invoking not only reinforcement theory within psychology but also exchange theory within sociology—we might view Busch's analysis from that perspective. To what extent do his ideas about the nature of a successful image of the future also suggest positive reinforcements instead of negative ones for individuals in a society? More specifically, to what extent does each of his seven characteristics of a successful image of the future promise positive versus negative reinforcement of individuals? If they do promise positive reinforcements, then this gives us an additional basis for accepting his hypothesis as a potentially fruitful one.

It appears that every single one of Busch's seven characteristics of a successful image of the future points toward the achievement of increased positive reinforcements. We might understand this most easily from the perspective of figure I.1, with its large gap between expectations and their fulfillment within modern society. That gap structures negative reinforcements, since expectations generally remain unfulfilled, whereas the ability to lower the top curve and/or raise the bottom curve increases the likelihood of positive reinforcement. As for (1), a successful image of the future must promise to bring those curves together for "*all* the problems plaguing the present." Concerning (2), here we have a specification of some of the particular problems that would have to be addressed at this particular time in history. With respect to (3), this requires the commitment of individuals to closing that gap. As for (4), Busch suggests that closing that gap must occur "in everyday life within the larger society," by contrast with retreat communes. His own article, with its implications for changes in the discipline of sociology, is an illustration of that approach, granting that he does not define this as part of a sweeping change in society's image of the future.

With regard to (5), Busch is suggesting that everyone begin to learn how to close that gap on their own in their everyday lives and, as a result of their successes, become motivated so as to continue to accomplish this. As for (6), Busch sees a successful structure for an image of the future as pointing the individual in the direction of closing that gap, just as these seven characteristics constitute at least a minimal structure. Finally, with regard to (7), closing that gap to an extent and receiving positive reinforcement as a result should not be a sometime thing. From moment to moment the individual in everyday life, pursuing mundane activities, has opportunities to close that gap and obtain positive reinforcement as a result. For example, simply by lowering his aspirations or expectations and learning to see one's momentary behavior as "sacred"—because it can help to change one's entire worldview—the individual is moving toward positive reinforcement. Also, by taking action in that very moment which conforms to the individual's priorities with respect to basic cultural values, the individual is raising his fulfillment. In both cases, the individual learns to bring those curves together and gain positive reinforcement. We might also note that an "image" of the future can help the individual perceive, from one moment to the next, just what behavior would in fact yield positive reinforcement.

## Some Implications

Van Vogt follows Korzybski's ideas that we moderns have huge problems of communicating with one another because we fail to understand how language works, resulting in our oversimplifying the actual complexity of phenomena. The increasing threats he sees in the universe indirectly support hypothesis (1). Oversimplification is illustrated, in his view, by our stratified behavior, yielding support for (2). Vidich and Bensman's detailed analysis of mechanisms like techniques of particularization, the falsification of memory and the externalization of self apparently apply not just to the Springdalers but also to everyone else, including social scientists and the authors of this book. *Small Town in Mass Society* succeeds in uncovering huge gaps between aspirations and their fulfillment. Yet Vidich's and Bensman's focus on Springdale and lack of comment on changes in modern society as a whole prevents their work from bearing on hypothesis (1). However, the mechanisms used by the Springdalers to repress their problems appear to be closely linked to a stratified worldview, leading to support for (2). Busch's guide to constructing the future aims to understand how fundamental social change comes about, avoiding any position with reference to hypothesis (1). Yet he sees nothing less than a very broad image of the future, by contrast with an oversimplified or stratified one, as essential if society is to solve a crisis, thus supporting (2).

On the basis of our analysis of the van Vogt and Busch pieces, it appears that it is possible to turn negative reinforcements into positive reinforcements for the individual. We saw this in Gosseyn's helping Ashargin look back at the scenes of personal humiliation in his past and learning to redefine them so that they were no longer harmful to his further development. We also saw this in the possibility of developing an image of the future for us moderns that would encourage positive versus negative reinforcements in our everyday lives. The implications of such procedures are vast. If indeed all of us moderns more or less are experiencing the gap portrayed in figure I.1, then it is indeed quite difficult for us to obtain positive reinforcements and avoid negative ones. Van Vogt and Busch, then, are opening up the possibility of reversing this situation by helping us to understand how to close that gap.

As for images or metaphors, Van Vogt's idea of "the cortical-thalamic pause" helps us to link "head" and "heart." We employ our cortex for thinking, and our thalamus is a seat for our emotions. When we pause in an effort to link them we give ourselves an opportunity which we would not have if we automatically reacted to events. Vidich and Bensman's ideas—"techniques of particularization," "falsification of memory" and "externalization of self"—are not very visual. Nevertheless, they manage to capture in a simple way fundamental procedures for the repression of inconvenient facts. Busch's idea of "constructing the future"—coupled with Polak's idea of "the image of the future"—conveys the optimistic notion that it is we humans who can proceed to build our own future, and not just build physical objects.

## CHAPTER 11

# "Hand"

## Conforming Behavior versus Praxis

IN THIS FINAL CHAPTER of part V we continue our situational focus by examining studies emphasizing the "hand," or action and interaction. "Praxis" derives from the Greek root "prak-," with "practical," "pragmatic" and "practice" also based on that root. It is a concept that Marx used to link the actions of the individual to changes in the structure of society, for he saw the two in interaction with one another. Mills's emphasis on "history and biography and the relations between the two within society" (chapter 6) also indicates the importance of the interaction between the individual and society. Neither should we forget Freire's interest in praxis (chapter 9): "But men's activity consists of action and reflection: it is praxis; it is transformation of the world."

Our own purpose here is much the same, given our emphasis on the interaction of all the concepts within the headings of these eleven chapters. The idea goes against the grain of much of sociology, where the emphasis is on how the individual is shaped by social structure, as illustrated by the concept of "conforming behavior." We can grant that social structure generally is far more powerful in changing individual structures than vice-versa, yet we can also assume that change can also be substantial in the reverse direction. Van Vogt's *Worlds* and *Players* (chapter 10) provide us with a fictional example, and Busch's guide to constructing the future gives us an argument based on historical examples of the initiation of fundamental changes in society by individuals and small groups. What is crucial for Busch is not the number of individuals initially involved in such changes but whether an image of the future has been developed with a number of characteristics favorable to its widespread acceptance and displacement of the old image of the future.

Greenstein's "Modifying Beliefs and Behavior through Self-Confrontation" presents the work of Milton Rokeach, a social psychologist whose theory is based on the idea that people are oriented to maintaining "cognitive consistency," following Festinger's theory of cognitive dissonance (introduced in chapter 6). He hypothesized that helping them to become aware of their own fundamental inconsistencies will yield changes in their behavior. Our own focus here is on the nature of the inconsistencies which Rokeach uncovered, since this will help us to understand the nature of existing gaps between aspirations or expectations and their fulfillment. For example, many of Rokeach's studies took place during the civil rights movement in the 1960s, where the subjects of his experiments—college students—were most concerned with egalitarian ideals. When Rokeach was able to show students their own departures from those ideals, that proved to be most effective in inaugurating changes in their behavior. We should note the significance of Rokeach's focus on values, which we took up in chapter 7 with our discussion of Robin Williams's *American Society.*

Our treatment of Joan V. Bondurant's *Conquest of Violence: The Gandhian Philosophy of Conflict,* centers on Gandhi's struggle in 1930 and 1931 to oppose the British Salt Acts along with his success in ultimately helping India achieve independence from Great Britain following World War II. The Gandhian approach to civil disobedience has been taken up in other efforts to achieve social change in a relatively peaceful way, as illustrated by the civil rights movement in the United States. We had a situation in India that figure I.1 depicts: a large gap between aspirations and their fulfillment. In this case the aspirations had to do with cultural values like "equality" and "freedom," and patterns of stratification were illustrated by the hierarchical relationship between British administrators of India and the people of India along with their governmental representatives. A crucial player in this conflict was the people of Great Britain, many of whom came out for Indian independence after learning of brutal police treatment of Indians during their non-violent protests.

George A. Lundberg's *Can Science Save Us?* (1947/1961) centers on the vast problems modern society faced in the postwar era and the idea that social science is by far the best tool we have for solving those problems. Those problems illustrate the gap between aspirations or expectations and their fulfillment, and we shall examine their nature. Yet modern society pays little attention to social science's possibilities and gives little support to developing such knowledge. At the beginning of his concluding chapter, Lundberg states: "Can science save us? Yes, but we must not expect physical science to solve social problems. We cannot expect penicillin to solve the employer-employee struggle, nor can we expect better electric lamps to illumine darkened intellects and emotions."

## Greenstein's "Modifying Beliefs and Behavior through Self-Confrontation"

Theodore N. Greenstein reviewed the work of the social psychologist Milton Rokeach in his "Modifying Beliefs and Behavior through Self-Confrontation" (1989). Rokeach had completed a series of studies that emphasize the importance of cultural values and which were much concerned with learning about how actual changes in behavior occur. Rokeach's "self-confrontation" theory developed out of his earlier investigations of rigid thought as well as Festinger's earlier work on the importance of "cognitive dissonance" (1957). For example, he brought together for two years three institutionalized individuals, each of whom believed that he was Jesus Christ (1964), seeking to maximize the degree to which they had to confront their most fundamental beliefs. By contrast with the many social psychologists centering on attitude change, he came to believe in the importance of basic values like "equality" and "freedom." More specifically, he concluded that "information about contradictions within one's belief system that is perceived to be incompatible with self-conceptions should motivate cognitive and behavioral change." What comes to be at stake for the individual is not merely some external stimulus but the individual's own awareness of personal contradictions having to do with his beliefs, values and behavior.

Rokeach's first experimental tests of self-confrontation theory, involving students at Michigan State University in 1966, proved to become the basis for many other studies that he and his colleagues performed in the 1960s, 1970s and 1980s:

> In the initial studies, a group of Michigan State University (MSU) students were first asked to rank the eighteen values of the Value Survey (Rokeach, 1967; see also Rokeach, 1968) in order of their "importance to you, as guiding principles in your life." Next, the students were shown results of a previous study examining the value rankings of MSU students. Then, the experimenter offered an interpretation of the value rankings of this comparison group.... The experimenter pointed out that the students in the comparison group ranked *freedom* first out of eighteen values, but ranked *equality* eleventh. At this point the experimenter attempted to arouse a state of self-dissatisfaction among the subjects by observing that the students apparently "value freedom far more highly than they value equality." This suggests that MSU students in general are much more interested in their own freedom than they are in freedom for other people....
>
> Students in the experimental groups increased their ranking for equality an average of 1.47 to 1.68 ranks three months after the experimental session. A second set of studies was then conducted, commencing in the

fall of 1967. These studies included posttest measures not only of values and attitudes but of behavior relating to civil rights as well.... Three to five months after the experimental session, all subjects received a solicitation (on NAACP letterhead) to join the National Association for the Advancement of Colored People. Experimental subjects were more than twice as likely as control subjects to respond favorably to this solicitation. Experimental subjects were significantly more likely to enroll in a special ethnic core program of coursework twenty-one months after the experimental session.... By 1979 Rokeach counted 23 published studies using the self-confrontation technique to induce long-term change (Greenstein, 1989: 400–402).

One further theoretical issue that was explored was the specific roles of self-conceptions or self image and values in behavior change. It was learned that the perceived inconsistency between behavior and self-conceptions, not necessarily mediated specifically through values, yielded the greatest change in behavior. Later, a question explored was whether such behavioral changes could be brought about by a television broadcast and not just under laboratory conditions. On February 27, 1979, with the aid of extensive publicity in newspapers, *TV Guide* and television spot announcements, a thirty-five–minute program—"The Great American Values Test"—was presented in the Tri-Cities area of eastern Washington State (Ball-Rokeach, Rokeach and Grube, 1984). The approach taken paralleled that used in the laboratory experiments, with a focus on the values of freedom and equality. Telephone interviews conducted immediately following the telecast determined who had watched the program, and questionnaires along with behavioral measures—requests for donations relating to racism, sexism—were mailed to them. Although there were no significant effects—compared with a control group—on the values of freedom and equality, the behavioral solicitations showed effects that were statistically significant for the experimental participants. Those effects proved to be strongest for those who had viewed the entire program without interruption.

Indirectly, these studies suggest a substantial gap between certain aspirations or expectations and their fulfillment, namely, with respect to the cultural value of equality. Subjects showed in one way or another their willingness to alter their behavior with reference to that value—whether by what they wrote in questionnaires or by specific actions they took—long after the relatively short experimental sessions or television program. By their performance on questionnaires they indicated their commitment to the cultural value of equality within the top curve of figure I.1. By changing their behavior, such as responses to solicitations, they demonstrated efforts to bring the bottom curve of figure I.1 closer to the top curve. Also, these studies suggest that certain expectations are more important than others. It was only after a great deal of preliminary work that these experiments focused on the values of equality and freedom, cultural values that appear to be fundamental within contemporary society (see for example Simmel, chapter 4). It could be argued, however, that this latter group was previously committed to the importance of the problems of racism and sexism, and it was that prior commitment—rather than the impact of the program—which at least partly explains their response to behavioral solicitations.

In addition, these studies open up several important directions for further study. For one thing, self image or self conceptions emerges as a central factor among the many structures within the personality structure. Our focus on gaps between aspirations and their fulfillment does not directly address the importance of self conceptions, and neither does our overall focus on the importance of personality structures. Another important direction for further study is the potential of the mass media for educational purposes. Greenstein and his colleagues opened a door to the possibility that even a short program has the potential for long-term behavioral repercussions. Further, these studies demonstrate the importance of cultural values in understanding human behavior. Rokeach's analysis supplements that of Williams (chapter 7) in explicitly distinguishing among a range of values, and he and his colleagues have succeeded in demonstrating that they have implications for behavior. Still further, such experimental work requires very close attention to exactly what is and is not done within a series of momentary scenes, e.g., just what the experimenter says and does, the specific nature of instruments given to the subjects, and exactly what their responses are. This parallels the close attention to the situation that we have discussed in detailed studies such as that of Scheff and Retzinger (chapter 9).

Further, if the work of Vidich and Bensman (chapter 10) succeeded in alerting us to a range of powerful forces preventing us moderns from facing our contradictions, then we certainly require studies which help us understand how our contradictions can be brought up to the light of day. Although Greenstein and Rokeach do not address this problem as a whole, they do at least illustrate procedures for addressing it in part. From the perspective of positive and negative reinforcements, their procedure appears to alert subjects to contradictions which would ordinarily constitute negative reinforcements. However, by giving those subjects an opportunity to change personal behavior which they had come to see in a negative light, they are then able to act so as to convert those negative reinforcements into positive ones. This suggests the question of how such conversions might be accomplished with reference to a wide range of contradictions which individuals have buried. For example, what might have been done by the Springdalers to obtain the kinds of positive reinforcements which would have enabled them to eliminate their techniques of particularization and their falsification of memory?

Although Greenstein and Rokeach succeed in opening up several valuable directions for further research, their studies suffer from the same kinds of problems that are shared widely throughout the social sciences, problems associated with a specialized and inadequately communicated approach. This is well exemplified by their failure to cite the work of Williams on cultural values, well known throughout sociology but not well known among psychologists. To suggest the implications of that failure, their list of values is not also a list of cultural values but rather appears to constitute goals based on a survey, such as "salvation" and "a world at peace." This misses out on the sociological and anthropological conception of cultural values as key elements of culture that are shared throughout society. For example, Williams based his selection on the conclusions of many observers of American culture over several centuries. Goals, by contrast, can be short-term phenomena. Also, the results of a survey are quite different from the accumulated wisdom of many social scientists over a long period of time. It is no accident that Rokeach emphasized two among their list of goals—freedom and equality—which Williams also listed as cultural values.

This narrowness can be illustrated as well by the existence of many other factors—as discussed in the foregoing chapters of this book—which convert the experimental situations analyzed by Rokeach and Greenstein into complex situations. For example, little attention was paid to the phenomenon of investigator effect. If the experimenters were perceived as favorable to the civil rights movement, then that would have pressured students toward conforming behavior regardless of their own personal contradictions that came to light. In the long run, such problems relating to the complexity of human behavior will not be solved unless investigators begin to question social scientists' approach to the scientific method itself along with the metaphysical stance which prevents such questioning.

## Bondurant on Gandhi in *Conquest of Violence*

One historical example of praxis is the achievement of Mohandas Gandhi, the prime mover in the development of independence for India. Why was he able to accomplish this monumental feat? Joan V. Bondurant's *Conquest of Violence: The Gandhian Philosophy of Conflict* (1965) provides at least some answers. To understand Gandhi's approach to conflict, let us focus on one particular conflict, namely, the salt campaign between 1930 and 1931 in response to the British Salt Acts providing for a salt tax, which was held to work a hardship on poor people for whom salt was a necessity. Gandhi and other leaders of the Indian National Congress decided on a civil disobedience campaign, beginning with a two hundred mile march to the sea from Ahmedabad to Dandi, where the volunteers would proceed to prepare salt from sea water. The salt campaign was viewed by them as part of the more general political movement for independence. The campaign was seen as a *satyagraha*, based on Gandhi's philosophy of nonviolence. Training courses were initiated for volunteers, who took this pledge:

1. I desire to join the civil resistance campaign for the Independence of India undertaken by the National Congress.
2. I accept the Creed of the National Congress, that is, the attainment of Purna Swaraj [complete independence] by the people of India by all peaceful and legitimate means.
3. I am ready and willing to go to jail and undergo all other sufferings and penalties that may be inflicted on me in this campaign.
4. In case I am sent to jail, I shall not seek any monetary help for my family from the Congress funds.
5. I shall implicitly obey the orders of those who are in charge of the campaign (Bondurant, 1965:92).

Gandhi wrote a letter delivered on March 2 to Lord Irwin, the British Viceroy, which reviewed the grievances of the people of India, conveyed the aims of the salt *satyagraha*, and included the specific plans for the march. Volunteers would be undertaking constructive work during the march, were forbidden to drink intoxicants, and were urged to overcome discrimination against Untouchables. On March 12 the march began, attracting nationwide attention, and the volunteers reached Dandi on April 5. The following day they broke the salt laws by preparing salt from sea water, encouraging people throughout India to follow suit, with the Congress Party publishing leaflets with instructions on how to manufacture salt. When leaders of the salt campaign were arrested, the overwhelming response throughout India was civil disobedience. Shops closed, Indian officials resigned in very large numbers, nonpayment of taxes was initiated, and new leaders took the places of those who had been arrested.

In response to outbreaks of riots in Karachi and Calcutta, Gandhi declared on April 17: "If non-violence has to fight the people's violence in addition to the violence of the Government it must still perform its arduous task at any cost" (Bondurant, 1965:95). On April 17 Gandhi sent a second letter to Lord Irwin explaining his intention to march on Dharsan and to occupy the salt depots located there unless the salt tax was repealed. He was arrested on May 5, but Congress officials proceeded with the march. As they were struck down by British police, fresh volunteers took their places, with first-aid units working to revive the victims. Volunteers did not strike back and did not even deflect the blows rained down on them, sometimes pleading with the police to join them. An American journalist, Negley Farson, recorded an incident in which a Sikh, blood-soaked from the assault of a police sergeant, fell under a heavy blow. Congress first-aid volunteers rushed up to rub his face with ice.

> [H]e gave us a bloody grin and stood up to receive some more.... [The police sergeant was] so sweaty from his exertions that his Sam Browne had stained his white tunic. I watched him with my heart in my mouth. He drew back his arm for a final swing—and then he dropped his hands down by his side. "It's no use," he said, turning to me with half an apologetic grin. "You can't hit a bugger when he stands up to you like that!" He gave the Sikh a mock salute and walked off (Bondurant, 1965: 96).

Publication of such stories reached the British public, and there was increasing political pressure on the British government to repeal the salt tax. The salt *satyagraha* was replaced by other campaigns after the monsoon season started. For example, there was an economic boycott of foreign products and widespread civil disobedience throughout 1930 with respect to new laws that were aimed at limiting the assembly of those in the independence movement. Lord Irwin and Gandhi met early in 1931 and finally reached the Gandhi-Irwin Agreement, published on March 5. The salt laws were not repealed, but a new interpretation of them allowed people in villages located where salt could be made to do so and sell salt for consumption in those villages. Amnesty was given to all individuals convicted of nonviolent offenses, and representatives of the Congress party would be invited to participate in the next Indian conference on such questions as constitutional reform, defense, external affairs and the position of minorities. In return, civil disobedience was to be ended along with non-payment of taxes and the encouragement of resignations from governmental posts.

Gandhi's approach to conflict, *satyagraha,* has been interpreted within the literature of conflict resolution as involving at least these eight elements:

1. Refraining from any form of verbal or overt violence toward members of the rival group
2. Openly admitting to the rival group one's plans and intentions
3. Refraining from any action that will have the effect of humiliating the rival group
4. Making visible sacrifices for one's cause
5. Maintaining a consistent and persistent set of positive activities which are explicit (though partial) realizations of the group's objectives

6. Attempting to initiate direct personal interaction with members of the rival group, oriented toward engaging in friendly verbal discussions with them concerning the fundamental issues involved in the social struggle

7. Adopting a consistent attitude of trust toward the rival group and taking overt actions which demonstrate that one is, in fact, willing to act upon this attitude

8. Attempting to achieve a high degree of empathy with respect to the motives, affects, expectations, and attitudes of members of the rival group (Janis and Katz, 1959: 86).

If we examine the history of the salt *satyagraha,* we can see these elements in play. Gandhi and the Congress party were firm in doing whatever they could to prevent the widespread civil disobedience from escalating into violent conflict. Gandhi's own relationship with Lord Irwin illustrated all of these ideals. Behind the success of Gandhi's campaigns were people-oriented cultural values shared by the British public and India's peoples, such as equality, freedom, individual personality and democracy. Thus, aggressive actions by Lord Irwin to punish non-violent protesters came to be viewed by the British public as unconscionable. Given the Nazi and Japanese threats during World War II, the Congress party did not push for independence immediately, but it was finally granted after the war. India continued its cultural and trade ties with Britain but gained control over its foreign policy and no longer required a British military force.

Looking closely at these eight components of the Gandhian *satyagraha,* we might assess their relationship to an interactive worldview and an interactive scientific method. They focus on situational behavior, although they also require certain individual and social structures to be present in order to succeed. More specifically, we can see them as involving "head," "heart" and "hand." As for the "head," verbal abuse of the rival group was forbidden. With respect to the "heart," there are efforts to achieve an attitude of trust along with a high degree of empathy with respect to the rival group. As for "hand," a great deal is involved: avoidance of overt violence, avoidance of acting so as to humiliate the rival group, attempting to initiate direct personal interaction with them, communicating one's plans and intentions to them, making visible personal sacrifices and engaging in positive or constructive activities. All of these situational efforts taken together yielded examples of praxis, where individual behavior in fact had enormous repercussions for fundamental changes in society.

Such situational behavior took place within the context of the personality and social structures operating at the time, and within the historical context that existed. For example, the religions of India to an extent were open to the idea that individuals might sacrifice themselves for the good of India. This openness was supplemented by training programs in exactly how the individual might learn to risk personal harm and even death. Cultural support of the values of equality, freedom, individual personality and democracy were important not only within India but within Britain as well, with patterns of social stratification being viewed with no more than limited justification. The economic strain on Britain due to its military efforts in India was another factor involved in the struggle along with the importance of continuing trade with India. Thus, there were pressures on Britain to give up its stratified relationship to India and develop a more egalitarian one.

For all of his accomplishments, Gandhi provided no more than a partial direction for the development of an interactive worldview, given his focus on situational factors as distinct from structural factors throughout modern society. If we look to figure I.1 we see some links between the Gandhian struggle for independence and the gap between aspirations or expectations and their fulfillment within that diagram. For example, the achievement of independence reduced the stratification between Britain and India, thus lifting the bottom curve upward. Further, Gandhi was successful in helping to reduce ethnic stratification within India. Yet the top curve of the revolution of rising expectations apparently has continued to rise within India along with the rest of the world—although unevenly—yielding an increasing gap between aspirations and their fulfillment. Also, social stratification apparently remains a major pattern within social structures throughout the world. From our own perspective, it is essential to confront the nature of our worldview if indeed we wish to confront our aspirations-gap.

## Lundberg's *Can Science Save Us?*

George A. Lundberg, a sociologist teaching at the University of Washington, wrote a small book—*Can Science Save Us?* (1947/1961)—just after World War II, revising it over a decade later. His focus was not on science in general but rather on social science, and we can glimpse Lundberg's ideas in his concluding paragraphs:

> A leader, however admirable in ability and intentions, attempting to administer centrally a large society today is somewhat in the position of a pilot trying to fly the modern stratoliner without an instrument board or charts. That is to say, it cannot be a very smooth flight. If he succeeds at all, it will be at the expense of much wreckage of men and materials. Successful piloting depends directly upon the adequacy and accuracy of the instruments in the machine, the charts by which a course can be pursued or modified, and the training of the pilot to read both aright. Only as a result of the development of the basic physi-

cal sciences can a large modern airplane either be built or flown. Only through a comparable development of the social sciences can a workable world order be either constructed or administered. The appalling thing is the flimsy and inadequate information on the basis of which even a conscientious executive of a large state is today obliged to act.

It comes down, then, to this: Shall we put our faith in science or in something else? ... If it is answered in the affirmative, then social research institutions will make their appearance, which will rank with Massachusetts and California Institutes of Technology, Mellon Institute, the research laboratories of Bell Telephone, General Electric and General Motors, not to mention several thousand others....

Finally, a word should be said to those who find the methods of science too slow. They want to know what we shall do while we wait for the social sciences to develop. Well, we shall doubtless continue to suffer.... We shall probably become much sicker before we consent to take the only medicine which can help us (1947/1961: 142-143).

Lundberg was what we would call today a "public intellectual," writing for such publications as *Harper's Magazine, The Scientific Monthly* and *The Humanist,* and addressing this book to a general audience. The above quote suggests the forcefulness of his prose along with the logic of his argument, which is representative of his book as a whole. His focus is on our urgent need to abandon building technologies for solving social problems on the basis of "the flimsy and inadequate information" that he believes presently is the basis for our fundamental decisions in all of our institutions. Metaphorically, Lundberg concludes that "successful piloting of the ship of state depends directly upon the adequacy and accuracy of the instruments in the machine, the charts by which a course can be pursued or modified, and the training of the pilot to read both aright." If social technologies are to become effective, they must build on social science knowledge, just as effective technologies like building airplanes are based on physical science knowledge. Further, just as pilots require extensive training in order to fly planes, Lundberg believes that we all—particularly our leaders—require education in social science in order to solve personal and world problems.

For Lundberg, the alternative to this approach is that "We shall probably become much sicker before we consent to take the only medicine which can help us." Here he is suggesting the existence of a substantial and increasing gap between our goals or aspirations or expectations and our ability to fulfill them. He wrote his revised book during the Cold War, and he argued that the gap between the development of physical science and social science has yielded a most dangerous situation for us all. Lundberg quotes from an article by Nikita S. Khrushchev in the October 1959, issue of *Foreign Affairs:*

> Is it possible that when mankind has advanced to a plane where it has proved capable of the greatest discoveries and of making its first steps into outer space, it should not be able to use the colossal achievements of its genius for the establishment of a stable peace, for the good of man, rather than for the preparation of another war and for the destruction of all that has been created by its labor over many millenniums? Reason refuses to believe this (1947/1961: 133).

In his opening chapters, "Prescientific Thoughtways in a Technological Age" and "Can Science Solve Social Problems?" Lundberg reviews arguments against the potential of the social sciences. He presents cogent responses to each of these arguments, concluding that there is no barrier whatsoever to our capacity to develop the social sciences, given the model of physical science achievements that we already have. Leaders along with educational initiatives are certainly required, but their effectiveness will depend on the social science knowledge on which they build. Technologies are only so good as their basis in knowledge. He argues that social scientists themselves "have hitherto lacked boldness and an adequate vision of the true task of social science." Instead of attempting to "formulate laws of human behavior which are comparable to the laws of gravity, thermodynamics, and bacteriology," research has been "for the most part a quest for superficial remedies, for commercial guidance, and for historical and contemporary 'human interest' stories."

Lundberg's ideas are most refreshing in that they take us back to a time when sociologists were still enamored with their possibilities. That was also the time when C. Wright Mills wrote his *The Sociological Imagination* (1959). Across the decades they are suggesting to us that perhaps the ideas of social scientists are in fact incredibly powerful, and that we somehow have failed to develop them sufficiently and communicate them effectively. Perhaps we have failed to follow the ideals of the scientific method. Perhaps we have not taken into account sufficiently the incredible complexity of human behavior. Perhaps we have not dipped deeply enough into the momentary situation. Perhaps we have not paid enough attention to powerful metaphors that can help us communicate to ourselves and others. Perhaps our very worldview or metaphysical stance is holding us back. Perhaps Lundberg and Mills are right about the potential of social science research, and perhaps our current ideas about its limitations are wrong.

Lundberg has a good deal to say about the failures of education along with our one-sided focus on physical science research, with the force of his feelings coming through. For example, he states:

To be qualified to pull a tooth or remove an appendix, we require people to study systematically for seven or eight years beyond high school. To keep nations from flying at each other's throats, any political hack will do. Human relations will improve when we undertake serious scientific study of how to improve them. In the meantime, we continue to rely on incantations, denunciations, exhortations, and exorcism exactly as our prescientific forefathers did regarding their physical maladjustments (1947/1961: 77).

He argues that what must be taught starting in the earliest grades is not just the content of social science findings but—far more important—the nature of the scientific method. He agrees with Robert Hutchins's diagnosis of the key problem of education: "that modern education suffers from the lack of a unifying discipline, such as theology provided in the Middle Ages." But he disagrees as to the remedy that Hutchins offers: reading a hundred or more "classic" works that have come down to us through the ages. He sees those classics as no more than "the ancient and medieval gropings of mankind to find its way about," and he proposes instead that the unifying discipline of modern education lies in modern science, which has resulted from the sifting of knowledge from all the epochs of history. For Lundberg, it is the scientific method even more than the substantive knowledge from biophysical and social science which must be taught. Such teaching must be bolstered by a great many times the amount of social science research than presently exists.

For Lundberg, the three principal defects of our educational system are (1) the failure to recognize that the scientific method can function as a unifying discipline for all of education; (2) the failure to develop an adequate understanding of that method even in college students and even in students of physical science, let alone in students in the earliest grades; and (3) the failure to give students an adequate understanding of the nature and uses of language. As for that third defect, a profound understanding of language not only is essential for understanding the scientific method. It is also essential for the effective communication of scientific knowledge, both inside the scientific community and outside of it. Lundberg paraphrased H. G. Wells's idea that human beings are in a race between education and catastrophe, and he looked toward newer modes of communication such as television to aid in that race.

Lundberg emphasized the scientific method as a unifying basis for social science in particular and education in general. To build on that idea, we require a fuller understanding of how the scientific method is actually being practiced by social scientists. For example, is it indeed the case that stratified metaphysical assumptions are holding back the social scientist's ability to follow the ideals of the scientific method? Is the failure of social scientists to be reflexive enough to address the problem of investigator effect preventing them from achieving rapid cumulative development? Is specialization and sub-specialization preventing social scientists from opening up to the complexity of human behavior? Do today's social scientists generally fail to move very far up language's ladder of abstraction in their research, and does this get in the way of the integration of social science knowledge? Is the failure of society to give much support to social science research largely responsible for the limitations of that research? The tragedies that Lundberg predicted are already upon us, yet there is almost no sign throughout contemporary societies of any support for Lundberg's emphasis on the scientific method within social science as a possible way to address our fundamental social problems.

## Some Implications

Neither the work of Greenstein and Rokeach nor that of Gandhi bears on hypothesis (1). Although Gandhi was deeply concerned about the failure of India to achieve independence, his efforts did help to convert his aim into a reality. Yet they support hypothesis (2). Greenstein's and Rokeach's self confrontation theory examines the potential impact of opening up to contradictions which formerly had been buried. They found that these contradictions can be resolved, enabling individuals to fulfill a wider range of their cultural values. Gandhi's approach to resolving conflict directly opposed the British policy of stratification and proved to be most effective in finding solutions for many of the problems which India faced.

Lundberg saw modern problems as increasing, in support of hypothesis (1). His commitment to the potential of the scientific method was sharply opposed to a stratified orientation, in support of (2). He appears to be a truly neglected figure in the history of social science. Others also saw the gap between the biophysical and the social sciences as central to the problems of modern society, and others also have seen education as our major hope in closing that gap and giving the modern world a chance to continue whatever development it has achieved. But few have focused so clearly and systematically on the nature of this possibility, the forces which oppose it, and the urgency of taking decisive action in this direction. For Lundberg, a central defect of education in the modern world is "our failure to recognize the dominant importance of the scientific method." Since Lundberg's time we have learned a great deal more about just how social scientists can learn to follow the ideals of the scientific method in their efforts to address the complexities of human behavior. Yet as has been argued throughout this book, any epistemological change such as this one invokes the metaphysical stance within which that epistemology is nested. Thus, the problem of addressing that defect becomes far more difficult. Yet if we fail to take this medicine, following Lundberg, "we shall probably become much sicker." Given the escalation of social problems throughout the world since Lundberg wrote *Can Science Save Us?* still the question remains as to whether we will "consent to take the only medicine which can help us."

As for images, from Gandhi's salt *satyagraha* we have the image of a blood-soaked Sikh continuing to raise his head for yet another battering by a police sergeant, who finally drops his club-wielding arm and walks off. And Lundberg's image of a leader attempting to fly the ship of state without an instrument board or charts is indeed a powerful one.

# PART VI

# Conclusions and Implications

Our task here is not an easy one, given the breadth of the preceding chapters. It is not difficult to draw conclusions based on our two hypotheses, for we have already drawn conclusions about each of the excerpts in the foregoing chapters within the chapter sections on "Some Implications." Our key problem, rather, is to develop the general implications suggested by all of the foregoing material. What will help us to accomplish this is to focus on an audience of sociologists and their students and, to a lesser extent, of other social scientists. This is the audience that we know best. As for other readers, we might suggest that expertise in sociology is no requirement for taking up these conclusions. In the most important ways—such as the enormous problem of addressing one's own fundamental assumptions or worldview, and also the problem of gaining awareness of the invisible crisis of modern society—we are all very much in the same boat. For example, our own intellectual background is Western rather than Eastern. Thus, it fails to take very seriously the insights developed within—for example—Hinduism, Buddhism, Confucianism, Taoism and Zen. Further, our own knowledge fails to encompass much much more, such as the literature of Islamic civilization as illustrated by the works of Ibn Khaldun (see for example Mahdi, 1957; Ahmed, 2005; Dhaouadi, 2005; Rosen, 2005). Moving toward such breadth will, however, enable us authors to move as well toward a better understanding of our own worldview.

## CHAPTER 12

# Connecting the Dots

WE BEGIN with a section on conclusions with respect to our two hypotheses. We have already indicated how each of the foregoing thirty-three contributions relates to those hypotheses in the paragraphs on implications at the end of each chapter. Here, we will pull those analyses together. But more than simply a numerical summary is required. Our overall approach in this book is to include a metaphorical or image-oriented use of language along with a dichotomous and gradational orientation. And those sections on implications include attention to images. Thus, in this section on conclusions we shall touch on a very few of the central images presented previously. Following this section on conclusions, our final section will be on implications.

## Conclusions

Our two hypotheses are:
1. *The gap between aspirations and their fulfillment is in fact increasing in contemporary society.*
2. *To the degree that a worldview or metaphysical stance is stratified versus interactive, there will be a large gap between aspirations and their fulfillment.*

As for hypothesis (1), sixteen of the thirty-three selections did not bear on the question of whether the aspirations-fulfillment gap is increasing, sixteen suggested or implied that the gap is indeed increasing, and one author thought it was in fact decreasing. The sixteen in support of the hypothesis were: Berger (chapter 2); Levin (chapter 3); Marx, Simmel, and Horney (chapter 4); Hesse (chapter 5); Mills (chapter 6); Durkheim and

Chua (chapter 7); Orwell and Illich (chapter 8); Hoyle, Scheff, and Freire (chapter 9); Van Vogt (chapter 10); and Lundberg (chapter 11). Much like Marx's description of a contradiction between the forces and relations of production, the evidence points toward a fundamental contradiction between our cultural expectations and our patterns of social organization limiting their fulfillment. Granting all of the limitations of this study, and granting the importance of further research, this is indeed substantial evidence in support of this hypothesis. Although we can speak of an increasing aspirations-fulfillment gap in a bland way, what we moderns appear to be facing is nothing less than an invisible crisis bearing down on us much like an invisible tsunami. It is a tsunami that is racing toward every single one of the institutions of contemporary society.

Concerning hypothesis (2), we might note that this hypothesis implies that an interactive worldview will be associated with a small gap between aspirations and their fulfillment. Bearing in mind the limitations of this study and the importance of further research, all of the thirty-three authors yielded substantial evidence in its favor. The basic argument is that we have a continuing revolution of rising expectations associated with our continuing scientific and technological revolutions. Yet our patterns of stratification and bureaucracy—which include patterns of social stratification—limit the fulfillment of those expectations so as to yield an increasing gap worldwide between what people want and are able to get. And it is our stratified worldview with its limited utilization of the capacities of language and limited fulfillment of scientific ideals which lies behind our growing problems. We see the stratified and interactive worldviews illustrated by (1) isolation versus interaction with respect to physical structures and (2) outward versus inward-outward perception with regard to biological structures. As for personality structures, those two different metaphysical stances are illustrated by (3) a stratified versus an interactive worldview, (4) alienation versus an expressive orientation, and (5) addiction versus pragmatism. With respect to social structures, these alternatives are exemplified by (6) the scientistic method versus the scientific method, (7) anomie versus cultural value fulfillment, and (8) social stratification versus egalitarian relationships. Turning to the situation, we have (9) labeling versus reflexive behavior, (10) negative reinforcement versus positive reinforcement, and (11) conforming behavior versus praxis.

Looking to some of the key images within the book, a number of them have to do with fundamental problems within contemporary society as a whole along with basic problems that we denizens of our world are facing as individuals. Here, the emphasis is on our first hypothesis pointing toward an increasing gap between aspirations or expectations and their fulfillment. From Karl Marx we have images of the worker (chapter 4) as "crude and misshapen," "feeble," "a slave of nature," living in "hovels," "deformed," and open to "privation," "stupidity" and "cretinism."

From Herman Hesse (chapter 5) we have the image of the Glass Bead Game played throughout the academic world, along with its "hubris, conceit, class arrogance, self-righteousness, exploitativeness." From George Orwell (chapter 8) we have an image of Big Brother as so powerful and cruel as to force Winston Smith and Julia into betraying one another, and to brainwash Winston into believing, at the close of the book, that "He loved Big Brother." From Ivan Illich (chapter 8) we have an indictment of the "schooling" of the individual by every one of society's institutions, carrying forward the abstract concept of social stratification. Thus, "The pupil is 'schooled' to confuse teaching with learning, grade advancement with education, a diploma with competence, and fluency with the ability to say something new.... Medical treatment is mistaken for health care, social work for the improvement of community life, police protection for safety, the rat race for productive work."

Other key images have to do with a focus on the individual along with the idea of the fundamental importance of the scientific method. Those images bear most directly on the second hypothesis with its emphasis on worldviews as a partial explanation for the problems addressed in the first hypothesis, namely, the gap between expectations and their fulfillment. Here, for example, we have Edwin Abbott's image of Flatland and Spaceland, elaborated by our own image of II Timeland (chapter 1). Our oversimplified Spaceland view of phenomena parallels the square's Flatland view, by contrast with a Timeland perspective that is much closer to the complexity of a scientific understanding. From George Kelly (chapter 2) we have a vision of "man-the-scientist ... ever seeking to predict and control the course of events ... test his hypotheses, and weight his experimental evidence." Jack Levin's experiment (chapter 3) contrasts "relative evaluation" with "self evaluation," suggesting a contrast between the see-saw world of a stratified metaphysical stance with the stairway world of an interactive stance. That stairway world does nothing less than point the individual toward following Peirce's dictum (chapter 6): "Do not block the way of inquiry." And Friedrich Nietzsche's *The Gay Science* (chapter 6) conveys an image of the union of art and science. He criticizes those who believe that "'where laughter and gaiety are found, thinking does not amount to anything': that is the prejudice of this serious beast against all 'gay science.' Well then, let us prove that this is a prejudice."

## Some Implications

We believe that we have opened a door to a focus on the importance of the fundamental or paradigmatic assumptions that shape not only social science research but also everyone's behavior in everyday life. On the one hand this is no more than a beginning for such research, and we hope that other social scientists will see not only the possibility and importance of further research in this area but also its urgency. For we believe that there is indeed an invisible crisis—along with the visible one that is all too evidently displayed by the mass media—that is descending on all of us, based on an increasing worldwide aspirations-fulfillment gap. And we also believe that such research can succeed in uncovering crucial—yet almost completely ignored—forces that are widening that gap as well as forces that might work to narrow it. On the other hand, we shall suggest implications of this research on the assumption that further research will corroborate these findings. This may or may not in fact occur. We would like to believe that there is indeed no invisible crisis confronting contemporary society. Yet even though the evidence presented here is no more than preliminary, we believe that it is sufficient to suggest an exploration of its implications.

The most important implication is the existence of fundamental contradictions within our present worldview or metaphysical stance, contradictions which an alternative worldview promises to resolve. This suggests the importance—indeed, the urgency—of efforts by social scientists to move toward such an alternative worldview. For our present worldview or metaphysical stance is sufficiently powerful so as to shape all of our behavior, including our conduct of the scientific method. Failing successful efforts to alter our present worldview, there is good reason to believe that the worldwide aspirations-fulfillment gap will continue to increase and continue to exacerbate the major social problems facing modern society. And there will come a time, perhaps near at hand, when our ability to cope with such increasing problems will prove insufficient to prevent them from overwhelming our defenses and yielding worldwide calamities.

Our second implication is the importance and urgency of shifting from our traditional stratified approach to the scientific method to an interactive orientation such as the Web and Part/Whole Approach. This suggests that it is possible for social scientists to move much closer toward fulfilling scientific ideals, including the Enlightenment vision of the classical sociologists. Such a change in our understanding and employment of the scientific method will require a great deal, such as pointing toward the integration of social science knowledge, increasing usage of secondary analyses, ever-increasing intellectual breadth on our own part, usage of language's dichotomous, gradational and metaphorical potentials, increasing optimism about the future of social science and society and continuing movement toward an interactive worldview or metaphysical stance.

Our third implication has to do with the communication of social science findings to the public at large. C. Wright Mills illustrated such a commitment through books addressed to the reading public and not just to other sociologists, and also through articles for widely read magazines. By so doing he was following democratic ideals calling for an educated public, if intelligent political decisions are to be made and if elected officials are to be held accountable for their actions. If social science knowledge is to have the impact it deserves to have on public policies, more and more social scientists must also become public intellectuals. Given the increasing understanding promised by a shift toward an interactive worldview and scientific method—the above two implications—audiences should become far more interested in what social scientists have to say. And social scientists have much to learn from such experiences. In particular, this can help them learn to shift their worldview and their approach to the scientific method.

Our fourth implication has to do with fundamental changes in contemporary society. An interactive worldview and scientific method points toward an interactive society by contrast with a stratified and bureaucratic one. To the extent that the above three implications are taken seriously by the community of social scientists, this will imply that such a basic change in society is indeed possible. Given a growing and worldwide gap between aspirations and their fulfillment, there will be an increasing demand for solutions to growing problems. In this situation, social scientists—given their increasing understanding and greater visibility—will be able to respond to that demand to an increasing extent. And to the extent that an interactive scientific method has been employed throughout social science, they will be in a position to address a wide range of social problems. Granting the great difficulties involved in altering paradigmatic structures, a scientific method that follows scientific ideals should prove a match for the great difficulties that would be involved.

The emphasis of these four implications is on our findings with respect to hypothesis (2), namely, a widening of the aspirations-fulfillment gap of a stratified worldview and the narrowing of that gap of an interactive worldview. A fifth implication centers on evidence for hypothesis (1), namely, an increasing aspirations-fulfillment gap in modern society. This is nothing less than an invisible crisis confronting our contemporary world. Its invisibility, based largely on its abstract or intangible as well as long-term nature, makes it all the more threatening. And since our basic social and personality structures are involved in that increasing gap, a genuine crisis is involved. Our fifth implication is the importance of our gaining awareness of the humongous threat to not only our way of life but also to our very survival. Without such awareness we social scientists cannot expect to gain the motivation to act on the above four implications. Even with the help of that motivation, there is no guarantee that we can indeed learn to address our invisible crisis in time to avoid catastrophe. Yet if we can learn to follow through on all five of these implications, we may well be able to escape catastrophe by the skin of our teeth.

Following the above third implication, if social scientists are increasingly to become public intellectuals, how will an interactive worldview or metaphysical stance guide them as they enter the political arena? And building on the above fourth implication, how will that worldview aid them in pointing toward a strategy for confronting fundamental changes in contemporary society? No quick and easy illustrations can be given here, since any fundamental social problem is a highly complex affair, especially following an interactive worldview which emphasizes such complexity. Building on our second implication, a long-term strategy is to work toward a changed worldview not just among social scientists but throughout society as a whole. Even in its early stages, such a strategy can help to guide short-term strategies. Those can focus on small steps which take into account the complexity of any given problem, such as a huge gap between expectations and their fulfillment.

For example, efforts to democratize the Middle East in a short time, such as by emphasizing America's military might, have yielded yet another example of what Merton called "the unanticipated consequences of purposive social action" (chapter 3). A slower process emphasizing actions that have the support of the world community along with moderates throughout the Middle East would pay more attention to a variety of key social structures. And it would also pay more attention to the egalitarian ideals within personality structures throughout the world. Further, it would increase possibilities for taking into account the complexities of momentary situations as they emerge. Overall, it could give due recognition to the large gap between aspirations for peace and democracy and existing patterns of social stratification throughout the Middle East and the world. Such a slower process would lower our short-term aspirations for achieving peace and democracy in the Middle East yet not abandon our long-term aspirations for fulfilling those ideals. And by reducing the short-term gap between our ideals and our ability to fulfill them, it could help us to achieve over time our long-term ideals.

Assuming the validity of our findings, and granting that we are by no means alone with respect to many of the ideas in this book, we can pose the question of whether we will follow through on the implications of this analysis. Will we social scientists learn to take seriously our responsibilities to our profession, to society, and to ourselves? Or will we continue to hide within our tried-but-untrue techniques of particularization, falsification of memory and externalization of self, failing to penetrate the complexity of human behavior at a time when that understanding is desperately needed? Will we move toward the kind of metaphysics, epistemology and theory that enables us to "connect the dots" and confront both the structural and situational basis for that complexity? Or will we choose to continue with the illusion that we are in fact following the ideals of the scientific method by continuing to go our separate ways? Will we, following Hesse (chapter 5), continue to play our glass bead game all the while that flames are spreading around us, illustrating the invisible and visible crises of contemporary society? Or can we, following Mills (chapter 6), develop the guts to become "plastic enough to change" our metaphysical, epistemological and theoretical ideas? Will we continue to avoid our responsibilities as citizens of the world by keeping our hands off any political implications of our research? Or will we begin to become public intellectuals who attempt to communicate widely the implications of our knowledge for understanding and confronting social problems, implications that appear to us to point to the suicidal course of contemporary society?

# References

Abbott, Andrew. *Time Matters: On Theory and Method.* Chicago: University of Chicago Press, 2001.

Abbott, Edwin A. *Flatland: A Romance of Many Dimensions.* New York, Dover, 1884/1952.

Abramson, Paul, and John Aldrich, "Decline of Electoral Participation in America," *American Political Science Review* 76 (1982): 502-521.

Adorno, T. W., et al. *The Authoritarian Personality.* New York: Harper & Row, 1950.

Agnew, Robert, 1992 "Foundation for a General Strain Theory of Delinquency." *Criminology* 30:47-87.

Agnew, Robert. "A Revised Strain Theory of Delinquency," *Social Forces* 64 (1985): 151-167.

Ahmed, Akbar S. "Ibn Khaldun and Anthropology: The Failure of Methodology in the Post 9/11 World," *Contemporary Sociology* 34 (December 2005), 591-595.

Ainslie, G. *Breakdown of Will.* Cambridge: Cambridge University Press, 2001.

Alexander, Jeffrey C. "The Binary Discourse of Civil Society," in Steven Seidman and Jeffrey C. Alexander, *The New Social Theory Reader.* New York: Routledge, 2001, 193-201.

Aronson, E. "The Theory of Cognitive Dissonance: A Current Perspective," in L. Berkowitz (ed.), *Advances in Experimental Social Psychology,* Vol. 4. New York: Academic Press, 1969.

Aronson, E. "The Return of the Repressed: Dissonance Theory Makes a Comeback." *Psychological Inquiry* 3 (1992), 303-311.

Ball-Rokeach, Sandra J., Milton Rokeach, and Joel W. Grube. *The Great American Values Test: Influencing Behavior and Belief through Television.* New York: Free Press, 1984.

Bannister, D., and Fay Fransella. *Inquiring Man: The Theory of Personal Constructs.* New York: Penguin, 1971.

Bardach, Janusz. *Man Is Wolf to Man: Surviving the Gulag.* Berkeley: Univ. of California Press, 1998.

Becker, Ernest. *The Denial of Death.* New York and London: Free Press, 1973.

Becker, Howard S. "The Politics of Presentation: Goffman and Total Institutions," in Bernard Phillips, Harold Kincaid and Thomas J. Scheff (eds.), *Toward a Sociological Imagination: Bridging Specialized Fields*. Lanham, Maryland: University Press of America, 2002, 293-304.

Bem, D. J. "Self-perception: An Alternative Interpretation of Cognitive Dissonance Phenomena." *Psychological Review* 74 (1967), 183-200.

Berger, John. *Ways of Seeing*. London: BBC and Penguin Books, 1985.

Bertalanffy, Ludwig von. "The Theory of Open Systems in Physics and Biology." *Science* III (1950), 23-29.

Bondurant, Joan V. *Conquest of Violence*. Berkeley: Univ. of California Press, 1965.

Boorstin, Daniel J. *The Image: A Guide to Pseudo-Events in America*. New York: Harper & Row, 1961.

Borgatta, Edgar F., and Rhonda J. V. Montgomery. *Encyclopedia of Sociology*. New York: Macmillan Reference USA, 2000.

Buckley, Walter. *Sociology and Modern Systems Theory*. Englewood Cliffs, N.J.: Prentice-Hall, 1967.

Busch, Lawrence. "Macrosocial Change in Historical Perspective: An Analysis of Epochs." Unpublished doctoral dissertation. Ithaca, New York: Cornell University, 1974.

Busch, Lawrence. "A Tentative Guide to Constructing the Future: Self-Conscious Millenarianism," *Sociological Practice* 1 (Spring 1976), 27-39.

Camerer, C., G. Loewenstein and M. Rabin (eds.). *Advances in Behavioral Economics*. Princeton: Princeton University Press, 2003.

Chua, Amy. *World on Fire: How Exporting Free Market Democracy Breeds Ethnic Hatred and Global Instability*. New York: Doubleday, 2003.

Cohen, Jere. *Protestantism and Capitalism: The Mechanisms of Influence*. New York: Aldine de Gruyter, 2002.

Dahrendorf, Ralph. *Society and Democracy in Germany*. Garden City, New York: Doubleday, 1967.

Dantzig. Tobias. *Number: The Language of Science*. New York: The Free Press, 1954.

Davis, Kingsley, and Wilbert E. Moore. "Some Principles of Stratification," *American Sociological Review* 10 (1945), 242-249.

Dewey, John. *Reconstruction in Philosophy*. Boston: Beacon Press, (1920/1948).

Dhaouadi, Mahmoud. "The *Ibar*: Lessons of Ibn Khaldun's Umran Mind," *Contemporary Sociology* 34 (December 2005), 585-590.

Duhem, Pierre. *The Aim and Structure of Physical Theory*. Princeton: Princeton University Press, 1954.

Durkheim, Emile. *Suicide*. New York: Free Press, 1897/1951.

Erikson, Kai. "On Work and Alienation," *American Sociological Review* 51 (February 1986), 1-8.

Farson, Richard E. "Why Good Marriages Fail," in Ronald Fernandez (ed.), *The Future as a Social Problem*. Santa Monica: Goodyear, 1977, 169-176.

Feffer, Andrew. "Sociability and Social Conflict in George Herbert Mead's Interactionism, 1900-1919," *Journal of the History of Ideas* 51 (April-June 1990), 233-254.

Festinger, Leon. *A Theory of Cognitive Dissonance*. Stanford: Stanford University Press, 1957.

Forrester, Jay W. *Principles of Systems*. Cambridge, Mass.: MIT Press, 1968.

Forrester, Jay W. *Urban Dynamics*. Cambridge, Mass.: MIT Press, 1969.

Forrester, Jay W. *World Dynamics*. Cambridge, Mass.: Wright-Allen Press, 1971.

Fransella, Fay, and Laurie Thomas. *Experimenting with Personal Construct Psychology*. London and New York: Routledge & Kegan Paul, 1988.

Freire, Paulo. *Pedagogy of the Oppressed*. New York: Herder and Herder, 1970.

Freire, Paulo. *Education for Critical Consciousness*. New York: Seabury, 1973.

Giddens, Anthony. *Central Problems in Social Theory: Action, Structure and Contradiction in Social Analysis*. Berkeley: University of California Press, 1979.

Giddens, Anthony. *The Constitution of Society*. Berkeley: University of California Press, 1984.

Goffman, Erving. "On the Characteristics of Total Institutions," in Goffman, *Asylums: Essays on the Social Situation of Mental Patients and Other Inmates*. Garden City, N.Y.: Anchor Books, 1961, 1–124.

Gould, Stephen Jay. *The Mismeasure of Man*. New York: Norton, 1981.

Gouldner, Alvin W. *The Coming Crisis of Western Sociology*. New York: Basic Books, 1970.

Gouldner, Alvin W. "The Politics of the Mind: Reflections on Flack's Review of *The Coming Crisis of Western Sociology*," *Social Policy* 5 (March/April 1972), 13–21, 54–58.

Greenstein, Theodore N. "Modifying Beliefs and Behavior through Self-Confrontation," *Sociological Inquiry* 59 (November 1989), 396–407.

Grusky, David B. "Social Stratification," in Edgar F. Borgatta and Rhonda J. V. Montgomery, *Encyclopedia of Sociology*. New York: Macmillan Reference USA, 2000, 2807–2821.

Habermas, Jürgen. *The Theory of Communicative Action,* Vol. 1. Trans. by Thomas McCarthy. Boston: Beacon Press, 1984.

Harman-Jones, E., J. Brehm, J. Greenberg, L. Simon, and D. E. Nelson. "Evidence that the Production of Dissonance is not Necessary to Create Cognitive Dissonance," *Journal of Personality and Social Psychology* 70 (1996), 5–16.

Heider, Fritz. *The Psychology of Interpersonal Relations*. New York: Wiley, 1958.

Herling, Gustav. *A World Apart*. New York: Roy Publishers, 1951.

Hesse, Herman. *The Glass Bead Game (Magister Ludi)*. New York: Bantam Books 1943/1969.

Hitler, Adolph. *Mein Kampf*. Boston: Houghton Mifflin, 1943.

Horney, Karen. *The Neurotic Personality of Our Time*. New York: Norton, 1937.

Howard, Judith A., and Danielle Kane. "Attribution Theory," in Borgatta, Edgar F., and Rhonda J. V. Montgomery, eds., *Encyclopedia of Sociology*. New York: Macmillan Reference USA, 2000.

Hoyle, Fred. *The Black Cloud*. New York: New American Library, 1957.

Huizinga, Johan. *Homo Ludens*. Boston: Beacon Press, 1950.

Huxley, Aldous. *Brave New World*. New York: Harper & Row, 1939.

Illich, Ivan. *Deschooling Society*. New York: Harper & Row, 1971.

Jacobs, Jane. *The Death and Life of Great American Cities*. New York: Random House, 1961.

Jacobsen, Chanoch. "The Process of Secularization: Toward a Theory-Oriented Methodology," in Bernard Phillips, Harold Kincaid, and Thomas J. Scheff (eds.), *Toward a Sociological Imagination: Bridging Specialized Fields.* Lanham, MD: University Press of America, 2002.

James, William. *Pragmatism: A New Name for Some Old Ways of Thinking.* New York: Dover, 1907/1995.

Janis, Irving L., and Daniel Katz. "The Reduction of Intergroup Hostility," *Journal of Conflict Resolution* 3 (March 1959), 85–100.

Johnson-Laird, P. N. "Mental Models," in Michael Posner (ed.). *Foundations of Cognitive Science.* Cambridge, Mass.: MIT Press, 1993, 469–499.

Jones, Edward E., and Keith E. Davis. "From Acts to Dispositions: The Attribution Process in Person Perception," *Advances in Experimental Social Psychology* 2 (1965), 219–266.

Jones, Edward E., and Daniel McGillis. "Correspondent Inferences and the Attribution Cube: A Comparative Reappraisal," in J. H. Harvey, W. Ickes, and R. F. Kidd (eds.), *New Directions in Attribution Research,* Vol. 1. Hillsdale, N. J.: Erlbaum, 1976.

Kaplan, Abraham. *The New World of Philosophy.* New York: Random House, 1961.

Kelley, Harold H. "Attribution Theory in Social Psychology," *Nebraska Symposium of Motivation* 15 (1967), 192–238.

Kelley, Harold H. "The Processes of Causal Attribution," *American Psychologist* 28 (1973), 107–128.

Kelly, George A. *The Psychology of Personal Constructs,* 2 vols. New York: W. W. Norton, 1955.

Kelly, George A. *A Theory of Personality: The Psychology of Personal Constructs.* New York: W. W. Norton, 1963.

Kincaid, Harold. *Philosophical Foundations of the Social Sciences.* New York: Cambridge University Press, 1996.

Kincaid, Harold, John Dupre, and Alison Wylie (eds.). *Value-Free Science: Ideal or Illusion?* Cambridge, UK: Cambridge University Press, 2006.

Kitagawa, Daisuke. *Issei and Nisei: The Internment Years.* New York: The Seabury Press, 1967.

Knottnerus, J. David. "Agency, Structure and Deritualization: A Comparative Investigation of Extreme Disruptions of Social Order," in Sing C. Chew and J. David Knottnerus, eds. *Structure, Culture and History: Recent Issues in Social Theory.* Lanham, MD: Rowman & Littlefield, 2002.

Knotterus, J. David. *Ritual as a Missing Link within Sociology: Structural Ritualization Theory and Research.* Boulder, Colo.: Paradigm, 2007.

Korzybski, Alfred. *Science and Sanity.* Garden City, N.Y.: Country Life Press, 1933.

Krugman, Paul R., and Maurice Obstfeld. *International Economics: Theory and Policy,* 6th ed. Boston: Addison-Wesley, 2003.

Kuhn, Thomas S. *The Structure of Scientific Revolutions.* Chicago: Univ. of Chicago Press, 1962.

Lakoff, G. *Woman, Fire, and Dangerous Things: What Categories Reveal about the Mind.* Chicago: University of Chicago Press, 1987.

Lauderdale, Pat, Steve McLaughlin, and Annamarie Oliverio. "Levels of Analysis,

Theoretical Orientations and Degrees of Abstraction," *American Sociologist* 21 (Spring 1990), 29–40.

Lerner, Daniel. *The Passing of Traditional Society.* New York: Free Press, 1958.

Levin, Jack. "The Influence of Social Frame of Reference for Goal Fulfillment on Social Aggression." Ph.D. Dissertation, Boston University, 1968.

Lewis, Bernard. *What Went Wrong? Western Impact and Middle Eastern Response.* New York: Oxford University Press, 2002.

Lipset, Seymour Martin, and William Schneider. *The Confidence Gap: Business, Labor, and Government in the Public Mind.* New York: Free Press, 1983.

Luhmann, Niklas. *Social Systems.* Trans. by John Bednarz. Stanford: Stanford University Press, 1984/1995.

Lundberg, George A. *Can Science Save Us?* New York: David McKay, 1947/1961.

Mahdi, Muhsin. *Ibn Khaldun's Philosophy of History: A Study in the Foundation of the Science of Culture.* Chicago: University of Chicago Press, 1957.

Mannheim, Karl. "On the Interpretation of Weltanschauung," *Essays on the Sociology of Knowledge.* New York: Oxford, 1952, 8–58.

Marx, Karl. *Early Writings.* Trans. and ed. by T. B. Bottomore, New York: McGraw-Hill, 1844/1964.

Marx, Karl. *Karl Marx: Selected Writings in Sociology and Social Philosophy.* New York: McGraw-Hill, 1849/1964.

Marx, Karl, and Friedrich Engels. "Manifesto of the Communist Party," in Robert C. Tuicker (ed.), *The Marx-Engels Reader.* New York: W. W. Norton, 1848/1972, 331–362. Matzner, David. *The Muselmann: The Diary of a Jewish Slave Laborer.* Hoboken, N.J.: KTAV Publishing House, 1994.

Mayton, Daniel M., Sandra J. Ball-Rokeach, and William E. Loges. "Human Values and Social Issues: An Introduction." *Journal of Social Issues* 50 (1994): 1–8.

Meadows, Donella H., Dennis L. Meadows, Jorgen Randers, and William W. Behrens III. *The Limits to Growth.* New York: Universe Books, 1972.

Merton, Robert K. "The Unanticipated Consequences of Purposive Social Action," *American Sociological Review* 1 (December 1936): 894–904.

Merton, Robert K. "Social Structure and Anomie," in Merton, Robert K., *Social Theory and Social Structure.* New York: Free Press, 1949, 125–149.

Messner, Steven F., and Richard Rosenfeld. *Crime and the American Dream.* Belmont, Calif.: Wadsworth, 1994.

Michels, Robert. *Political Parties.* New York: Free Press, 1949.

Mills, C. Wright. "The Professional Ideology of Social Pathologists," *American Journal of Sociology* 49 (September 1943), 165–180.

Mills, C. Wright. *The Sociological Imagination.* N. Y.: Oxford University Press, 1959.

Mills, C. Wright. *Sociology and Pragmatism*: The Higher Learning in America. New York: Oxford University Press, 1964.

Moberg, David O. *The Church as a Social Institution.* Englewood Cliffs, N.J.: Prentice-Hall, 1962.

Nietzsche, Friedrich. *The Gay Science.* Trans. by Walter Kaufmann. New York: Random House, (1887) 1974.

Orwell, George. *Nineteen Eighty-Four.* New York: Harcourt Brace Jovanovich, 1949.

Osgood, Charles, et al. *The Measurement of Meaning*. Urbana: Univ. of Illinois Press, 1967.

Pappas,Theodore (ed.). *Britannica Concise Encyclopedia*. London: Encyclopedia Britannica, 2002.

Pappenheim, Fritz. *The Alienation of Modern Man*. New York: Monthly Review Press, 1959.

Passas, Nikos, and Robert Agnew (eds.). *The Future of Anomie Theory*. Boston: Northeastern University Press, 1997.

Peirce, Charles S. "The Fixation of Belief," in Peirce, Charles S., *Philosophical Writings of Peirce*. New York: Dover, 1877/1955, 5-22.

Peirce, Charles S. "How to Make Our Ideas Clear," in Peirce, Charles S., *Philosophical Writings of Peirce*. New York: Dover, 1878/1955, 23-41.

Peirce, Charles S. "The Scientific Attitude and Fallibilism," in Peirce, Charles S., *Philosophical Writings of Peirce*. New York: Dover, 1896/1955, 42-59.

Peirce, Charles S. "Concerning the Author," in Peirce, Charles S., *Philosophical Writings of Peirce*. New York: Dover, 1897/1955, 1-4.

Peirce, Charles S. "The Approach to Metaphysics," in Peirce, Charles S., *Philosophical Writings of Peirce*. New York: Dover, 1898/1955, 310-314.

Phillips, Bernard. *Worlds of the Future: Exercises in the Sociological Imagination*. Columbus, Ohio: Charles E. Merrill, 1972.

Phillips, Bernard. *Sociology: From Concepts to Practice*. New York: McGraw-Hill, 1979.

Phillips, Bernard. "Paradigmatic Barriers to System Dynamics," *Proceedings of the International Conference on Cybernetics and Society*. Cambridge, Mass.: IEEE, October 1980, 682-688

Phillips, Bernard. *Sociological Research Methods: An Introduction*. Homewood, Illinois: Dorsey Press, 1985.

Phillips, Bernard. "Toward a Reflexive Sociology," *American Sociologist* (Summer 1988): 138-151.

Phillips, Bernard. "Simmel, Individuality, and Fundamental Change," in Michael Kaern, Bernard Phillips, and Robert S. Cohen (eds.), *Georg Simmel and Contemporary Sociology*. Dordrecht/Boston/London: Kluwer, 1990.

Phillips, Bernard. *Beyond Sociology's Tower of Babel: Reconstructing the Scientific Method*. New York: Aldine de Gruyter, 2001.

Phillips, Bernard, "Prejudice: The Levin Experiment," in Bernard Phillips, Harold Kincaid and Thomas J. Scheff (eds.). *Toward a Sociological Imagination: Bridging Specialized Fields*. Lanham, Maryland: University Press of America, 2002, 199-226.

Phillips, Bernard, "Mills, C(harles) Wright (1916-1962)," in John R. Shook (ed.), *Dictionary of Modern American Philosophers*. Bristol, UK: Thoemmes Press, 2004.

Phillips, Bernard (ed.). *Understanding Terrorism: Building on The Sociological Imagination*. Boulder, Colo.: Paradigm, 2007.

Phillips, Bernard, Harold Kincaid, and Thomas J. Scheff (Eds.). *Toward a Sociological Imagination: Bridging Specialized Fields*. Lanham, Maryland: University Press of America, 2002.

Piven, Frances Fox, and Richard A. Cloward. *Why Americans Don't Vote*. New York: Pantheon, 1988.

Polak, Fred L. *The Image of the Future,* 2 vols. Leyden: A.W. Sythoff, 1961.

Polak, Fred L. *The Image of the Future.* San Francisco: Jossey-Bass, 1973.

Postman, Neil. *Amusing Ourselves to Death: Public Discourse in the Age of Show Business.* New York: Penguin, 1985.

Putnam, Robert D. *Bowling Alone: The Collapse and Revival of American Community.* New York: Simon & Schuster, 2000.

Quine, W.V. O., and J. S. Ullian. *The Web of Belief,* New York: Random House, 1970.

Quinn, N., and D. Holland. "Introduction," in D. Holland and N. Quinn (eds.), *Cultural Models in Language and Thought.* New York: Cambridge University Press, 1987, 173-192.

Rafalovich, Adam. "Assessing the Terrorist Movement: Anomie and the Fractured American *Weltanschauung,*" chapter 4 in Bernard Phillips (ed.), *Understanding Terrorism: Building on The Sociological Imagination.* Boulder, Colo.: Paradigm, 2007.

Raushenbush, Hilmar S. *Man's Past: Man's Future.* New York: Delacorte, 1969.

Rees, Martin. *Our Final Hour: A Scientist's Warning: How Terror, Error, and Environmental Disaster Threaten Humankind's Future in This Century—On Earth and Beyond.* New York: Basic Books, 2003.

Retzinger, Suzanne. *Violent Emotions: Shame and Rage in Marital Quarrels.* Newbury Park, Calif.: Sage, 1991.

Riesman, David. *The Lonely Crowd.* New Haven: Yale University Press, 1961.

Roberts, Nancy, David Andersen, Ralph Deal, Michael Garet, and William Shaffer. *Introduction to Computer Simulation: The System Dynamics Approach.* Reading, Mass.: Addison-Wesley, 1983.

Rokeach, Milton. *The Three Christs of Ypsilanti.* New York: Knopf, 1964.

Rokeach, Milton. *Value Survey.* Sunnyvale, Calif.: Halgren Tests, 1967.

Rokeach, Milton. *Beliefs, Attitudes, and Values.* San Francisco: Jossey-Bass, 1968.

Rokeach, Milton. *The Nature of Human Values.* New York: Free Press, 1973.

Rosen, Lawrence. "Theorizing from Within: Ibn Khaldun and His Political Culture," *Contemporary Sociology* 34 (December 2005), 596-599.

Ross, D. *Economic Theory and Cognitive Science: Microexplanation.* Cambridge, Mass.: MIT Press, 2005.

Scheff, Thomas J. *Being Mentally Ill: A Sociological Theory.* Chicago: Aldine, 1966.

Scheff, Thomas J. "The Labelling Theory of Mental Illness," *American Sociological Review* 39 (June 1974), 444-452.

Scheff, Thomas J. *Microsociology: Discourse, Emotion, and Social Structure.* Chicago: University of Chicago Press, 1990.

Scheff, Thomas J. *Bloody Revenge: Emotions, Nationalism, and War.* Boulder, Colo.: Westview, 1994.

Scheff, Thomas J. *Emotions, the Social Bond, and Human Reality: Part/Whole Analysis.* Cambridge: Cambridge University Press, 1997.

Scheff, Thomas J. *Goffman Unbound! A New Paradigm for Social Science.* Boulder, Colo.: Paradigm, 2006.

Shaffer, Stephen D. "A Multivariate Explanation of Decreasing Turnout in Presidential Elections, 1960-1976," *American Journal of Political Science* 25 (1981): 68-95.

Simmel, Georg. "Metropolis and Mental Life," in *Georg Simmel on Individuality and Social Forms,* ed. by Donald N. Levine. Chicago: Univ. of Chicago Press, 1903/1971, 324-339.

Simmel, Georg. "Subjective Culture," in in *Georg Simmel on Individuality and Social Forms,* ed. by Donald N. Levine. Chicago: Univ. of Chicago Press, 1908/1971, 227-234.

Sjoberg, Gideon. *The Preindustrial City.* New York: Free Press, 1965.

Skocpol, Theda. *States and Social Revolutions.* New York: Cambridge University Press, 1979.

Smith, Peter B., and Shalom Schwartz. "Values," in J. W. Berry, M. H. Segall, and C. Kagiticibasi (eds.), *Handbook of Cross-Cultural Psychology,* vol. 3. Boston: Allyn and Bacon, 1997.

Snow, C. P. *The Two Cultures.* New York: Cambridge University Press, 1959.

Sommer, Robert. *Tight Spaces: Hard Architecture and How to Humanize It.* Englewood Cliffs, N.J.: Prentice-Hall, 1974.

Stebbins, Robert. *Between Work and Leisure: The Common Ground of Two Separate Worlds.* New Brunswick, N.J.: Transaction Publications, 2004.

Taylor, Shelley E., and J. Crocker. "Schematic Bases of Social Information Processsing," in E. T. Higgins, C. P. Herman, and M. P. Zanna (eds.), *Social Cognition: The Ontario Symposium.* Hillsdale, N.J.: Erlbaum, 1981.

Thomas, William I. *The Unadjusted Girl.* Boston: Little, Brown, 1923.

Turner, Jonathan H. *Face to Face: Toward a Sociological Theory of Interpersonal Behavior.* Stanford: Stanford University Press, 2002.

Udy, Stanley H., Jr. "'Bureaucracy' and 'Rationality' in Weber's Organization Theory," *American Sociological Review* 24 (1959): 591-595.

Vaughan, Diane. "Anomie Theory and Organizations: Culture and the Normalization of Deviance at NASA," in Nikos Passas and Robert Agnew (eds.), *The Future of Anomie Theory.* Boston: Northeastern University Press, 1997, 95-123.

Veblen, Thorstein. *The Theory of the Leisure Class.* New York: Mentor, 1963.

Vidich, Arthur, and Joseph Bensman. *Small Town in Mass Society: Class, Power, and Religion in a Rural Community.* Garden City, N.Y.: Doubleday, 1960.

van Vogt, A. E. *The World of Null-A.* New York: Berkley Publishing, 1945/1970.

van Vogt, A. E. *The Players of Null-A.* New York: Berkley Publishing, 1948.

Wallerstein, Immanuel. *The Modern World-System.* New York: Academic Press, 1974.

Wallerstein, Immanuel. *The Capitalist World-Economy.* New York: Cambridge University Press, 1979.

Wallerstein, Immanuel. "The Annales School: The War on Two Fronts." *Annales of Scholarship* 3 (Summer 1980), 85-91.

Wallerstein, Immanuel." Beyond Annales?" *Radical History Review* 49 (Winter 1991), 7-15.

Weber, Max. *The Protestant Ethic and the Spirit of Capitalism.* New York: Scribner's, 1905/1958.

Weber, Max. *From Max Weber: Essays in Sociology,* ed. by H. H. Gerth and C. W. Mills. London and New York: Oxford University Press, 1946.

Weber, Max. *The Theory of Social and Economic Organization.* New York: Free Press, 1964.

Wesolowski, Wlodzimierz. "Some Notes on the Functional Theory of Stratification," *Polish Sociological Bulletin* 3 (1962), 28-38.

Wiener, Norbert. *The Human Use of Human Beings: Cybernetics and Society.* Garden City, N.Y.: Doubleday Anchor, 1954.

Willer, David, and Murray Webster, Jr. "Theoretical Concepts and Observables," *American Sociological Review* 35 (August 1970): 748-757.

Williams, Robin M., Jr. "Major Value Orientations in America," *American Society, 3rd ed.* New York: Knopf, 1970, 452-500.

Wilson, Edward O. "Back from Chaos," *The Atlantic Monthly* (March 1998), 41-62.

Wilson, James Q. *What Government Agencies Do and Why They Do It.* New York: Basic Books, 1989.

Wright, Erik Olin, Andrew Levine, and Elliot Sober. *Reconstructing Marxism.* London: Verso, 1992.

Wright, Robert. *Nonzero: The Logic of Human Destiny.* New York: Pantheon, 2000.

Wrong, Dennis H. "The Functional Theory of Stratification: Some Neglected Considerations," *American Sociological Review* 24 (1959), 772-782.

# Index

# About the Authors

**Bernard Phillips,** a student of C. Wright Mills at Columbia, received an M.A. from Washington State University, and a Ph.D. from Cornell, studying with Robin M. Williams Jr. Phillips taught at the University of North Carolina and University of Illinois before teaching at Boston University. He co-founded ASA's Section on Sociological Practice and founded the Sociological Imagination Group, which has had annual conferences since 2000. Phillips initiated a series of monographs, "Advancing the Sociological Imagination," first with Aldine and then—along with his coeditor, Harold Kincaid—with Paradigm Publishers. His most recent books are *Beyond Sociology's Tower of Babel: Reconstructing the Scientific Method,* the edited volume *Toward a Sociological Imagination: Bridging Specialized Fields,* and the edited volume *Understanding Terrorism: Building on the Sociological Imagination.* Excerpts from his work are on the website *www.sociological-imagination.org.* His e-mail address is *berniefelps@aol.com.* He lives in Longboat Key, Florida, and Provincetown, Massachusetts, with his wife Marjorie.

**Louis C. Johnston,** Fellow of the American College of Physicians, received B.S. and M.D. degrees from Northwestern University and an M.S. from the University of Illinois. He has a background in biological and medical research, having published some two dozen refereed articles on oxygen and heat metabolism as well as on hypertension. He was medical director of a large Chicago hospital where he established educational and training programs for students and practicing physicians. As a former associate professor of medicine and preventive medicine in Chicago (Northwestern, Illinois, and Rush), he is currently writing on the embedding of sociology within medicine and biology. He believes that today's doctor-patient relationship could be substantially improved by educating and training physicians and health-care administrators to develop an interactive or nonstratified worldview along with the Web and Part/Whole Approach to the scientific method. He lives in Longboat Key, Florida, with his wife Anne and puppy Zoe. His e-mail address is *ljohnston04@comcast.net.*

For Product Safety Concerns and Information please contact our EU
representative  GPSR@taylorandfrancis.com
Taylor & Francis Verlag GmbH, Kaufingerstraße 24, 80331 München, Germany

www.ingramcontent.com/pod-product-compliance
Lightning Source LLC
Chambersburg PA
CBHW050415280326
41932CB00013BA/1863

9 781594 513725